The Which? Guide to Shares

About the author

Jonquil Lowe is a freelance journalist and former head of the Money Group at *Which?* magazine. She is the author of several other books on personal finance, including *The Which? Guide to Pensions*, *The Which? Guide to Giving and Inheriting* and *Be Your Own Financial Adviser*, all *Which?* books.

The Which? Guide to Shares

Jonquil Lowe

 CONSUMERS' ASSOCIATION

Which? Books are commissioned and researched by
Consumers' Association and published by
Which? Ltd, 2 Marylebone Road, London NW1 4DF
Email address: books@which.net

Distributed by The Penguin Group:
Penguin Books Ltd, 27 Wrights Lane, London W8 5TZ

First edition March 1998

British Library Cataloguing in Publication Data
A catalogue record for this book is available from the British Library

ISBN 0 85202 692 7

For a full list of *Which?* books, please write to Which? Books, Castlemead, Gascoyne
Way, Hertford X, SG14 1LH, or access our web site at
http://www.which.net

Cover and text design by Kyzen Creative Consultants

Typeset by Business ColorPrint
Printed and bound in England by Clays Ltd, Bungay, Suffolk

Contents

★ An asterisk next to the name of an organisation or a publication in the text indicates that the address can be found in this section

Introduction

PRIVATE shareholders once dominated the UK stock market, but the 1960s and 1970s saw their place being taken by the big shareholder institutions – insurance companies, pension funds, unit trust companies and the like. By 1979, only 3 million people had their own direct shareholdings and the myth had grown that shares were just for the rich. Less than twenty years later, the popularity of privatisation issues and the impact of windfall shares from building society conversions have well and truly smashed that myth: some 16 million individuals are now thought to hold shares.

Britain may have become a nation of share-owners, but they are not like the shareholders of the past. Many people own shares in just one or two companies. Often, these shareholdings are out on a limb and play no role in the individual's overall financial planning. Yet shares are multi-talented, sophisticated investments which can help you to achieve your financial ambitions and even give you a lot of fun as well.

However, there are pitfalls too. Shares are 'risk investments'. Their value can – and does – fall as well as rise. If you had sold shares in October 1997, when stock markets worldwide tumbled in response to problems in Asia, you could have lost a lot of money. It is essential that you understand the risks of shares and never invest money that you might need back at short notice or at a set time. You must have the scope to leave your money invested if the market does turn down. Provided you can sit out a general slump, the market will almost certainly recover. But individual shares might not – a company could go bust which, in many cases, means that shareholders lose their whole investment. So you need to understand how to alter risk and how to match different levels of risk to your investment aims.

From the outside, the stock market may seem a confusing, fast-moving world with no place for the small investor. Once you step over the threshold, though, you realise that shares are intrinsically very simple. You own a slice of a company which you can sell to someone else in a marketplace, full of bustle, noise and colour, which is driven by the fundamental laws of every market: supply and demand.

It is hard to become a share investor without feeling the excitement of the marketplace, but shares are also a cornerstone of sound financial planning. Over the long run, the return on shares will outstrip the amount you could earn in the building society or from other 'safe' investments, such as British Government stocks. If you are to stand a realistic chance of achieving long-term goals, such as financing children through school and college, building up an adequate retirement fund, accumulating a sizeable nest egg and so on, you should have at least some of your money invested in shares.

Whether you do this by handing over your money to an institution or by accumulating your own portfolio of shares depends largely on two factors – how much you have to invest and whether direct share ownership appeals to you.

If you are a very small investor, running your own portfolio of shares could be prohibitively expensive. Once you have a few thousand pounds to invest, direct share ownership becomes feasible, but it still might not be the best option. You should first have your basic finances in order and many advisers would warn against direct share holding unless you have £30,000 or more to save. Below that level, it will often make more sense to use investments such as unit trusts. Alternatively, you could join forces with others to form an investment club.

Provided you have enough to invest, the decision to opt for direct investment in shares now rests with you: do you have the temperament, the time, the access to information? This book aims to help you make your decision. It shows how shares can fit into your particular financial strategies; it explains how they work and how they are taxed; it describes where to find the main sources of information about companies and their shares; and it shows you how to interpret what you discover – and, of course, it tells you how to buy and sell shares, including the options facing small investors in the electronic age of the stock market.

With this book as your starting point, you can build on your handful of privatisation issues and windfall shares to create one of the soundest and most fascinating investments you will ever make.

Chapter 1

Who are the share owners?

ALTHOUGH you might not realise it, shares play a central role in most people's financial plans. When you buy insurance or contribute to a pension plan, a substantial part of your money usually finds its way on to the stock market. You might have investments in unit trusts or investment trusts – perhaps through a personal equity plan – and, with these, your return is linked to a fund of shares and other investments.

But share ownership does not have to be so remote. At the end of 1996, it was estimated that around 9.5 million individuals in the UK held shares direct. By value, they held approximately one fifth of the ordinary shares quoted on the London Stock Exchange, accounting for about one tenth of the total wealth of the personal sector. In 1997, share ownership became even more widespread.

The growth of popular capitalism

Private individuals have a substantial presence in today's stock market. This is a far cry from the late 1970s when they numbered just three million people and share ownership was viewed as the preserve of the sophisticated and well-heeled. The rise in popularity of direct share ownership since then has been due most recently to building society conversions but before that owed much to the former Conservative government's specific policy of promoting wider share ownership, described by the Chancellor, Nigel Lawson, in 1986 as a move to 'create a popular capitalism, in which more and more men and women have a direct stake in British industry and businesses'. This had three main strands.

Chart 1.1: Who owns shares in the UK

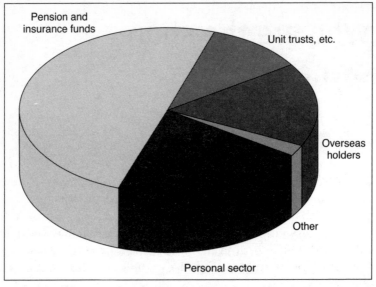

Source: Financial Statistics, Office for National Statistics, Crown Copyright 1998

Chart 1.2: How people in the UK invest their savings

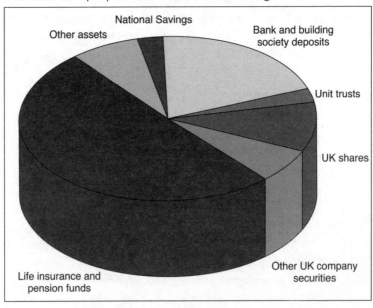

Source: Financial Statistics, Office for National Statistics, Crown Copyright 1998

Privatisations

The sale of shares in previously nationalised industries was largely an exercise in raising money to enable the government to keep its accounts in order, but it also became an important expression of Thatcher ideology. Shares were not simply sold off to big private institutions, but the offers were deliberately structured to woo the small investor: minimum investments were small; the price could often be paid in instalments; individuals were given priority over institutions in the allocation of shares; bonus shares to be handed out at a later date were used as an incentive for holding on to the original shares; and some of the largest issues were heavily advertised on TV and through the popular press. Most importantly, the share price was nearly always pitched on the low side with the result that immediate profits were likely.

The stream of privatisations continues and these same aspects that were designed to attract small investors have become expected features. Bearing this in mind and, in particular, given the price advantage, it is not surprising that most privatisation issues have so far proved to be excellent investments – see Table 1.1.

Employee share schemes

Special schemes, giving tax perks to employees who take up shares in the company they work for, were introduced by the Labour government in the late 1970s, but it was in the Thatcher years that these schemes expanded and flourished. In 1979, there were just 30 such schemes. By March 1996, there were more than 9,000.

Personal equity plans (PEPs)

These were introduced on 1 January 1987 as vehicles to encourage direct ownership of shares. Later, they were adapted and investment in PEPs became possible wholly via unit trusts or investment trusts (and were subsequently further amended to allow investment in bonds). By March 1997, over 11 million plans had been taken out.

The great year of conversions

Dramatic though the rise in share ownership between 1979 and 1996 might seem, it is nothing compared with the explosion of share ownership which took place in 1997 as the result of a single factor: the conversion of mutual organisations into companies.

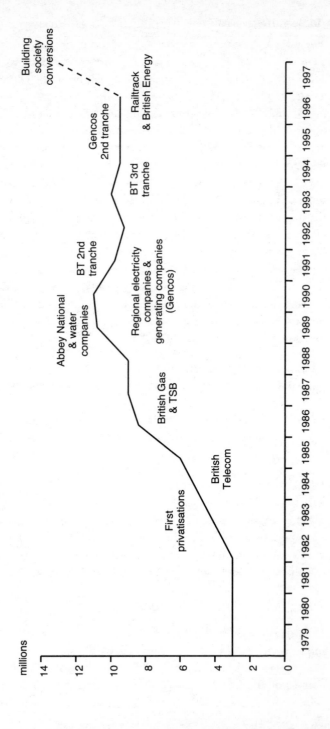

Chart 1.3: Rising number of share owners since 1979 with key issues/events shown

Table 1.1: Privatisations – a good deal for shareholders

Company	Date of privatisation	Issue price	Price at end February 1997	Increase in share price since issue
Amersham International	February 1982	142p	1299p	815%
Associated British Ports	February 1983	14p	313p	2,136%
	April 1984	33.75p		827%
British Aerospace	July 1981	150p	1277.5p	752%
	September 1985	375p		241%
British Airports Authority	July 1987	122.5p	532p	334%
British Airways	February 1987	630.5p	630.5p	404%
British Energy	July 1996	100p	142p	42%
British Gas[1]	December 1986	135p	236.25p	75%
British Petroleum	June 1977	70.4p	679.5p	865%
	October 1979	121p		462%
	September 1983	145p		369%
	October 1987	330p		106%
British Steel	December 1988	125p	150.5p	20%
British Telecom	December 1984	130p	425.5p	227%
	December 1991	335p		27%
	July 1993	410p		4%
Cable and Wireless	November 1981	28p	498.5p	1680%
	November 1983	68.75p		625%
	March 1985	146.75p		240%
Enterprise Oil	June 1984	185p	622p	236%
National Power	March 1991	175p	489p	179%
	February 1995	340p		44%
Northern Ireland Electric	June 1993	220p	380p	73%
PowerGen	March 1991	175p	616p	252%
	February 1995	370p		66%
Railtrack[2]	May 1996	190p	453.5p	139%
Rolls Royce	May 1987	170p	233p	37%
Scottish Power	June 1991	240p	351p	46%
Scottish Hydro	June 1991	240p	355.5p	48%
Water companies:	November 1989			
Anglian Water		240p	651.5p	171%
Northumbrian		240p	1,179p	391%
United Utilities		240p	667.5p	178%
Severn Trent		240p	715p	198%
Southern Water		240p	1,050p	338%
South West Water		240p	688.5p	187%

Thames Water		240p	688p	187%
Hyder		240p	831.5p	246%
Wessex Water		145p	362.5p	150%
Yorkshire Water		240p	716p	198%
Regional electricity companies:	November 1990			
Eastern Electricity		240p	975p	306%
East Midlands		273p	670p	145%
London Electricity		280p	705p	152%
Manweb		240p	990p	313%
Midlands Electricity		120p	420p	250%
Northern Electric		240p	651p	171%
Norweb		240p	1,190p	396%
Seeboard		120p	535.4p	346%
Southern Electric		240p	793.5p	231%
South Wales		240p	940p	292%
South Western		240p	965p	302%
Yorkshire		240p	894p	273%
National Grid[3]	December 1995	204p	207.5p	2%

[1] Including Centrica
[2] In partly paid form
[3] Allotted to shareholders in most of the regional electricity companies

Source: Proshare, *Individual share ownership facts and figures, 1997*

Mutual organisations grew up, mainly in the nineteenth century, as self-help bodies owned by their members. As time passed and the organisations grew, the members ceased to feel like members of a club and became more like ordinary customers, but the legal relationship had not changed. The customers still owned the organisation.

There are many mutual organisations in the UK. Some are insurance companies, some are friendly societies, but the most dominant of all have been building societies. Until 1997, the vast majority of the adult population had at least one savings account with a building society. Millions of people had mortgages from building societies. Most (but not all) of these customers were members with a share in the ownership of the organisation with whom they saved or from whom they borrowed.

Over the last decade or so, building societies have operated in an increasingly competitive world, facing challenges in their traditional areas of saving and lending as well as in new areas of financial activity which opened up after a change in the law in 1987 broadened the powers of building societies. To compete effectively, the larger societies embarked on programmes of modernisation, expanding their range of products, responding more rapidly to customers' demands, entering new fields and promoting themselves more aggressively.

But many societies lacked sufficient capital to make this transformation. Merging with other societies was one possible solution. Another route was to abandon their mutuality. For some societies, mutual status was becoming a handicap, because an organisation owned by its members cannot raise new capital from outsiders. By contrast, if a company wants to raise extra capital it can sell new shares to anyone.

If a mutual body decides to convert to become a company, it must first seek the consent of its members. Provided they agree to the conversion, the members' ownership rights must be bought out either for cash or by exchanging them for ownership rights (in other words, shares) in the new company. Abbey National was the first building society to shed its mutual status and become a bank in 1989. Suddenly, people who had viewed themselves solely as customers of a building society found that they had all along been unwitting owners of a valuable asset and were now delighted recipients of windfall shares which they could either keep or sell for cash. Around a quarter of the former members sold their shares immediately. The rest chose to hold on to their shares, many becoming direct share-owners for the first time.

It was clear that other building societies would follow suit, but not which ones or when. Many smaller building societies merged – this required members' consent but did not release any windfalls. Then, in May 1994, it was announced that the Cheltenham & Goucester would be taken over by Lloyds Bank the following year and that former members would receive a cash sum. At the end of 1994, it was the turn of the Halifax and Leeds Permanent building societies to announce their intended merger and subsequent conversion to company status.

The ball had finally started to roll. A new breed of building society investor sprang to life: the carpetbagger. Carpetbaggers invest, usually the minimum they can, in a savings account which confers membership rights, in the hope that the mutual organisation will convert to a company or be taken over by another company. The year 1997 was the best to date for carpetbaggers and long-term members alike, with several takeovers and four building societies and two insurance companies releasing windfall shares and/or cash on conversion.

Many of the remaining building societies are vociferous defenders of mutuality, pointing out that, without shareholders to feed, the mutual societies can pass on greater benefits to customers through higher savings rates and lower borrowing rates. Despite this, experts within the industry predict that the larger societies – those with assets of over £1 billion, say – will continue to be targets for the carpetbaggers and that further conversions are likely. A forecast from one of the banks, HSBC, predicted that, following on from the £35 billion of windfalls up to 1997, there could be a further £25 billion of windfalls from converting building societies and insurance companies over the next five years.

In general, around three-quarters of the recipients have so far held on to their new shares. As a direct result of conversion from mutual status to company, it is reckoned that the number of individuals holding shares direct climbed by several million in 1997 although the total number of small shareholders now in existence is uncertain.

The new shareholdings

At the time of writing, the full impact of the new shareholdings created by building societies had not been documented. Returning to the 9.5 million individual share-owners in existence at the end of 1996, a very large proportion held the shares of just one or two companies – likely to be privatisation issues.

The building society conversions will almost certainly have increased the prevalence of share-owners with only one or two holdings. This is worrying, because shares are by nature a risky

Table 1.2: Number of people receiving conversion shares in 1997

Date	Conversion	Number of people allocated shares
April 1997	Alliance & Leicester	2.2 million
May 1997	Colonial Mutual	250,000
June 1997	Halifax	7.6 million
June 1997	Norwich Union	2.9 million
July 1997	Woolwich	2.5 million
October 1997	Northern Rock	885,000

Table 1.3: Remaining building societies with assets over £1 billion

Building society	Total assets 1996/7 (in billions)
Nationwide	£40.453
Bradford & Bingley	£17.038
Britannia	£16.060
Yorkshire	£7.144
Birmingham Midshires*	£6.838
Portman	£4.011
Coventry	£3.741
Skipton	£3.259
Chelsea	£3.016
Leeds & Holbeck	£2.648
Derbyshire	£2.017
West Bromwich	£1.851
Norwich & Peterborough	£1.668
Cheshire	£1.641
Principality	£1.564
Newcastle	£1.560
Dunfermline	£1.126
Staffordshire	£1.060
Nottingham	£1.048

Source: Moneyfacts
* To be taken over by Royal Bank of Scotland in 1998

investment. Conventional wisdom says that the risk should be spread by holding the shares of at the very least half a dozen companies and probably more (see Chapters 8 and 9). Yet fewer than a fifth of share owners have a balanced portfolio.

The most popular companies, in terms of numbers of shareholders, are shown in Table 1.5. As expected, privatisation issues feature heavily.

Table 1.4: Number of share holdings, 1996

Number of companies in which shares are held	Percentage of shareholders
1	38%
2 to 3	28%
4 to 5	11%
6 to 10	11%
10 or more	8%
Not known	4%

Source: Proshare, *Individual share ownership facts and figures, 1997*

Table 1.5: Companies most popular with share owners, 1996/early 1997

Company	Number of ordinary shareholders
Abbey National	2,690,000
British Telecommunications	2,395,396
British Gas	1,670,275
Lloyds TSB	1,133,574
PowerGen	983,267
National Power	969,077
BAA	490,961
Scottish Hydro-Electric	441,547
British Petroleum	411,992
British Energy	390,000
Rolls-Royce	381,030
Railtrack	349,400
Marks & Spencer	307,600
Shell Transport & Trading	c. 300,000
Southern Electric	297,603
British Airways	c. 240,000
Thames Water	c. 240,000
Imperial Chemical Industries	223,444
British Steel	183,000
United Utilities	158,684
Eurotunnel/Eurotunnel SA	136,859

Source: Proshare, *Individual share ownership facts and figures, 1997*

Chapter 2

The role of shares in your financial planning

IN an investors' Utopia, all investments would earn you fantastic returns without your running any risks. The real world is very different, with a trade-off between risk and return. Invariably, you face a choice: play it safe but put up with a low return on your investment or savings, or go for a better return but accept some degree of risk.

Quite where you strike the balance depends on a variety of factors:

- what you are hoping to achieve through your savings and investments
- what other savings and investments you already have
- how easily you can replace or do without any money you lose
- whether you are comfortable with the idea of risk.

Types of investment risk

When people talk of 'risk' in the context of investment, they usually mean the risk of losing some or all of their money. But that is just one type of investment risk. There are several:

- **capital risk**: the possibility of losing some or all of your original capital
- **income risk**: on the one hand, if you invest for a variable income, that income might fall. On the other hand, if you invest for a fixed income, you may be locked in while incomes from competing investments are rising
- **inflation risk**: although your original capital may seem to be intact, its value in terms of what you can buy with it will fall if the return is not high enough to compensate you for the effect of rising prices.

One reason for giving shares a place in your financial planning is to overcome inflation risk, but this means taking on some degree of capital risk. Once again, it is a case of striking a balance between the various types of risk. The specific types of capital risk you run when investing in shares are looked at in more detail in Chapter 8.

Risk and return

Shares do not simply give you a means of out-running inflation. Historically, they have also turned in much higher returns than 'safer' investments (in other words, those that do not expose you to any capital risk, typically deposits, such as bank and building society accounts) – so much so that for many long-term investment aims the only way to achieve your goal is to accept the capital risk inherent in shares. Opting for safer investments simply would not produce high enough returns. But sometimes you just cannot afford to run the capital risk and must make do with the lower returns from safer investments.

Chart 2.1: Shares give higher returns over the long term

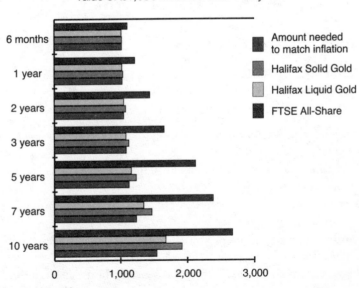

Value of £1,000 invested until 1 July 1997

Source: *Money Management*

A financial plan

Nearly everyone works towards financial goals. For example, money left over after meeting essential spending might be put into a savings account to go towards a future holiday or household project; if you can afford it, you might be paying a regular sum into a savings plan for your children's future use; and, if you are an employee, you are quite probably paying automatically into a pension scheme.

Without a formal plan, your saving and investing can be very haphazard, with the result that some goals may be only partially met and others overlooked. A proper financial plan forces you to clarify:

- your financial goals
- the resources you have available to meet your goals
- the priority you attach to each goal
- the most appropriate means for achieving your goals.

You can think of your goals as being a ladder with the most essential goals being the lowest rungs. The more resources you have available, the higher up the ladder you can climb. If your resources decline, you have to step down a few rungs of the ladder, abandoning some financial goals.

The rest of this chapter takes a whistle-stop tour through the process of financial planning to show how shares can be used to meet some of your goals. For a more in-depth look at this whole area, see *Be Your Own Financial Adviser,*★ also published by Which? Books.

Your financial goals

Since we are all individuals we might be expected to have different financial targets but, in practice, there are certain goals which are common to many people, some depending on the stage of life they have reached.

Everyone should have an emergency fund. This is a pool of money which can be drawn on at short notice to cope with the unexpected, such as urgent car or house repairs or perhaps a sudden opportunity to do something special. The size of the required fund will vary from person to person or family to family, but it is likely to be around £1,000 as a minimum.

Everyone should have some protection against loss of earnings through illness or becoming disabled. The state provides only limited

Chart 2.2: Achieving your financial goals

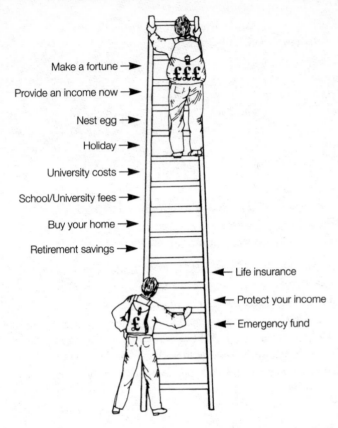

- Make a fortune →
- Provide an income now →
- Nest egg →
- Holiday →
- University costs →
- School/University fees →
- Buy your home →
- Retirement savings →

- ← Life insurance
- ← Protect your income
- ← Emergency fund

help if you cannot work. If you are an employee, you might have cover through your job. If you are self-employed, you will have to organise your own protection, for example, by taking out permanent health insurance.

Everyone should also look ahead to retirement and start to save as early as possible for their pension.

Anyone who has dependants – such as a wife or husband or children still at home – should have, as a goal, protecting them financially in the event of death. Again, employees often have life cover provided as part of the rewards for their work. If you are self-employed, you need to arrange your own life insurance. Even if you do not work, you should consider insurance, if dependants left behind would need to pay for cleaning and childcare, say, which you used to provide.

Another common goal is owning your own home. This is often a particular preoccupation of young families.

Resources and priorities

Clearly, if your funds were unlimited, you would have no problem in meeting all your financial goals. But, when income and capital are restricted, you have to make choices. This means attaching priorities to your goals. Some – an emergency fund and, say, life cover – may seem essential. Others, such as retirement planning, may seem less important when you are young but are likely to have a higher priority as you get older.

Different people will have different priorities, but Chart 2.2 shows a fairly typical ranking. (Interestingly, insurance against loss of earnings through illness is often given a lower priority than logically it should have: it is costly, and people mistakenly believe that the state will look after them, quite apart from taking the 'it will never happen to me' view of life.)

Achieving your goals

Having established your goals, you have to decide on the best way to realise them. Although a vast range of financial products is available, the nature of the goal sometimes limits you to a fairly narrow choice. For example, an emergency fund must be reasonably accessible and you need to be certain that its value is fairly stable. An instant access bank or building society account is ideal. A notice account would also be suitable, if you could fund an immediate financial crisis using a credit card, say.

But shares would be totally unsuitable for an emergency fund because, at the time you needed your money, you might find that the stock market had slumped with the effect that your shares had fallen in value. Even worse, the company whose shares you hold might go bust, leaving you with worthless shares and no emergency fund to fall back on.

By contrast, when it comes to retirement planning, you are investing for growth over a long period. If you were hoping that a building society account would eventually produce a generous pension, you would need to set aside very large sums indeed. You can reduce the amount of capital you need to put into your pension investments if you opt for shares, or investments linked to shares, since – assuming historical trends continue – the performance of shares will be far superior to the performance of deposit accounts. With long-term investment, it does not matter that the share prices can go down as well as up, because you can ride out any slumps and wait for the stock market to bounce back. Only as you get near to the point of retirement does it become important to switch to investments without capital risk.

With most medium- to long-term financial goals, there is no single right or wrong solution to meet the goal. Instead, there will be many options. Which you choose often comes down to your personal attitude towards risk. Some people are very averse to risk and reluctant to expose their capital at all. If you would lose sleep worrying about the stock market, direct investment in shares is not going to be a good choice for you. This does not necessarily mean avoiding share-based investments altogether. There are halfway houses – for example, with-profits funds and guaranteed equity products – that let you enjoy some

---

Shares – a toe in the water

If shares seem too risky but you are attracted towards stock market returns, a medium-risk option would be to invest on a with-profits basis. You do this by taking out a **with-profits insurance policy**. The policy guarantees you a certain minimum return which will be paid out either at the end of the policy term (for example, five, ten, twenty-five years, depending on the policy you choose) or in the event of your death. Each year, bonuses (called 'reversionary' bonuses) are added to your policy. Once added, the bonuses cannot be taken away, so the value of your policy steadily grows. At the end of the term, a terminal bonus is also added which can be substantial, perhaps amounting to a third or even a half of the whole policy value.

The size of the bonuses is linked to the profitability of the insurer and is determined by a host of different factors, such as the cost of getting new business, the amount paid out in claims, whether there are shareholders to be paid a dividend, the size of reserves, and the insurer's attitude towards smoothing bonus levels from year to year. But the major factor behind the bonuses will be how well premium income has grown when invested on the stock market and in other investments. In this way, with-profits

---

of the returns from the stock market without exposing you to all the risks – see Box.

You do not necessarily need to look for a single product to meet your financial goal. By mixing products, you can often strike an acceptable balance of risk and reward. For example, if you are investing for growth, you could put all your money into shares. But, if you want to guard against a general slump in the stock market, it would be a good idea to split your capital and put some in shares, and some into other types of investment, such as British Government stocks, which generally tend to do well when shares are in the doldrums. Similarly, if you are investing to provide an income now, you cannot simply choose high-income products. Usually, you will need to ensure that the value of your capital is maintained so that it will go on providing an income in the future. Moreover, if the income is to continue over a long period, you need at least to keep pace with inflation.

policies give you some of the return from shares without exposing you to all the risks.

Another possibility is to invest in the so-called **'guaranteed equity investments'**. These are set up in various ways but they generally make the same promise: you invest for a given period – generally five years – after which you get back your original investment plus some proportion of the growth in the stock market (usually measured as the change in the FTSE 100 Index). Even if the stock market falls, you are still guaranteed the return of your original capital, so you cannot lose – or can you?

These investments are not so good as they might seem at first sight. You are protected from the downside risk of shares, but you pay a price. The return on shares is made up of two parts: capital gain and income. Although a guaranteed equity investment lets you share in the capital growth of shares, you do not share in the income. And do you really need this protection at all? Although share values fall as well as rise in the short term, over the long term they tend to grow, reflecting the increasing value, at least in line with inflation, of the underlying businesses. Over most five-year periods, a direct investment in a balanced portfolio of shares will have increased in value rather than have fallen.

Having fun

Not all financial goals are driven by sense and responsibility: investment can also be pure fun. Shares and other stock market investments are ideal vehicles for speculation. 'Playing the market' gives you the pleasure of pitting your wits against the professionals, of spotting the opportunities others have overlooked and of taking enormous risks which, if they pay off... Of course, it is in the nature of speculation that gambles do not always pay off. Fun money should be money which you can afford to lose.

Chart 2.3: Matching investments to your financial goals

Financial goal	Main characteristics required to meet goal	Examples of financial products which could be suitable
Emergency fund	• You can get your money back instantly (or at short notice if you have access to credit) • No capital risk	• Bank or building society instant access account or notice account • National Savings investment account
Replacement earnings if you could not work because of illness or disability	Definitely available whenever need arises	• Sick pay scheme through your job • Permanent health insurance
Lump sum and/or replacement income for dependants if you were to die	Definitely available whenever need arises	Life insurance through your job or arranged privately
Adequate income in retirement	• Good growth prospects • Must beat or keep pace with inflation • Moderate capital risk acceptable (except as retirement draws near) but cannot afford to lose all capital	• Pension scheme through job • Personal pension scheme • Unit trusts, investment trusts, spread of shares held in a PEP or, from 1999, in an ISA

Financial goal	Main characteristics required to meet goal	Examples of financial products which could be suitable
Purchase of your own home	• Means of spreading cost of purchase (unless you are a cash buyer)	• Repayment mortgage • Interest-only mortgage linked to an investment – e.g. investment-type insurance or PEP/ISA
Financing school or university fees and costs	• Money needs to be available at set time in the future • Must beat or keep pace with school fees inflation • Moderate capital risk acceptable while fund builds up. Capacity for capital risk reduces as fees and costs become payable	• With-profits funds • Unit trusts, possibly switching to deposit-based investments as fees and costs become payable
Short-term savings – e.g. for a holiday, home improvements, etc.	• Access to money at some set time • No capital risk	• Bank and building society notice and term accounts • National Savings investment account • Local authority bonds • Range of investments held in an ISA (from April 1999)
Long-term investment – e.g. to top up retirement income, build up nest egg	• Good growth prospects • Moderate capital risk acceptable	• National Savings certificates • British Government stocks • Corporate bonds • Unit trusts, investment trusts, spread of shares held in a PEP or, from 1999, in an ISA • Unit trusts, investment trusts, spread of shares outside a PEP/ISA

Financial goal	Main characteristics required to meet goal	Examples of financial products which could be suitable
Providing an income now	• Reliable income • Must beat or keep pace with inflation over longer term • Maintain or enhance value of capital to ensure future income	• National Savings income bonds and pensioners bonds • British Government stocks • Permanent income-bearing shares • Corporate bonds • Preference shares • Unit trusts • Investment trusts • Spread of blue chip shares • Annuities • Range of investments held in an ISA from April 1999
Chance to make a fortune	• Possibility of substantial windfall profits • Capital risk acceptable	• Premium bonds (no capital risk with these) • Venture Capital Trusts • Shares in new venture companies, e.g. via Enterprise Investment Scheme • Penny shares • National Lottery • Traded options • Futures contracts

Chapter 3

The London Stock Exchange

SHARES are bought and sold through stock exchanges. In the UK, the main exchange is the London Stock Exchange (LSE), more formally entitled the International Stock Exchange of the United Kingdom and Republic of Ireland. This is made up of a main market, called the Official List, and a junior market, the Alternative Investment Market (AIM), for small, young and growing companies which do not have the required track record or funds to seek a full listing. AIM started up in 1995, largely replacing the role of an earlier junior market, the Unlisted Securities Market (USM). The LSE now provides a highly organised and stringently regulated market for shares and other stocks, but it evolved from very informal beginnings.

The birth of shares in the UK

The earliest English companies were set up in the sixteenth century to explore the possibilities of sea-borne trade with the New World and the Far East. The latter posed a particular challenge. Eastern luxuries

Table 3.1: The London Stock Exchange

Statistics for 1996	Main market		AIM
	UK shares	International shares	
Number of companies listed	2,171	533	252
Average number of deals each day	43,159	18,087	727
Average value of shares traded each day	£943.4 million	£797.1 million	£21.6 million

Source: London Stock Exchange

29

had been reaching Europe for centuries via a tortuous combination of sea and overland routes. In Europe, this lucrative trade was dominated by the Italians. By the end of the fifteenth century, the Portuguese, spurred on by the possibility of vast profits, had successfully completed an all-sea voyage to India and back via the Cape of Good Hope. But there was a feeling that there must be a shorter route to the East via Northern waters – at that time, the vastness of the polar ice cap was unimagined.

The very first 'joint stock company' was founded in 1553 under the headship of Sebastian Cabot, a veteran explorer. Cabot had failed to find either a North-West passage to the East or a route to the South Seas along the Rio de la Plata in Uruguay. In his old age, he became determined to see a North-East passage opened up.

A company was set up to raise money to provision three ships, optimistically named the Bona Speranza, Bona Confidenza and Edward Bonaventura. Their task was to search out a North-East passage and return with goods from the East which would provide the shareholders with their profits. The sum of £6,000 was raised through the sale of £25 shares and the ships set out on 10 May 1553.

In the event, the ships were separated in a storm. Two found shelter in a frozen bay on the Northern tip of Scandinavia, where all hands died from cold and starvation. The third ship, captained by Richard Chancellor, succeeded in reaching Archangel. The ship's officers then made a long sleigh journey across the frozen wastes of Russia to Moscow to meet the Tsar, Ivan the Terrible.

At that time, the Russians had their own trading links with the East via the Caspian Sea but no access to North European trade, having fallen out with the German Hanseatic League. Chancellor was able to exploit the situation and strike up a valuable trading agreement. Although he had not reached the Far East, he returned home a hero because of this deal, which led to the formation of the Muscovy Company.

In the beginning, companies issued shares on a voyage-by-voyage basis, with shareholders either being paid off completely on the return of the ships or closing their losses if the venture failed. One of the most famous of the early companies was the East India Company. Although established in 1600, it did not issue permanent share capital until 1692.

In 1694, King William III came to the stock market to raise money to finance war against France. The Bank of England organised an issue of loan stock which was readily taken up by the public. This became a regular way of financing government activities and, by 1711, the national debt had grown to some £9 million.

The South Sea Bubble and other madness

At this point, another raison d'être for the company arose – that of gaining a monopoly over some area of trade. The South Sea Company was formed to take over the national debt in return for being granted a monopoly over trading with South America and the Pacific region. This company caught the public imagination for several reasons: there was a genuine belief that excellent profits were to be made from South Seas trade; at the outset it was possible to buy government stocks for around £55, substantially less than their par value of £100, and to exchange them at par for stock in the new company, producing instant paper profits; there were relatively few opportunities for equity investment; and as demand for stock outstripped supply, the share price rose strongly, further whetting the appetite of investors.

Over the next few years, the shares were buoyant and the issued capital was twice increased, but it was in 1719 that the share price really began to take off on a suggestion that the company should take over the whole outstanding national debt of £31 million. In 1720, an Act of Parliament was passed to enable this. Demand for the shares soared. The South Sea Company issued further shares, some in partly paid form, which meant that investors had initially only to pay a deposit of as little as a tenth of the full share price. The increase in share price was therefore magnified into a huge gain on the amount of money actually invested.

Unfortunately, the company itself was spectacularly unsuccessful at trading and, inevitably, the bubble had to burst. In September 1720, the share price plummeted from a peak of £1,050 for each £100 par of stock. Those investors who got out before the crash, including the Prince of Wales, made a fortune. But many more, left with worthless stock and debts for money they had borrowed to invest, faced financial ruin.

The South Sea Company was not the only 'bubble company' during this time. Enthusiastic investors ploughed money into all manner of dubious ventures, including companies whose only published aim was to pursue 'an undertaking which shall in due time be revealed', expecting the shares to rocket. Between September 1719 and August

1720, there were 190 new issues. It has been estimated that, in 1720, the value of money invested in bubble companies was around £500 million, which was equivalent to five times all the cash in Europe. Given the fantastic scale of the speculative madness, it is not surprising that the government passed the Bubble Act in 1721, which banned the formation of joint stock companies other than by royal charter (which was costly and difficult to obtain). Shares, therefore, became relatively scarce until the repeal of the Act in 1825.

Nineteenth-century industrial expansion

Shares came back into their own with the growth of the UK's industrial base in the nineteenth century. Great ventures, such as the building of the railways, could not be financed by individuals. This led to a boom in the sale of railway shares to the public in the 1840s. The ability to form companies and get the public to subscribe for shares was an important factor in helping the industrial revolution to gather pace.

From that time onwards, shares have become a widely used method of raising finance for business ventures. Their popularity with investors is in large part due to the existence of the 'secondary market' where shares can be sold after they have been issued. This allows investors to turn their investment back into cash easily and pocket any profits by selling their shares to someone else.

The origins of the Stock Exchange

New issues of shares in the early companies were bought through brokers, who generally traded in commodities too. Existing shares could also be sold and bought through the brokers – an important facility, bearing in mind that sea voyages sometimes lasted many years and the original investor might not be able to wait so long to see a return on the investment.

Commercial brokers of all types congregated in and around the Royal Exchange in the heart of London. As the volume of trade in shares increased rapidly in the 1690s, specialist stockbrokers developed. By all accounts they were a rowdy bunch: having been banned from the Royal Exchange, they began to meet in the coffee houses in Change Alley, in particular at Jonathan's and Garraway's.

In 1762, a group of brokers tried unsuccessfully to get exclusive use of Jonathan's. They then formed a subscription club, raising enough money to buy their own coffee shop, New Jonathan's, in nearby Threadneedle Street. This continued to be a subscription club, with members being charged sixpence a day entrance. In 1773, the members of New Jonathan's voted to change its name to the Stock Exchange Subscription Room.

The Stock Exchange was born. However, the premises were rather small and, amid some resistance from the owners of the coffee shop, the decision was taken to move to a larger site. A further subscription raised £20,000, which was used to take over derelict buildings in Capel Court in 1801. This has remained the site of the London Stock Exchange ever since.

The Stock Exchange started as an exclusive club and remained largely unchanged until the 1980s. Members were individuals, although in due course they joined together to form partnerships. Dealing was carried out at the Stock Exchange premises. Those with particular types of stocks to trade would tend to congregate in specialist groups, while others would mill around getting quotes and identifying the best deals before striking a bargain.

As the early trade in shares developed, brokers who dealt in shares were meant to be licensed by the Lord Mayor of London and the Aldermen of the City. This rule applied to all agents dealing in commodities and the like. To be licensed, brokers were meant to be of good behaviour and were supposed to carry a silver medal as evidence of the licence. Jobbers, who were dealers buying and selling shares on their own account, did not have to be licensed. Whether licensed or not, all could be members of the developing Stock Exchange.

In general, an investor did not deal direct with a jobber but went to a broker who would act as agent. The separation of the broking function from jobbing was a useful protection for investors, removing the possibility of a conflict of interest between the customer's business and the broker's own. But, at this early stage, brokers could also act as jobbers. Although there was a tendency to adopt one role or the other, it was possible for brokers to switch to being jobbers, and vice versa.

Later on, the government imposed a new system of licensing and introduced a number of rules, including a ban on brokers acting as jobbers, a ceiling on the commission that brokers could charge and a requirement to record details of all deals. This attempt to regulate stockbroking was not particularly effective and it is probable that there were many unlicensed brokers and other breaches of the rules.

Tightening the rules

Brokers' licences finally disappeared in 1886. By then, the market in foreign shares, particularly South African and American stocks, was booming. There was a great deal of trading after hours and often brokers would in effect act as jobbers, striking up their own deals away from the Stock Exchange trading floor. Similarly, jobbers actively touted their prices outside the Stock Exchange, trying to drum up business in a similar way to the brokers. This was a chaotic period for the Stock Exchange which, after much debate, resulted in the adoption in 1908 of a new rule book and a tougher approach to rule enforcement.

The 1908 rule book for the first time prohibited jobbers from dealing direct with investors and banned brokers from setting share prices. Stock Exchange members had to declare whether they were brokers or jobbers and were not allowed to switch without the consent of the Stock Exchange's ruling committee. Some jobbers tried to evade the rules and deal direct with the public through a 'dummy broker' (either a co-operative real broker or an artificial split of the firm into a jobbing and a broking side). In 1912, minimum commission scales were introduced, which made deals through dummy brokers unprofitable and so 'single capacity' – the division of jobber from broker – was finally imposed.

A new exchange

The volume of share trading increased enormously as the century progressed, in part due to the increasing importance of pension funds and insurance companies. Yet the structure of the Stock Exchange and of share dealing remained largely unchanged until the mid-1980s.

In 1961, it was decided to demolish the old Stock Exchange buildings and erect a new tower block with a trading floor and extensive office space. The new building was opened in 1972. A glazed public gallery overlooked the trading area, revealing a hectic scene which, at that time, seemed to be the very essence of the stock market. Jobbers operated from hexagonal stands, giving their prices on request to brokers who busily milled around the trading floor. A broker would not reveal whether he (or, very occasionally, she) was a buyer or a seller and the jobber would quote his spread of prices for the given size of deal. Having toured the jobbers' pitches, the broker might refer back to the office trading desks via the telephones at the side of the trading floor. If the deal was to go ahead, the broker would return to the jobber who gave the best price. A verbal agreement would be made and both jobber and broker would make a rough note of the bargain to be settled up later. A small cinema attached to the public gallery made periodic showings of the Stock Exchange film entitled *My Word is My Bond*, the motto of the Stock Exchange ('*dictum meum pactum*').

'Big Bang'

This gentlemanly way of doing business came under increasing strain during the 1970s and 1980s. The London Stock Exchange faced intense competition from foreign stock markets, especially after the abolition of exchange controls in 1979, which enabled the big institutional investors to invest abroad more easily. Overseas brokers were not hampered by minimum commission charges and could aggressively undercut London brokers on price. Moreover, many stocks quoted in London were also listed on stock exchanges abroad, particularly on the New York exchange, so London could be bypassed altogether.

The Stock Exchange had also fallen under the scrutiny of the Office of Fair Trading (OFT) which, in 1978, started a challenge against the Stock Exchange rule book under restrictive practices legislation, which had recently been extended to cover services. The exclusion of non-members from the Stock Exchange and the minimum commission agreement (deemed to be an example of price-fixing) were among the main targets.

The final nail in the coffin of tradition was the pace of technological change. Advances in computer capacity, information technology and telecommunications meant that business could be conducted more rapidly and cheaply via electronic means and could be carried on just as easily with a financial centre many thousands of miles away as it could through the domestic stock market. Trading was becoming global. But it was also becoming round-the-clock, which meant there was still a need for a first-rate European market to handle dealing while New York and Tokyo slept.

The Stock Exchange was determined to secure for itself the role of European leg in the global market, but it was hampered by its own rule book. In particular, the rules restricted membership to individuals and did not allow outsiders to own a stake in the member firms, yet traditional partnerships of jobbers and brokers did not, on their own, have the necessary capital to compete on an international basis. New sources of substantial capital were essential.

The Stock Exchange would probably have taken steps sooner to relax its rule book had it not been preoccupied with the OFT's challenge. The Exchange was forced into a defensive position and could not be seen to weaken. The case slowly dragged on and, eventually, in July 1983, the Stock Exchange and Cecil Parkinson, the then secretary of state for trade, reached an out-of-court agreement: the OFT charges would be dropped, provided the Stock Exchange reformed its most restrictive rules by dropping the minimum commission agreement and allowing outsiders to become members. The Stock Exchange was given three years to implement these reforms.

It soon became clear that the abolition of fixed commissions and the aggressive competition that would be unleashed would bring about even more fundamental changes. Jobbers had already been forced to respond to the chill winds of competition in order to stop orders bypassing London and going through overseas markets instead. They had cut their margins (the spread between selling and buying prices which provided the jobbers' earnings) to compete more keenly on price. And, realising that to stay in business they needed more capital to act as a buffer against the risks of market-making, jobbing firms had been merging to form larger partnerships. But the number of jobbing firms was reaching such a low level that it was no longer certain that a competitive market could be maintained in all shares. With the abolition of fixed commissions, brokers too would see their profit margins squeezed.

It seemed unlikely that the market could continue to support both specialised jobbing firms and the brokers acting as middlemen. The only solution was to abandon single capacity (the division between jobbers and brokers), which previously had been so fiercely upheld. Brokers would be able to act as market-makers. But, to do that, they would need additional capital to finance their portfolios of shares and to cover the risks of trading on their own account – yet another incentive to allow outsiders to join the Stock Exchange.

Big Bang – the day the Stock Exchange was reformed – came officially on 27 October 1986. But by then the stock market had already changed dramatically. In 1982, the Stock Exchange had taken the pre-emptive step of allowing outsiders to own up to 29.9 per cent of a member firm. This was increased to 100 per cent in March 1986. Foreign banks and dealing houses, British High Street banks and merchant banks were all hungry to take a slice of the action, and the largest jobbing and broking firms quickly passed into their hands, creating large financial conglomerates able to carry on all aspects of City business. Where conflicts of interest were possible within these new giants, 'Chinese walls' – artificial barriers between departments – were erected to prevent sensitive information from passing into the wrong hands.

Big Bang was also important as the day on which the Stock Exchange turned on its screen-based information system, Stock Exchange Automated Quotations (SEAQ). Instead of brokers physically trailing around the jobbers' pitches to collect quotes, they could now call up the full range of quotes for any listed share on a computer screen at a desk. For a time, the Stock Exchange trading floor remained open, but dealers and brokers quickly switched to dealing via their telephones and computer screens and the trading floor fell quiet.

The electronic age

At the start of 1997, SEAQ was still the backbone of Stock Exchange trading. SEAQ screens carried the prices of over 2,000 securities direct into the offices of brokers and institutional investors both in the UK and around the globe. These are current prices, showing bid and offer from all the market-makers dealing in the particular stock, with the best prices automatically highlighted. Dealing is either by phone or direct through member firms' computer systems. A further 500 securities listed on foreign exchanges are quoted on SEAQ International.

On 20 October 1997, the Stock Exchange took another major step into the electronic age with the introduction of the Stock Exchange Electronic Trading Service (SETS). This replaced SEAQ as the main way of trading in the shares of the UK's major companies, initially those which comprise the FTSE 100 Index, later to be extended to a further 250 stocks. The London Stock Exchange has been relatively slow to embrace electronic trading. Several exchanges abroad have already gone down this route and the big institutional investors, for which exchanges compete most hotly, have shown a preference for this method of dealing.

Fundamental to SETS is a shift from quotation-driven dealing to order-book dealing. The dealers' computer screens show an order book for each share. Buyers and sellers enter their desired purchases and sales, complete with the prices they are seeking, into the electronic order book. SETS then automatically matches buyers to sellers, enabling deals to be transacted completely electronically. Once teething problems have been resolved, this should dramatically cut costs, because there is no market-maker involved. It has been estimated that, as a result, the spread between buying and selling prices could halve.

The impact of SETS on the private investor is as yet unclear. The majority of deals done by small share owners will not be traded through SETS, which is restricted to deals of 500 or more shares where they are priced at £5 or more each, or deals of 1,000 shares where they are priced at less than £5. (The reason for this is to stop the system becoming clogged up with a high volume of very small orders.) Instead of going to the order book, your broker will contact a 'retail service provider' – basically a market maker – who must quote the best prices from the order book. In this way, it is hoped that small investors, as well as the large institutions, will benefit from the keener prices possible under SETS.

Some pundits are pessimistic. They argue that small trades are inevitably less profitable and that it is only a matter of time before small share orders have to accept wider prices than they would under SETS. But the Stock Exchange is confident that the system will work for small investors and is closely monitoring the situation. If it does look as if small investors are getting a raw deal, the Stock Exchange has contingency plans, in the first instance, to bring small deals within the order book system and, in the longer run, to set up a parallel order book for small trading if that proves necessary.

Another fear is that small investors may be unable to deal when the market is busy. SETS will match bargains very rapidly and details of most deals struck will be posted on the system instantaneously. This means that the market will move very fast when trading is heavy. Some experts have said that it will move so fast that it will be impossible for the retail service providers to give up-to-date quotes. The result is that small investors may either have to deal blind or not deal at all. These fears may be overstated – only time will tell.

In the early days, another problem emerged. At certain times – especially early in the morning when many private client brokers like to carry out their customers' orders – trading has tended to be very 'thin'. With little activity in the market, the spreads between buying and selling prices have been much wider than usual. It is to be hoped that such problems will be ironed out once SETS 'beds in'.

The SEAQ system continues for shares outside the order book system which, although due to expand, is unlikely to be appropriate for shares which are not traded frequently. Electronic advances have also had a great impact on the way in which share deals are settled. For more about this aspect, see Chapter 4.

The Stock Exchange rivals

For centuries, the London Stock Exchange has been dominant in the UK but, for most of its existence, it has not been the only stock exchange available to investors. In the nineteenth and early twentieth centuries, more than 20 provincial stock exchanges operated around the UK. These were eventually merged into the London Stock Exchange in 1973.

With the globalisation of markets and the advance of technology, London has had to compete with stock exchanges in other countries, particularly the New York Stock Exchange and the US NASDAQ (National Association of Security Dealers Automated Quotation system) exchange, but also with rivals closer to home, in Frankfurt and Amsterdam, for instance. There are also exchanges which span across national borders, such as EASDAQ (European Association of Security Dealers Automated Quotation system), a pan-European exchange so far dominated by high-technology stocks.

The Stock Exchange also faces competition closer to home. In 1995, Tradepoint (itself a company listed on the AIM) was set up to provide an alternative UK stock exchange and from the start it has used electronic order-driven trading. However, Tradepoint has so far failed to capture the volume of trade it needs to break even. At the time of writing, it had just completed a reorganisation which it hoped would boost its trade to a profitable level over the next two years.

Chapter 4

How to buy and sell shares

FOR many people, their first experience of acquiring shares is through a new issue when a state concern is privatised or a building society converts to a bank. This is a relatively simple process which does not involve a stockbroker or any dealing charges. If you have held the shares for a time, the business of selling them or of buying others may seem something of a mystery, and a particular problem, if your shareholdings are fairly small, is how to keep down the costs of buying and selling.

Stockbrokers' services

Unless you are buying newly issued shares, you will have to deal through a stockbroker or other financial adviser (who in turn will have to use a stockbroker). Stockbrokers are middlemen who act as your agent. They may be traditional broking firms but, these days, are often departments or subsidiaries of banks and building societies. Before you can start to buy or sell, you will usually have to register with a broker. This is a simple process which involves providing a few details about yourself. The broker may run a check on your creditworthiness at this stage.

Once you have registered, you are ready to give your instructions for specific deals. Depending on the service, you might do this in person (for example, at a High Street branch), by post, by fax, over the Internet or, most commonly, by phone.

In general, your broker will deal for you 'at best' – i.e. if you are a buyer, the broker will secure the lowest price, and if you are a seller, the highest price. Your broker might allow you to set a 'limit', which is a price above which you will not buy or below which you will not sell. Typically, the limit holds for 24 hours, but some brokers will accept a limit for longer periods, although there may be a charge.

Once you have placed your order, your broker sets to work. Your order may be handled in one of three ways.

- If you are buying shares included in the FTSE 100 Index (see page 94) and your order is reasonably large, it will be dealt with through the order book under the trading system known as SETS (see page 37). The broker will feed into a computer the shares you wish to buy or sell, the size of your deal, the pricing instruction (for example, 'at best') and the time limit after which the order is to lapse if it has not been met. The computer system then automatically matches your deal with other trades on offer. For example, if you want to buy 1,000 Unilever shares at best, the system will match you to the seller(s) of Unilever asking for the lowest price. If you are selling 1,000 Unilever shares at best, the system matches you to buyer(s) offering the highest price. All deals through the order book must be settled within five days (due to be reduced to three days at some time in 1998).

- If you are buying FTSE 100 shares but your trade is relatively small (fewer than 500 shares where they are priced at £5 or more each, or fewer than 1,000 shares where they are priced at less than £5 each), or you want longer than five days (three days from 1998) in which to settle, your deal will be handled 'away from the order book'. Your broker will go to a 'retail service provider' (basically, a market maker) who will buy or sell your shares at the best price you would have got had you been eligible to deal through the order book.

- If the shares are not included in the FTSE 100 Index, SETS does not apply. Instead, your broker will phone up one or more market makers who will quote their best buying and selling prices for those shares and the quantity in which you are trading. Your broker will then strike a deal with whichever market maker gives the best quote.

(At the time of writing, SETS has only just started up and the Stock Exchange has said that order book trading will be extended from the FTSE 100 shares to the next 250 shares in due course.)

Your broker sends you a contract note confirming the deal and showing the amount due to be paid or due to be received. The contract note is your proof of sale or purchase. Keep it safely, as you may need to refer to it for tax purposes (see Chapter 5). If you have bought shares and have opted to receive a share certificate, this will be sent to you by the registrar of the company in which you have invested. In theory, the certificate could arrive within a few days but, in practice, it often takes longer. This is a nuisance if you want to sell the shares again: although it is not essential to have the share certificate, most brokers will probably be unwilling to deal for you without it. This problem is avoided if you opt for your broker to act as your nominee (see page 48) or if you are able to register the shares in your own name electronically (see page 51).

How much you pay for the dealing service varies from broker to broker and depends also on the type of service you choose. There are four options:

- execution-only service
- execution and advice
- portfolio management
- financial planning.

Execution-only

An execution-only service (also called a dealing-only service) is the most basic and cheapest way to buy and sell shares. In its simplest form, the broker just carries out your instructions without offering any comment or advice on what or when or for how much you should buy or sell. In practice, many execution-only services offer information (albeit falling short of advice), which can range from current prices to reports on individual companies and markets.

Not all execution-only services are comprehensive. Some of the cheapest only sell for you; they do not buy. With some, there are limitations on the range of shares in which you can deal – e.g. only privatisation stocks or FTSE 100 shares.

The cheapest execution-only services are often postal. The snag with these is that you do not know precisely when your purchase or sale will be made, nor at what price. But even a phone-based service will not necessarily allow you to deal instantly, because some services group together lots of smaller deals and just trade three or four times a day, instead of dealing immediately you place your order. The best execution services put you directly in touch with dealers and trade instantly.

Just a few brokers run High Street operations where you can walk in and deal immediately on production of a share certificate or payment. The largest brokers of this type are run by the High Street banks. In the USA, dealing over the Internet is commonplace. In the UK, Internet dealing has yet to take off in any big way, but you can send orders to a broker (as opposed to linking direct to the dealing systems) through the Internet using the dealing gateways available through ESI★ and Infotrade.★

Some execution-only brokers offer you a choice of services. Typically, there will be a standard service, which is appropriate if you deal only occasionally, plus one or more services aimed at investors who trade more frequently. The latter usually have lower dealing charges for each transaction (e.g. a lower percentage rate, lower minimum commission or even a flat-rate dealing charge) but may include a one-off or annual joining fee. Which type of service will suits you depends on how often you expect to buy and sell and the usual size of your deals.

Execution-only services are very straightforward and particularly appropriate if you want to make a one-off sale of a fairly small holding of privatisation issues or former building society stocks. They are also a good choice if you have the time, inclination and confidence to carry out your own research, tracking and share selection.

Table 4.1: Example of execution-only dealing commissions

Broker	Type of service*	Commission	Examples
The Share Centre	Standard telephone/Internet service	For FTSE 100 and privatisation shares, 1% of value of deal, minimum £2.50 for purchases, £7.50 for sales	£5 to buy or £7.50 to sell £500 of shares £10 to buy or sell £1,000 £50 to buy or sell £5,000
		Non-privatisation shares outside FTSE 100 charged at 1.25%, minimum £2.50 for purchases and £11.25 for sales	£6.25 to buy or £11.25 to sell £500 of shares £12.50 to buy or sell £1,000 £62.50 to buy or sell £5,000
		Deals over £5,000, quotations on request	

* Your shares must be held in a nominee account – see page 48.
Source: The Share Centre

Execution and advice

Execution and advice is the traditional stockbroking service. It generally costs a little more than execution-only, but is worthwhile if you need some guidance and particularly if you are new to investing in shares.

When you first get in touch with the broker, you will be asked for certain details, including your investment aims and your attitude towards risk. This provides the broker with the framework he or she needs to be able to give you suitable advice. Check what form the advice takes, as it varies from broker to broker. It could be informed comment on your intentions or advice on request; the firm might take the initiative in contacting you with suggestions; you might receive published reports about companies, sectors, the Budget, and so on.

Table 4.2: Example of execution and advice dealing commissions

Broker	Commission		Examples
James Brearley & Sons	First £7,000:	1.65%	£22 to buy or £16.50 to sell
	Next £8,000	0.6%	£1,000 of shares
	Excess	0.5%	£82.50 for £5,000
	Minimum £22 on purchases, £6 on sales		£133.50 for £10,000

Source: APCIMS Directory

Portfolio management

With a portfolio management service, your broker takes over all the administration of your portfolio. The service comes in two forms: advisory and discretionary.

If you opt for an **advisory service**, you still make the decisions about what shares to hold, when to buy and sell and so on, but with the benefit of advice from your stockbroker. The broker will not make any trades without first seeking your approval.

With a **discretionary service**, the broker takes over the complete running of your portfolio, making the decisions about which stocks to hold, buying and selling and so on. This will be done within the framework of your particular circumstances and overall investment aims, and only after completion of a detailed 'fact find' as required under the Financial Services Act. For example, if you needed an income from your portfolio of shares, your broker would select shares partly to provide a good stream of dividend income now and partly for capital growth to ensure a continuing income in the future. As the performance of individual shares alters and stock market conditions change, the broker might adjust the shareholdings in the portfolio but always with the same financial objectives in mind.

The advantage of a discretionary service is that your broker has a free hand to take advantage of good opportunities as they arise. Since markets can move very fast, the opportunities might be missed if the broker had first to get in touch with you. You can limit your broker's discretion by specifying, for example, particular types of shares (e.g. tobacco stocks) that you do not want to hold, certain shares in your portfolio that you do not want sold, the maximum size of any one holding, and so on.

With both advisory and discretionary services, you receive regular portfolio valuations and reviews.

The style of charging for portfolio management services varies greatly from one firm to another. Most make some form of annual charge, either at a flat rate or as a percentage of the value of your portfolio. This is usually on top of dealing charges each time shares are bought or sold, which may be levied at the normal rate or at a special flat rate. A few make no regular charge, but you do of course pay dealing charges, sometimes at a rate that is higher than that for the normal dealing and advice service.

Table 4.3: Example of portfolio management charges

Broker	Type of service	Management charge		Examples
P. H. Pope & Son	Discretionary	0.25% a year, minimum £200 plus normal dealing commissions of:		£200 a year for £80,000 portfolio
		First £7,000	1.65%	£250 for £100,000
		Excess	0.5%	plus dealing
		Minimum	£20	charges

Source: APCIMS Directory

Portfolio management is usually suitable only if you have a sizeable sum to invest. Many brokers specify a minimum amount for share portfolio management, for example £25,000, £50,000 or £100,000. Some accept smaller portfolios but for investment in unit trusts and investment trusts, rather than direct in shares.

A special case of portfolio management is where a broker acts as a manager of a personal equity plan (PEP). Unlike unit or investment trust PEPs run by trust management companies, brokers usually levy specific charges for the single company PEPs or self-select PEPs they manage. The nature and scale of charges is generally different from those applying to normal portfolio management and usually includes charges associated with the running of a nominee account (see page 48).

Financial planning

As well as trading in stocks and shares, many brokers offer a full financial planning service. Following a detailed fact-find, the broker can help you to build an overall strategy for achieving your financial objectives, which typically will not be just investment objectives, but might also include protecting your family, ensuring that your income continues in case of illness, and so on. Investment in shares or share-based investments, such as unit trusts, might form part of the strategy, but so too will deposits and insurance policies. Chapter 2 gives a broad outline of financial planning. For a more detailed approach, see *Be Your Own Financial Adviser,*★ also published by Which? Books.

Stockbrokers give independent advice – in other words, they are not tied to any one product provider and their advice is based on the full range of financial products and companies available. Unlike many independent financial advisers, stockbrokers are not paid by commissions from companies whose products they sell. Instead, you pay a fee to the broker for the planning service. This means that there is no risk of an in-built tendency for the level of product-related commissions to influence the advice given.

Additional costs

Some brokers add a compliance charge – e.g. £2.50 or £10 – to the costs of each deal, which goes towards the costs of regulation (see Chapter 17). If you use a nominee account (see page 48), there may be additional charges. No VAT is charged on stockbrokers' commissions, but is usually levied on other charges and fees, such as for portfolio management.

When you buy (but not when you sell) shares, other than new issues, you must pay stamp duty of 0.5 per cent. This is automatically added to your bill and is shown on the contract note.

For purchases and sales over £10,000, there is a small Panel on Takeovers and Mergers (PTM) levy which goes towards funding the cost of regulating takeovers and mergers to ensure fair conduct.

Using a stockbroker

The major High Street banks and some building societies offer stockbroking services and you can get details from their branches or by phone. Most traditional stockbrokers and some banks which specialise in private clients (as opposed to big institutional clients) belong to a trade body called the Association of Private Client Investment Managers and Stockbrokers (APCIMS),★ which produces a free directory listing its members and their services. Another useful guide is the *Investors Chronicle Directory of Stockbrokers and Investment Managers.*★ To find a broker who can offer PEP management, see the *Chase de Vere PEP Guide.*★ The London Stock Exchange★ has also compiled a list of member firms offering sharedealing services to the public, particularly in connection with building society conversions.

Rolling settlement

For 300 years up to July 1994, when you bought or sold shares you did not pay the bill or receive your money straight away. The Stock Exchange calendar was divided into accounts which lasted two (or occasionally three) weeks. Deals made within an account were totted up or set against each other, with the total becoming payable several days after the end of the account. Like so much of Stock Exchange tradition, this system became increasingly out of step with the high-volume, rapid dealing of the modern world and had to change.

From July 1994, in line with major stock markets abroad, the Stock Exchange moved to a system of 'rolling settlement'. Initially, this operated so that, when you bought or sold shares, payment was due or made ten business days later – this was called 'T+10'. From June 1995, once the system had settled down, the time lag was shortened to just five days – 'T+5' and, from 1998, T+3 is due to be introduced.

In the old days, you had plenty of time to unearth your share certificate and fill in a transfer form, or write a cheque, and pop a package in the post to your broker. As the speed of settlement has increased, this method of settling your account has become increasingly unreliable. With the advent of Crest, it has also become unnecessary.

Crest

Crest is an electronic system for settling share transactions in which share certificates are 'dematerialised'. Instead of holding a paper ite, you have an electronic entry on a company's share register, in the same way that your current account is logged at your bank.

A shareholding is bought or sold, the payment and transfer of shares happens simultaneously by electronic means with no physical delivery of paper at all. This enables settlement to take place very rapidly.

Crest replaced the old paper-based system of settlement, Talisman. The switch was completed in April 1997 and now trading for around 90 per cent of all stocks is settled through Crest. The securities for which transactions are settled outside Crest (called 'residuals') tend to be those of very small companies where the shares are traded infrequently.

The private investor can adapt to this changing world in several ways, discussed below.

Stay 'in paper'

You do not have to switch to electronic shareholdings. Under Crest, there are still arrangements for settling deals involving share certificates, but you will have to make sure that your broker has the certificate in his or her hands in time for settlement. If not, the broker will be fined by Crest and in all likelihood will pass the fine on to you.

Many brokers let you deal for delayed settlement, using the old T+10 system or even T+25. But this requires special arrangements and additional administration, so expect to pay extra for this service.

Use a nominee account

Traditionally, as a shareholder in a company, your name would be entered on the company's share register and you would receive a certificate showing details of your shareholding. You can still hold shares in this way, but an alternative is to use a nominee account.

Typically, your broker or some third party firm acts as the nominee. Your shareholding is registered in the name of the nominee. Usually this will be an entry on an electronic share register but the nominee might be issued share certificates which they hold on your behalf. In either case, there is no need for you to prove you own shares when you come to sell – your broker has the proof and all the necessary details by virtue of being your nominee, and can deal immediately on your instructions.

An additional benefit is that the nominee handles all the administration involved with the shares, such as collecting dividends, receiving documents about share re-organisations and alerting you to your choice of actions, and so on.

If you have various shares in the nominee account, the dividends can be collected together and paid over to you in one lump, together with a single tax credit (see Chapter 5). If this involves some delay in paying out dividends to you, you should expect to receive interest on the delayed payments.

Some brokers offer their nominee service at no extra charge, as a standard way of handling share transactions more quickly and efficiently. Others charge for the service, in a variety of ways. There may be a regular management fee, at a flat rate, per shareholding or as a percentage of the value of shares held. There may be a charge for specific events, such as collecting dividends, sending you annual reports and so on. Finally, there may be a charge if you transfer your shares out of the nominee account.

To some extent, broker nominee accounts are being undercut by nominee services offered by large companies whose shares are held by investors. For example, several of the former building societies that have converted to companies have set up their own nominee accounts. They often use the lure of cheap selling costs to encourage investors to take up this route.

However, there are drawbacks to using a nominee account. It places an additional tier between you and the company in which you have invested. The nominee is the legal owner of the shares, although these are held beneficially for you. (This is very similar to a trust, where trustees own property but only for the benefit of others.) Two types of nominee account exist:

- **pooled accounts**, where the nominee appears on the share register of the company just once and the holding represents the amalgamation of all the nominee's clients' holdings
- **designated accounts**, where the nominee makes multiple appearances on the share register under a different code corresponding to each underlying investor.

The distinction has no relevance to the legal position. As the owner of the shares, the nominee – not the underlying shareholder – is entitled to all the rights and privileges associated with share ownership. This means that the shareholder may lose the right to vote, attend general meetings, speak at meetings, receive the annual report and accounts, receive share perks, and so on. Apart from distancing the ultimate shareholder from the company, this can cause real financial loss. For example, holders of permanent income-bearing shares (PIBS) in building societies have been entitled to windfall cash or shares on conversion of the society to a company, but where PIBS were held through a nominee account, it was the nominee who became so entitled. A problem arose because the nominee qualified for just one entitlement even though they represented many PIBS holders who, had they held the PIBS direct, would each have been entitled to a windfall.

Proshare,* an organisation which exists to promote private share ownership and represent shareholders, has drawn up the Proshare Nominee Code, which aims to protect the rights of underlying shareholders. The code advocates that:

- charges should be clearly disclosed
- shareholders should be able to receive company information if they choose, attend meetings, speak at meetings and receive any perks
- nominees should state how the investors' shareholding is safeguarded
- nominees should provide a statement outlining their complaints procedure and what compensation/insurance arrangements exist.

The code has received a mixed reception. Not all companies have agreed to it, though most of the larger ones have done so. Among brokers, only a few of the larger players have signed up. The trade body, APCIMS,* is pressing for a change in company law to give nominee shareholders exactly the same rights as direct shareholders and views the Proshare code as 'an unhappy halfway house which will inevitably be less effective than a proper reordering of company law'.

Some of the fears about nominee accounts have probably been exaggerated. Investors have voiced concerns that unscrupulous brokers might transfer the contents of the nominee account into their own hands and skip the country to live off their ill-gotten gains. But, in other areas, we are quite happy to accept certificate-less ownership provided safeguards are adequate – for example, in the case of bank accounts, where a regular statement is enough to reassure us that our assets are intact. Moreover, it is a legal requirement that PEP holdings are in nominee accounts. Millions of people are PEP holders and security has not been an issue.

However, the loss of shareholders' rights that nominee status can entail is a cause for concern. In November 1996, the government issued a consultation paper inviting ideas on how such rights could be protected and warning that statutory powers might be used if companies and brokers could not devise their own solutions.

Become a sponsored member of Crest

Normally, to hold shares electronically, you would use a nominee account as described above, with your broker arranging settlement through his or her membership of the Crest system. However, you can hold your shares directly in electronic form if you yourself become a member of Crest. This must be arranged through a broker who acts as your sponsor and opens a sponsored membership account for you with Crest. At the time of writing, a few brokers offered free sponsored membership, but most charge a fee ranging from around £20 (which is the amount your broker has to pay for each sponsored member to the company running Crest) up to £100 or more. Sponsored membership is suitable only if you are an active shareholder.

Paying on time

As important as transferring your shares on time when you sell is paying up on time when you buy your shares. If you rely on posting cheques, you will probably have to wait until your cheque has been cleared before your broker agrees to act on your buying instructions. However, there are ways to avoid such a delay:

- deal face-to-face, such as at an 'off-the-pavement' high street broker – where you can make payment on the spot – e.g. by credit card
- deal by phone, paying by debit card (Switch or Delta). A routine credit check is carried out and an instant debit is made against your current account
- many brokers offer their own money management facilities. You open a special deposit account, either with the broker or with a bank. Your broker has direct access to the money in the account so that he or she can pay in or draw out money on your behalf to settle your share deals. Some accounts even have an overdraft limit built in, so that you can buy using 'margin trading' where, in effect, you put down a deposit for the shares you are buying and pay the remainder of the full price later. The overdraft or loan might be secured against shares you hold in the broker's nominee account.

Chart 4.1: How to hold your shares

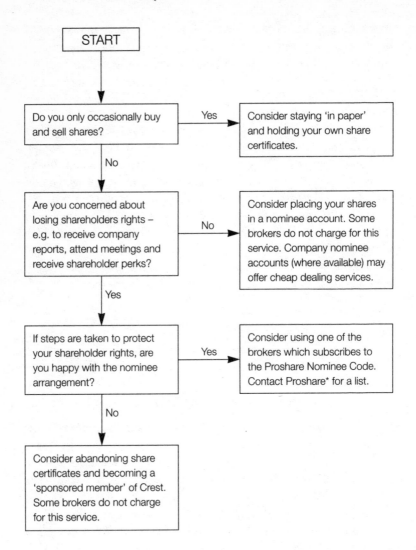

START

Do you only occasionally buy and sell shares? — Yes → Consider staying 'in paper' and holding your own share certificates.

No

Are you concerned about losing shareholders rights – e.g. to receive company reports, attend meetings and receive shareholder perks? — No → Consider placing your shares in a nominee account. Some brokers do not charge for this service. Company nominee accounts (where available) may offer cheap dealing services.

Yes

If steps are taken to protect your shareholder rights, are you happy with the nominee arrangement? — Yes → Consider using one of the brokers which subscribes to the Proshare Nominee Code. Contact Proshare* for a list.

No

Consider abandoning share certificates and becoming a 'sponsored member' of Crest. Some brokers do not charge for this service.

Buying new issues

Buying newly issued shares has always been a favourite with some investors, especially because of the scope for making a quick profit through 'stagging' – gambling that you sell your shares at a profit to the offer price as soon as trading starts. The privatisation programme gave a tremendous boost to the popularity of new issue trading and elevated stagging to something of a national sport.

Investors who have experienced new issue trading only through privatisations and building society conversions may, however, have a distorted view of this branch of share investment. The privatisation issues were nearly always priced on the low side in order to ensure a successful market debut. As a result, with a few notable exceptions (such as British Energy), you stood an excellent chance of making a quick killing.

Building society conversions have inevitably been a source of easy profits because the shares were free. Moreover, the profits that could be realised by selling the shares as they opened on the stockmarket were boosted by institutional investors (pension funds, insurance companies and so on) scrambling to build up adequate holdings in these stocks. The large former building societies have become constituents of the FTSE 100 index. Most institutions have some funds which aim to hold a wide spread of FTSE 100 stocks; this is particularly so in the case of 'tracker funds', which mimic the movement of a selected stock market index.

Not all new issues are so profitable. Indeed, some experts suggest that you are more likely to make a loss on a new issue than on a holding of established shares. They argue that a company newly launching on the stock market is anxious to raise as much capital as possible. The company and its advisers will try to choose a launch date when the stockmarket is buoyant and will pitch the price as high as they dare. If the company gets it right, you end up buying shares at a relatively high price, making losses – at least in the short term – more probable.

The new issue process

A company seeks a listing on the main market or the Alternative Investment Market (AIM) in order to raise new cash from the public for use in the business. To obtain a listing, the company must meet various requirements – to ensure that a fair and liquid market can be established in its shares – and must be sponsored by a broker. The company usually employs an issuing house – generally a merchant bank – to handle the issue. In most cases, the issuing house will arrange for other financial institutions and merchant banks to act as 'underwriters'. For a fee, they agree to take up unsold shares at a given price if the new issue is not a success. In that way, the company is guaranteed a minimum amount of capital, and the risks of the issue being a flop are borne by the underwriters, not the company.

Until 1995, companies worth more than £50 million which were newly seeking a stock market listing were obliged to offer some of their shares to the public. This requirement has been dropped and many new issues are no longer open directly to small investors. Instead, the whole of a new issue is often placed with institutional investors.

How to apply

If a new issue is open to the public, you can make your own application for shares. Instructions for applying are given in any advertisements in the press and in the company's prospectus (see Chapter 12) obtained from the issuing house and/or sponsoring broker. There is no fee or charge when you apply direct for newly issued shares.

With privatisation issues, various share shops have generally been set up to spread the workload and to ensure that the public has easy access to the share offer. Share shops are brokers, usually including the broking divisions of the High Street banks. To apply for shares, you register with a share shop and make your application through them. Once again, there is no charge.

Where the issue is not open to the public (which is increasingly the case), you may still be able to apply for shares through one of the many brokers which now offer a new issue service. The broker collates individual investors' applications and applies for a slice of the new issue in the same way as an institution.

Having registered for a broker's new issue service, you will usually be contacted with details of all new issues for which your broker is willing to apply, regardless of whether they are offered direct to the public or not. Some brokers cover all issues, some exclude small issues or concentrate on listings on the main market. There may be a charge for the service, most often an annual flat fee.

Proshare★ publishes a list of brokers who offer new issue services.

The allocation

If applications exceed the total of shares to be issued, the offer is 'over-subscribed'. In that case, applicants might not get all, or even any, of the shares they had hoped for. If the issue was by tender, the allocation is decided automatically. With a tender, you bid for your chosen number of shares at or above a given price. Successful applicants all pay the same price (called the 'striking price'), which is generally set at the highest level at which all the shares can be sold. Anyone who has bid below the striking price does not get any shares. Everyone who bid at or above the striking price gets their full application or a scaled-down amount.

Where the offer for sale is at a fixed price, the issuing house has to decide how the available shares will be rationed. This can be done in one or more ways:

- **scaling down** – you might get only a proportion of the shares you had applied for
- **ballot** – applicants are selected at random. Those who are successful in the ballot receive either their full application or a scaled-down amount. Those who are unsuccessful receive no shares at all
- **cut-off point** – people and institutions who have applied for very large quantities of shares might be excluded from the allocation.

The issuing house does not announce the basis on which shares will be allocated until after the closing date for applications. If you suspect that an issue might be over-subscribed, you might want to adjust your application – for instance by bidding for more shares than you otherwise would have.

DIY buying and selling

You do not have to use a stockbroker if you are transferring shares to or from a known person – e.g. a member of your family. First, get a stock transfer form (e.g. from the registrar of the company whose shares you hold). Do not use the transfer form, if any, on the reverse of the share certificate – this is used only for sales on the stock market. Send the completed form to the Stamp Office together with a cheque for stamp duty of 0.5% of the agreed market value of the shares. When the Stamp Office returns the form, duly stamped, send it with the old share certificate to the registrar of the company who will issue a new certificate.

Chapter 5

Tax and shares

THE return on shares comes in two forms: regular dividends and a profit or loss when you finally sell the shares. In general, both these elements are taxable. In this chapter, we look at the basics of how dividends and gains are taxed. Chapter 6 covers special schemes which allow you to invest in shares tax-efficiently.

Tax on dividends

Dividends count as income and are subject to income tax. The company has already paid tax (advance corporation tax) on the profits which it pays out as dividends. In recognition of this, the dividend that you receive is treated as a net-of-tax amount; it is accompanied by a tax credit for the amount of tax you are deemed to have already paid. Along with your dividend statement, you receive a tax voucher for the amount of the credit.

In the 1997–8 tax year, the tax credit is worth 20 per cent. If you are a lower rate or basic rate taxpayer, you do not have any further tax to pay. If you are a higher rate taxpayer, you have further tax at a rate of 20 per cent to pay on the grossed up amount of the dividend (i.e. the dividend plus the tax credit). Individuals who are non-taxpayers can use the tax credit to reclaim the tax already paid.

From 6 April 1999
From that date the rules are to change. The value of the tax credit is due to fall to 10 per cent. As before, lower rate and basic rate taxpayers will have no further tax to pay. Higher rate taxpayers will have further tax to pay on the grossed up amount of the dividend. The higher rate tax on dividends is to be set at a special level of 32.5 per cent – i.e.

Example

On 25 July 1997, Gill received a dividend of 5.7p per share from Alpha plc. Gill has 4,000 shares, so the total dividend came to 4,000 x 5.7p = £228. The dividend was accompanied by a tax credit for £57. This represents 20 per cent tax on the grossed up dividend of £228 + £57 = £285. Gill is a non-taxpayer and can use the tax credit to reclaim the £57 tax already paid. In total, Gill receives £228 + £57 = £285.

Gill's husband, Ralph, also has a holding of Alpha plc shares. He received a dividend of £570 on his 10,000 shares, together with a tax credit of £142.50. Ralph is a higher rate taxpayer, so has extra tax to pay. The gross dividend comes to £570 + £142.50 = £712.50. Tax at 40 per cent would be £285, but Ralph can set the tax credit of £142.50 against this, leaving just £142.50 still to pay. In total, Ralph receives £570 – £142.50 = £427.50 after tax.

---

further tax to pay of 22.5 per cent – in order to ensure that higher rate taxpayers are left with the same after-tax income as they would have received under the old rules. However, non-taxpayers will lose out because they will no longer be able to reclaim the tax already paid.

Example

Suppose the Alpha plc dividend received by Gill and Ralph had been paid on 25 July 1999. Under the new rules, this would be the position:

- Gill would receive a dividend of 4,000 x 5.7p = £228, together with a tax credit of £25.33 (representing 10 per cent of the gross dividend of £228 + £25.33 = £253.33). Gill would not be able to reclaim the tax already paid, despite being a non-taxpayer. Therefore, Gill would have an after-tax amount of £228 – i.e. £57 less than under the old rules.

- Ralph would receive a dividend of 10,000 x 5.7p = £570, together with a tax credit of £63.33. Higher rate tax at a rate of 32.5 per cent would be due on the gross dividend – i.e. 32.5% x £633.33 = £205.83. Ralph would be able to set the tax credit against this, leaving a further £142.50 to pay. The total dividend Ralph would get after tax is £570 – £142.50 = £427.50. In other words, he would receive the same as he would have done under the old rules.

Foreign income dividends

When a dividend is paid out, until April 1999 the company has to pay advance corporation tax (ACT). The ACT paid can be deducted from the mainstream corporation tax, which becomes payable later on when the company settles the tax bill on its profits for the year as a whole.

A company which has substantial overseas earnings (generally subject to tax in the country in which the earnings have been made) may find that it has little or no mainstream corporation tax to pay. This means that some or all of the ACT cannot be reclaimed and has to be carried forward in the hope that there will eventually be some mainstream corporation tax at a future date. To eliminate this problem, the previous Conservative government allowed for the payment of 'foreign income dividends' – also known as FIDs.

When a company pays out a foreign income dividend, it still pays ACT, but any ACT that cannot be offset against mainstream corporation tax for the year is refunded. The special treatment is carried through to the way that shareholders are taxed: when you receive a foreign income dividend, you do not get a proper tax credit – instead you receive a 'notional tax credit'. If you are a lower rate or basic rate taxpayer, there is no further tax to pay, but if you are a non-taxpayer, you cannot reclaim any tax against this notional credit. By contrast, higher rate taxpayers have extra tax to pay in the usual way. Your dividend statement should state the amount of the notional tax credit which you need to know to work out the higher rate tax if it is due.

In its July 1997 Budget, the Labour government announced that from April 1999 the special rules for foreign income dividends would cease. Subsequently, it announced that ACT itself would be abolished from 1999, making the special foreign income dividends rules redundant. Shareholders are unaffected by these changes – from 1999 onwards, they will not be able to reclaim tax credits on dividends anyway.

Stock or scrip dividends

Sometimes, instead of paying a cash dividend, a company offers shareholders extra shares in the company – a stock or scrip dividend. The new shares count as income for tax purposes. Tax is worked out on the following amount:

- where you have a choice between receiving cash or shares, the value of the shares for tax purposes is the cash equivalent
- where there is no cash alternative or where the cash equivalent works out to be substantially above or below the market value of the shares, the market value is used instead ('substantially above or below' means 15 per cent give or take 1 or 2 per cent).

If you are a lower rate or basic rate taxpayer, there is no tax to pay on the value of the shares received. If you are a higher rate taxpayer, the value of the shares is grossed up as if you had already paid tax at 20 per cent in 1997–8 (10 per cent from April 1999) and extra tax is due. Non-taxpayers cannot claim back any tax notionally paid. Your dividend statement will tell you the cash value of the shares for tax purposes and the notional tax credit.

Example

Harold holds 2,000 shares in Bravo plc. Bravo runs a scheme whereby shareholders can elect to receive all their dividends in the form of extra shares. Alternatively, they can carry on receiving dividends in cash. The scheme works as follows: the scrip shares are valued at the normal mid-market share price for Bravo shares on the day when the shares are first quoted 'ex-dividend' (see page 170). The cash dividend (excluding the value of the tax credit) is converted to shares at that price. Only whole shares can be issued. Any fraction of a share is left as cash and paid as a remaining cash dividend.

For example, in May 1997, Bravo announces a final dividend of 13.2 pence per share. The ex-dividend price of the shares is 280 pence per share. 280/13.2 = 21.21212. Therefore Bravo offers an alternative of one new share for every 21 shares already held.

Harold has opted to receive shares rather than cash dividends. He gets 95 new shares equivalent to the dividend on 95 x 21 = 1,995 shares. On the remaining 2,000 – 1,995 = 5 shares, Harold receives the cash dividend, i.e. 13.2p x 5 = 66 pence (together with a tax credit of 16.5 pence).

The cash value of the new shares for tax purposes is 95 x 21 x 13.2p = £263.34, and they come with a notional tax credit of £263.34/0.80 x 0.2 = £65.84. Harold is a basic rate taxpayer, so has no further tax to pay.

Bonus shares

With privatisation issues, in particular, your original shares often carry a right to receive further shares – bonus shares – provided you hold the original shares for a minimum length of time. When you receive the bonus shares they are treated for tax purposes as if they are a stock dividend and so there may be tax to pay on them as described above if you are a higher rate taxpayer. Your dividend statement states the cash value of the shares for tax purposes.

Tax on profits

If you make a profit when you sell some shares, there may be capital gains tax to pay. If you make a loss, you may be able to set the loss against gains made elsewhere, so reducing the tax bill.

The basics of capital gains tax

In general, the first step in working out the capital gain, if any, on an asset is to deduct the 'initial value' – what you paid or its value at the time you acquired it – from the 'final value', which is the sale proceeds or the asset's value at disposal. Making a profit does not automatically result in a capital gains tax bill, because:

- you can deduct various expenses
- gains due purely to inflation are ignored
- you can often deduct losses made in the same year or carried forward from an earlier year
- you have an allowance (£6,500 in 1997–8), which means that the first slice of chargeable capital gains made each year is tax-free.

Initial value and final value

Special rules apply to shares (see page 64), but broadly shares are valued in the following ways:

- if you buy and sell shares, in general you value them at the price you paid or received. But if the deal was at an artificial price, for example the result of a special arrangement between you and a close relative, market value will be used
- if you are given or give away shares, or acquire or dispose of them in some other way which does not involve actual buying and selling, the market value will be used.

The market value of **quoted shares** is worked out in one of two ways, whichever produces the lower result.

The first method is to use the 'quarter-up rule'. You take the lower of the two prices quoted in *The Stock Exchange Daily Official List* for the relevant date and add on one quarter of the difference between the two prices.

Under the second method, you take the average of the highest and lowest prices for normal dealing in the shares on the relevant date. If the stock market was closed on the date the shares changed hands, you use the price information for the last previous day of trading or the first subsequent day of trading, whichever produces the lower result.

With **unquoted shares**, you may have to enter into some negotiation with your tax office. The aim is to establish the price at which the shares would trade in an open market between an unconnected buyer and seller, assuming they had all the relevant information needed to strike a fair deal.

Allowable expenses

The general rule for capital gains tax is that you can deduct expenses incurred in acquiring, disposing of and improving an asset. In the context of shares, this means that you can deduct, for example, dealing costs when you buy and sell. If there was a dispute over who owned the shares, you could deduct legal costs paid as a result of attempts to prove your title to the shares.

If you buy shares which are only 'partly paid' – i.e. only part of the full share price has been paid, with further instalments outstanding – the payments you make later are treated as allowable expenses.

Indexation allowance

You are not taxed on gains which result from inflation since March 1982. To strip out the inflationary increases, the initial value and each allowable expense have to be increased by the amount of inflation from the time the cost was incurred (or 31 March 1982 if this is later) up to the time when you sell or dispose of the asset.

This is done by adding on an indexation allowance, which is found by multiplying each relevant cost by an inflation factor. The inflation factor is found by working out the following formula:

$$\frac{Rd - Ri}{Ri}$$

where Rd is the Retail Prices Index for the month in which you dispose of the asset and Ri is the Retail Prices Index for the month in which you acquired the asset or incurred the expense. The factor is rounded to the nearest third decimal place. Table 3.1 shows the Retail Prices Index figures from March 1982 to date.

You do not have to calculate the indexation factor for yourself. Tables of factors are available from tax offices and are also printed each month in the personal finance sections of many newspapers and magazines.

The indexation allowance can be used to reduce a gain, even to zero. However, since 30 November 1993, the indexation allowance cannot be used to create or increase a capital loss.

Example

Jayne bought 536 shares in Charlie Group plc at 280 pence a share in August 1983. Her dealing costs were £18. She sells the shares in June 1997. The indexed value of her initial outlay and associated dealing costs is:

Initial value: 536 x 280p	£1,500.80
Dealing costs	£ 18.00
Un-indexed costs	£1,518.80
Retail Prices Index for August 1983	85.68
Retail Prices Index for June 1997	157.5
Indexation factor (157.5 – 85.68)/85.68	0.838
Indexation allowance: 0.838 x £1,518.80	£1,272.75
Indexed value of costs £1,518.80 + £1,272.75	£2,791.55

Assuming Jayne has just this one holding of Charlie Group shares and she sells them at 623p per share, the amount on which tax might be payable is:

Final value (536 x 623p)	£3,339.28
less indexed value of costs	£2,791.55
Chargeable gain	£ 547.73

Jayne has no losses to set against her chargeable gain of £527.73 but as it is covered by her tax-free allowance of £6,500 for the year, she has no capital gains tax to pay.

Table 5.1: Retail Prices Index

Year	Jan	Feb	Mar	Apr	May	June	July	Aug	Sept	Oct	Nov	Dec
1982			79.44	81.04	81.62	81.85	81.88	81.90	81.85	82.26	82.66	82.51
1983	82.61	82.97	83.12	84.28	84.64	84.84	85.30	85.68	86.06	86.36	86.67	86.89
1984	86.84	87.20	87.48	88.64	88.97	89.20	89.10	89.94	90.11	90.67	90.95	90.87
1985	91.20	91.94	92.80	94.78	95.21	95.41	95.23	95.49	95.44	95.59	95.92	96.05
1986	96.25	96.60	96.73	97.67	97.85	97.79	97.52	97.82	98.30	98.45	99.29	99.62
1987	100.0	100.4	100.6	101.8	101.9	101.9	101.8	102.1	102.4	102.9	103.4	103.3
1988	103.3	103.7	104.1	105.8	106.2	106.6	106.7	107.9	108.4	109.5	110.0	110.3
1989	111.0	111.8	112.3	114.3	115.0	115.4	115.5	115.8	116.6	117.5	118.5	118.8
1990	119.5	120.2	121.4	125.1	126.2	126.7	126.8	128.1	129.3	130.3	130.0	129.9
1991	130.2	130.9	131.4	133.1	133.5	134.1	133.8	134.1	134.6	135.1	135.6	135.7
1992	135.6	136.3	136.7	138.8	139.3	139.3	138.8	138.9	139.4	139.9	139.7	139.2
1993	137.9	138.8	139.3	140.6	141.1	141.0	140.7	141.3	141.9	141.8	141.6	141.9
1994	141.3	142.1	142.5	144.2	144.7	144.7	144.0	144.7	144.7	145.2	145.3	146.0
1995	146.0	146.9	147.5	149.0	149.6	149.8	149.1	149.9	150.6	149.8	149.8	150.7
1996	150.2	150.9	151.5	152.6	152.9	153.0	152.4	153.1	153.8	153.8	153.9	154.4
1997	154.4	155.0	155.4	156.3	156.9	157.5	157.5	158.5	159.5	159.5	159.6	

63

Losses and tax-free allowance

A capital loss on one asset is set against gains made on other assets in the same year. Losses which cannot be used up in this way are carried forward and may be set against future gains. When using up carried forward losses, you use only as much of the losses as is necessary to reduce your chargeable gains to the amount of the tax-free allowance for the year.

Since the introduction of self-assessment, you must tell your tax office that you have made a loss within five years and ten months of the end of the year in which the loss occurred; otherwise, you will lose the right to set off the loss against your gains. It is up to you to notify your tax office, even if you do not receive a tax return.

Example

Pat has had the following pattern of capital gains and losses over the last three years:

Tax year	Gains	Losses	Net gains/losses	Tax-free allowance
1995–6	£2,053	£3,513	Loss: £1,460	£6,000
1996–7	£8,267	£1,000	£7,267	£6,300
1997–8	£4,424	nil	£4,424	£6,500

In 1995-6, Pat made a net loss of £1,460. Her tax-free allowance was totally wasted because she had no gains to set it against. In 1996-7, she did much better, making a net gain of £7,267. She set £967 of the loss carried forward from the previous year against her net gains, reducing them to £6,300 – i.e. just the amount of her tax-free allowance. This meant no tax to pay and a remaining loss of £1,460 – £967 = £493 to carry forward. In 1997-8, Pat makes net gains of £4,424. This is more than covered by her tax-free allowance, so there is no capital gains tax to pay. She continues to carry forward the loss of £493.

Special rules for shares

When you sell an antique chair, it is clear just what item you are selling and it should be relatively straightforward to establish the value of that particular chair at the time you first acquired it. Matters are not so simple when it comes to shares. Shares of the same sort in the same company are identical. If you have bought or been allocated the same type of shares at several different times, how can you decide which shares you are dealing with if you sell part of your holding? To cope with this problem, special rules have been devised.

When you sell or dispose of some of the shares of one type that you hold, the shares that are sold are matched to the shares you hold in the following order of priority:

- first they are deemed to be shares of the same type you bought on the same day if you made any purchases that day. As you might expect, there is no indexation allowance in this case
- next, they are matched to any shares of the same type that you have bought within the previous nine days. You cannot claim any indexation allowance
- next they are matched to any shares within your 'new holding' for that type of share, if you have one – see below
- next they are matched against your '1982 holding' for those shares, if you have one – see below
- finally, they are matched with any shares you bought before 7 April 1965, matching to your most recent purchases first and working back in time.

'New holdings' and '1982 holdings'

If you have held the shares you are selling for more than ten days, the problem of identifying which shares are being sold is solved by pooling all the shares of one type. In fact, because of changes in capital gains tax legislation over the years, there are two pools:

- the '**new holding**' made up of shares you have bought or acquired from 6 April 1982 onwards (the start of the first full tax year from which you could claim indexation allowance – see below
- the '**1982 holding**' made up of shares you bought or acquired between 7 April 1965 (when capital gains tax was first introduced) and 5 April 1982.

Shares in the same pool are all given the same value, which is an average (more technically, a 'weighted average') of the share prices actually paid. The indexation allowance that you can claim when you dispose of some of the shares is a proportion of the allowance for the pool as a whole. The value of the pool and the indexation allowance are worked out each time there is a change to the number of shares in the pool.

Example

Scott first bought shares in Delta plc in June 1992. In March 1995, the company made a 1 for 5 rights issue (see page 182) which Scott took up and, in April 1997, following a prolonged rise in price, Scott sold some of the shares to realise the profits:

Date	Purchases (number of shares)	Purchase price	Sales (number of shares)	Selling price
June 1992	10,000	104p		
March 1995	2,000	120p		
April 1997			5,000	184p

The Delta shares are all pooled to form a 'new holding'. The value of the share pool and the indexation allowances available to Scott are worked out as follows:

June 1992 Scott's pool is newly formed. It contains 10,000 shares worth 10,000 x 104p = £10,400. The indexed value of the pool is the same.

Date	Unindexed value of pool	Indexed value of pool
June 1992	£10,400	£10,400

March 1995 2,000 new shares (as a result of the rights issue) are added to the pool. This is a trigger for Scott to calculate the indexation allowance to date. First, he finds the indexation factor using the RPI figures for June 1992 and March 1995. This comes to (147.5 – 139.3)/139.3 = 0.059. The indexation allowance is 0.059 x £10,400 = £613.60. The value of the new shares (2,000 x 120p = £2,400) is added to his pool.

Date	Unindexed value of pool	Indexed value of pool
June 1992	£10,400	£10,400
March 1995 indexation allowance	–	£ 613.60
March 1995 new shares	£2,400	£2,400
TOTAL	£12,800	£13,413.60

April 1997 Scott sells some of the shares for £9,200. Once again, this is a trigger for him to work out the indexation allowance for his pool. Using RPI figures for April 1997 and March 1995, the indexation factor comes to (156.3 – 147.5)/147.5 = 0.060. This gives an indexation allowance of £13,413.60 x 0.060 = £804.82. This is added to the indexed pool to give new values as follows:

Date	Unindexed value of pool	Indexed value of pool
March 1995	£12,800	£13,413.60
April 1997 Indexation allowance		£804.82
TOTAL	£12,800	£14,218.42

5,000 of the total 12,000 shares in the pool are sold. To find the unindexed value of the shares he sells, he multiplies the unindexed value of the pool by 5,000/12,000 – i.e. 5,000/12,000 x £12,800 = £5,333.33. To find the indexation allowance, first he takes the same fraction of the indexed pool – i.e. 5,000/12,000 x £14,218.42 = £5,924.34 and subtracts from the result the unindexed value of the shares – i.e. £5,924.34 - £5,333.33 = £591.01. The chargeable gain on the 5,000 shares is then £9,200 (i.e. the sale proceeds) – £5,333.33 – £591.01 = £3,275.66. The new values for Scott's pool are:

Date	Unindexed value of pool	Indexed value of pool
April 1997	£12,800	£14,218.42
less shares sold	£5,333.33	£5,924.34
TOTAL	£7,466.67	£8,294.08

Shares held on 31 March 1982

The rules allowing you to claim an indexation allowance against gains that are due to inflation affect gains built up since March 1982 only. Where you have held your shares since before that date, unless you make an election to the contrary (see below), your gain or loss is worked out in one of two ways:

- using the rebased value – from the final value, you deduct the value of the shares on 31 March 1982, ignoring any expenses incurred before that date

- using the original value – from the final value, you deduct the initial value of the shares on the date you first acquired them and expenses even if incurred before 31 March 1982.

The same allowance for inflation is used with both these methods. The indexation allowance is the higher of the figure produced by indexing the 31 March 1982 value and the figure produced by indexing (from March 1982 onwards) the original value and allowable expenses incurred before 31 March 1982. Bear in mind that the indexation allowance cannot be used to create or increase a loss.

Once you have worked out the gain or loss under both methods, you use what is called the 'kink test' to decide on the final figure, as follows:

- if both methods produce a gain, it is the smaller of the two gains
- if both methods produce a loss, it is the smaller of the two losses
- if one method produces a gain and the other a loss, you are treated as having made neither a gain nor a loss, so there is no tax to pay but no loss relief either. For the purpose of this comparison, where any indexation allowance cannot be used because it would create a loss (see page 62), you are treated as if you would have a loss – see Example below
- if the method using the original value produces neither a gain nor a loss, then you are treated as having made neither a gain nor a loss, regardless of the result using the rebased value method.

Instead of going through a double calculation each time you sell shares that you owned on 31 March 1982, you can elect to use just the rebased value. In effect, you are treated as if you first started to own the shares on 31 March 1982: both the initial value and the indexation allowance are based on the value of the shares on 31 March 1982. However, you cannot make the election just for one shareholding or one asset: the election applies to all assets you owned on 31 March 1982 and, once you have made the election, you cannot change your mind. You have up to two years following the date of the sale of the shares or other assets to make the election, which then applies to all disposals made after that date.

There is no special form to fill in – get in touch with your tax office.

Stock or scrip dividends

If you receive shares instead of a cash dividend, the new shares are added to your share pool. You are treated as if the value of the shares (normally the amount of the cash dividend given up – see page 59) is the price you paid for them.

Example

Janice bought some Echo shares back in January 1979 for £3,000, incurring costs of £20. On 31 March 1982, these shares were worth £3,800. In May 1997, she sold the shares for £6,820. Her gain for tax purposes is worked out as follows:

Indexation allowance

Retail Prices Index for March 1982	79.44
Retail Prices Index for May 1997	156.9
Indexation factor (156.9 – 79.44)/79.44	0.975
Indexation allowance using	
31 March 1982 value	0.975 x £3,800 = £3,705
Indexation allowance using	
pre-March 1982 costs	0.975 x (£3,000 + £20) = £2944.50
Higher of the allowances	£3,705

Method 1: Rebased value

Final value	£6,820
Value at 31 March 1982	£3,800
Unindexed gain	£3,020
Indexation allowance	£3,705
Taxable gain	nil

Method 2: Original costs

Final value	£6,820
Initial value	£3,000
Allowable expenses incurred pre- 31 March 1982	£ 20
Unindexed gain	£3,800
Indexation allowance	£3,705
Taxable gain	£ 95

The calculations produce a gain under the second method but a loss (because of the unused indexation allowance) under the first method, so Janice is treated as having made neither a gain nor a loss. There is no tax to pay.

For the purpose of working out the unindexed value of your shares, the new shares are added to the original holding as if they had been acquired the same date as the original shares. For working out the indexation allowance, the value of the shares is treated as an allowable expense incurred on the day you became entitled to the extra shares.

Other types of share reorganisations

If you receive bonus shares or new shares through a rights issue, or your shares are split or your shareholding is reorganised in some other way – see Chapter 14 – this is generally treated as an adjustment to your original shareholding. For example, new shares acquired under a rights issue are added to your original shares as if they had been acquired on the same date as the original shares. For the purpose of working out your unindexed gain or loss, any payment you have to make is treated as an allowable expense incurred on that date. However, for working out your indexation allowance, the payment is indexed from the date on which payment actually became due (i.e. it is not related back to the date on which the original shares were bought).

Share reorganisations do not generally count as disposals for capital gains tax purposes, so normally there is no tax bill to pay at the time a reorganisation is made. This is the case even when a quoted company buys back its own shares – no capital gains tax is payable but the cash received from the company is treated in the same way as a dividend and subject to income tax.

Building society conversions, takeovers and mergers

The 1990s have turned out to be a decade of rationalistion for the building society sector. Many societies have launched a staunch defence of their mutual status, but others have abandoned the traditional ownership by their members in favour of ownership by shareholders. This has come about in two ways – conversion or takeover – both of which have resulted in the issue of shares or payment of cash to the former members. The tax treatment of these windfalls is as follows:

- **Conversion from a building society to a bank** (e.g. Abbey National). Your membership of the former society is treated as if it were an asset which you had acquired at no cost. If you receive cash at the time of conversion, it is as if you had sold the asset, so capital gains tax is chargeable on the full amount of cash. If you receive shares, it is as if you had converted the asset from one form to another, so there is no capital gains tax at the time you receive the shares. If you subsequently sell the shares, capital gains tax is chargeable. If the shares were completely free, the initial value of the shares is zero. If you had to pay something for the shares, what you paid is taken to be the initial value

- **Takeover of a building society by a company** (e.g. the takeover of Cheltenham & Gloucester by Lloyds Bank). This is similar to a conversion. Any cash payment is taxable as a capital gain. Any shares are treated as having been acquired at zero value if they were free (or at an initial value equal to what you paid if they were not free), and there may be capital gains tax to pay if they are subsequently sold.

Some building societies retain their mutual status but decide to merge to form a larger society. Sometimes this results in the payment of surplus reserves to the members. Such cash payments do not come within the scope of capital gains tax. However, they are taxable as income.

Chapter 6

Tax-efficient investment in shares

SEVERAL schemes exist which offer a tax-efficient route for investing in shares. Some were developed as a way of rewarding employees, some to encourage sources of capital for new and growing companies and one to foster wider long-term investment in shares. Plans have also been announced for new Individual Savings Accounts (ISAs), due to be launched in 1999.

Employee share schemes

If you are an employee or a director and you receive shares in your company as a standard part of the reward for your work, there could be income tax to pay. If you have to pay less for the shares than their market value, tax is charged on the difference between the market value and what you pay. If the shares count as a fringe benefit you are taxed slightly differently, but there could still be income tax to pay at the time you receive the shares. Your employer can tell you whether your shares count as pay or as a fringe benefit.

For purposes of capital gains tax, assuming the company has newly issued the shares, you are treated as having paid nothing for them, so you could well face a capital gains tax bill when you eventually sell the shares.

Various schemes allow you to receive shares in your company without having to pay income tax at the time you are given the shares.

Priority shares in a public offer

Suppose the company you work for makes an offer of shares to the general public but reserves some of the shares to be allocated to the employees at either the fixed offer price or the lowest tender price (see page 55). As an employee, you are not taxed on the value of any shares you receive as a result of the priority allocation, provided:

- the allocation for employees does not come to more than 10 per cent of the total shares on offer
- all employees are entitled to shares on the same terms. This does not mean that everyone has to receive the same number of shares: the entitlement could be based on length of service or salary
- the offer is not restricted to directors and/or employees earning above a given level.

If you get the shares at a discount to the issue price, the discount may also be free of income tax, provided the discount is available to everyone taking up the shares, including members of the public.

For capital gains tax, you are treated as having acquired the shares at the price you actually paid (i.e. nil, if they were free).

Approved profit-sharing scheme

Under this scheme, you are given shares in your company but they are held in trust for you for a minimum period of time. There is no income tax on the gift of the shares to you, provided certain rules are kept, including:

- the scheme must be open to all employees, although the company can set a qualifying period of service provided this is no longer than five years
- all employees must participate on the same terms
- the entitlement must be to ordinary shares in the company
- the maximum value of shares that can be allocated to you is £3,000 a year or, if greater, 10 per cent of your earnings, up to an overall maximum of £8,000 for the year
- the shares must be held in trust for at least two years (except where you reach retirement, are made redundant or have to stop work for health reasons), and they must remain in the trust for at least three years (five years before 29 April 1996) for the gift to be tax-free.

While the shares are held in trust, if there are any share reorganisations (share exchanges, bonus issues, and so on), you can tell the trustees what action you want them take on your behalf.

Once the trustees have handed the shares over to you, they become taxable in the normal way – i.e. dividends are taxed as described on page 56 and you may have a capital gains tax bill when you come to sell. The initial cost of the shares is their market value at the time you took over the shares from the trustees. However, you can put shares from an approved profit sharing scheme into a personal equity plan (see page 80).

Share option schemes

Rather than being given shares outright, you can instead be given the right (i.e. the option) to buy your company's shares at some future date(s) for some set price (as specified in the terms of the scheme). If at that time the market value of the shares is greater than the price at which you can exercise the option, you stand to make a profit. In the normal way, there would be income tax to pay on that profit (less anything you paid for the option itself) because it would count as a reward for doing your job. But if you receive the option under an approved share option scheme, no income tax is payable. Several different schemes exist.

You may have received your option before 17 July 1995 under what was called an 'executive share option scheme' (ESOP). No income tax is payable, provided the price at which you exercise the option is the market value of the shares at the time the option was granted (if it is less, there will have been tax to pay on the discount at the time you took up the option) and the option must be exercised some time within three and ten years of being granted.

From 17 July 1995 onwards ESOPs were replaced by very similar schemes called 'company share option plans' (CSOPs). CSOPs work in basically the same way as ESOPs except that the price at which you can exercise the option must be the same as the market value of the shares at the time the option is granted (i.e. no discount is allowed) and the maximum value of the shares over which you have an option is set at a much lower level of £20,000 (£100,000 for ESOPs).

A third type of tax-efficient share option scheme is the savings-related share option scheme. With this, you save regularly in a special save-as-you-earn (SAYE) account for a set period of time. At the outset, you are given the option to buy shares in your company at a set price some years in the future, using the money from your SAYE account. At the end of the period a tax-free bonus is added to your savings. Provided the scheme is approved and you do indeed take up the option using the SAYE money, you do not have to pay income tax either at the time the option is granted or at the time it is exercised. SAYE accounts can be set up to run for seven, five or three years. The minimum regular saving is £5 a month, the maximum £250 a month. Shares you receive under a savings-related share option scheme can be transferred to a personal equity plan (see page 80).

Investing in new ventures

A company which is just starting out or one which is expanding has three possible sources of finance: internal money either put in by the owner or saved back from profits; borrowed money, such as a bank loan; and external risk capital, raised by selling shares in the company to other people. Borrowed money can be a significant drag on a new or growing company, with hefty interest payments to meet on a regular basis. Selling shares has a distinct advantage: the people who buy the shares become part-owners in the company. Unlike a bank, the shareholders cannot demand their money back or force the company to close down if they fail to earn anything on their investment. They hope to share in the company's good times, but they are also committed to riding out the bad times.

Viewed from the other side of the fence, if you invest in new and expanding companies you are making a risky investment – a gamble. If the company takes off, you stand to make fantastic gains but, if it fails, you could see your whole investment wiped out. Even if the company does well and you are showing a profit on paper, you have no guarantee that you will be able to sell your shares to realise the profit because there might not be any willing buyers.

In recognition of these drawbacks, several tax breaks are available to encourage you to play the business angel and provide venture capital for business start-ups and expansions. The tax incentives apply mainly to investment in UK trading companies - i.e. excluding those dealing or speculating in, say, land, shares or commodities – and the companies must not be quoted on the Stock Exchange. The Inland Revenue treats companies on the Alternative Investment Market as unquoted.

The two main schemes for investing tax-efficiently in these companies are the enterprise investment scheme and venture capital trusts. Below, we describe how both of the schemes worked in 1997–8. However, in its July 1997 Budget, the government announced that it would be keeping both schemes 'under close review' and intended to introduce changes in the Spring 1988 Budget to ensure that the schemes genuinely remained ways of raising venture capital.

Enterprise investment scheme (EIS)

The enterprise investment scheme (EIS) gives you special tax advantages if you invest in the newly issued shares of an unquoted trading company. You can also become a director of a company you invest in through the EIS (but you may not invest through the scheme if you are already a director), giving you the chance to take an active role in the new ventures you are backing financially. Provided you invest for at least five years, the EIS gives you the following tax breaks:

- **income tax relief** at the lower rate (20 per cent in 1997–8) on the amount you invest, up to a maximum of £100,000 in any one tax year. Where you make your investment before 6 October any year, up to half the investment (up to a maximum of £15,000) can be treated as if it had been made in the previous tax year, assuming you have enough unused EIS limit for the previous year
- **no capital gains tax** on profits from selling the shares.

The EIS rules try to ensure that the tax rewards really are linked to taking a risk. Companies which cannot qualify for the EIS include those involved in leasing or letting, financial activities, oil extraction or any activity which is not genuine trading. The most a company can raise through the EIS is £1 million (£5 million for ship charter companies), restricting the EIS to relatively small companies.

Venture capital trusts

An investment in a venture capital trust (VCT) gives you broadly the same tax breaks as investing through the EIS, but it is not quite as risky because a VCT is a fund which is set up to invest in a range of unquoted trading companies. Furthermore, the VCT itself is a quoted company, so you may be able to sell its shares more easily than you could sell the shares of the individual companies held by the VCT.

Provided you hold the VCT shares for at least five years, the following tax breaks are given:

> **Example**
> Gregory is a higher rate taxpayer, earning some £70,000 a year. His finances are in good shape and he likes to invest some money each year more or less for fun. He likes the challenge of trying to spot a company that will be a winner but is not unduly upset if he sometimes gets it wrong and loses his stake.
>
> Recently, his eye was caught by Foxtrot, a company about to launch on the Alternative Investment Market which had developed equipment to boost the performance of mobile phones. He successfully subscribed for £10,000 worth of shares in the company. Gregory paid the full £10,000 for the shares and received a form EIS3 from the company. The EIS3 certifies that the company is eligible for the EIS. Gregory claims tax relief of £2,000 through his tax return, reducing the overall cost to him to £8,000. Provided he holds the shares for five years, he will keep the tax relief and any gain he makes on selling the shares will be tax-free. Under the self-assessment rules, Gregory does not have to send the form EIS3 to his tax office but he must be able to produce it if asked, so he should keep it in a safe place.

- **no capital gains tax** on any gains the VCT makes on shares held in the fund
- **income tax relief** at the lower rate (20 per cent) on the amount you invest in VCT shares up to a maximum £100,000 a year
- **tax-free income** if the VCT pays out dividends on its shares
- **tax-free gains** when you sell the VCT shares.

General tax breaks

Two further tax reliefs exist which are part of the general rules for capital gains tax and/or income tax. They are:

- **loss relief** – under the normal capital gains tax rules, if you make a loss on an investment, you can use it to reduce tax on gains made on other assets either during the same tax year or in future years. Where the loss is made on shares in an unquoted UK trading company (including companies you have invested in through the EIS but not via a VCT), you can instead, if you choose, use the loss to reduce an income tax bill in the same or the previous tax year, provided the company has been trading for at least six years (or various other conditions are met)

- **re-investment relief** – if you make a capital gain when you sell an asset, you can put off paying any tax due if you invest the proceeds in the shares of an unquoted trading company (including EIS companies, VCTs or another company set up to hold shares in eligible companies). The investment must be made within a period running from one year before you make the gain up to three years afterwards. If the company ceases to be eligible within three years of your making the investment, you will have to pay the tax after all.

Table 6.1: Tax breaks for investing in new ventures

Type of investment	Income tax relief on amount invested	Tax-free income	Tax-free gains	Income tax relief for losses	Re-investment relief from capital gains tax
Direct investment in shares of unquoted trading companies	✗	✗	✗	✓	✓
Enterprise investment scheme	At 20%	✓	✓	✓	✓
Venture capital trust	At 20%	✓	✓	✗	✓

Wider share ownership

Personal equity plans (PEPs) were first announced in the 1986 Budget as a measure to encourage direct share ownership by private individuals. The first plans went on sale from January 1987. Initially, the bulk of your money had to be invested in quoted shares, with only a maximum one quarter of your plan invested in unit trusts. The concept has been adapted over the years and now PEPs can be used for a much wider range of investments. However, the days of the PEP are now numbered. In December 1997, the government issued a consultative document outlining a new Individual Savings Account (ISA) which is due to replace PEPs – and TESSAs – as the main vehicle for tax-favoured investment from April 1999 onwards. The proposals for ISAs are outlined on page 84.

What is a PEP?

PEPs are not investments in their own right, but a tax-efficient 'wrapper' which can be used to enhance the returns you get from investments in shares and bonds, either directly or through unit and investment trusts. There are two types of plan: general PEPs and single company PEPs.

You can use a general PEP to invest up to £6,000 each year in UK ordinary shares, similar shares quoted on a recognised stock exchange in another European Union (EU) country, certain types of corporate bond and preference shares, and qualifying unit and investment trusts – the trust management company will be able to tell you which of its unit of investment trusts is 'PEP-able'. In addition, you can put up to £3,000 a year into a single company PEP which invests in the shares of a single company.

To take out a PEP, you must invest via a plan manager, who could be, for example, a unit or investment trust management company (where you are investing in trusts), a stockbroker, or a specialist investment management company. Each year in which you decide to make PEP investments, you take out a separate PEP with your chosen plan manager. You can choose a different manager each year and you can switch an existing PEP to a different plan manager, but you cannot have more than one general PEP and one single company PEP for each year. If you already have a general PEP with one plan manager, you might get a discount if you were to take out a single company PEP with the same manager.

Ways of investing in a PEP

PEPs were designed to encourage new investment in shares, so usually you must pay cash into your plan; the plan manager will then organise the purchase of the required shares. If you already own shares which you want to include in a PEP, usually you will need to sell them, invest the proceeds in your PEP and then buy the shares back.

But there are two occasions when you can put shares you own into your PEP: when you have just acquired the shares through a new issue and when you have received shares under certain employee share schemes.

If you succeed in getting some shares through a new issue – such as when a nationalised business is privatised or when a building society converts to a company – you have up to 42 days from the day the shares

Table 6.2: Maximum investment in PEPs

Year to:	Maximum investment in:	
	General PEP	Single company PEP
31 December 1987	£2,400	not available
31 December 1988	£3,000	not available
31 December 1989	£3,000	not available
5 April 1990	£4,800	not available
5 April 1991	£6,000	not available
5 April 1992	£6,000	£3,000
5 April 1993	£6,000	£3,000
5 April 1994	£6,000	£3,000
5 April 1995	£6,000	£3,000
5 April 1996	£6,000	£3,000
5 April 1997	£6,000	£3,000
5 April 1998	£6,000	£3,000

are allotted to you during which you can transfer them into either a general PEP or a single company PEP. The price you paid for the shares counts towards your PEP limit for the year. If the shares were free, they have a nil value and you still have the full PEP allowance to use for other shares. If the newly issued shares are partly paid, you will have to pay subsequent instalments out of the funds in the same PEP. This means that you will either have to pay in enough cash (by the end of the tax year in which you were allocated the shares) to meet the further payments or your plan manager will have to sell shares within the PEP in order to raise enough money to meet the payments.

Example

Holly works for Golf Insurance plc, which runs a profit-sharing scheme. In 1993, Holly was allocated 1,000 shares in the scheme; on 31 August 1997 she opts to have the shares transferred from the trustees. Golf has arranged a corporate PEP for its shares.

Instead of transferring them into her own name, Holly arranges for them to be transferred direct to the building society which acts as the PEP manager. The transfer takes place on 10 October, when the share price is 282 pence. The value of the shares is 1,000 x 282p = £2,820, comfortably inside Holly's PEP limit of £3,000 for a single company PEP.

If you receive shares through a profit-sharing scheme (see page 73) or savings-related share option scheme (see page 74) run by your employer, you have up to 90 days to transfer them into a single company PEP. (You cannot transfer shares acquired in this way into a general PEP.) For the purpose of working out your remaining PEP allowance, the shares are valued at their market value on the day they are transferred to the PEP (not their value on the date you acquired them).

Different types of PEP

'**Managed PEP**' is most often taken to mean a PEP invested in unit trusts or investments trusts. But it can also mean a PEP where a manager, such as a stockbroker or specialist PEP management company, selects a portfolio of shares (and perhaps trusts, too) aimed, for example, at producing high growth or a regular income.

Another type of managed PEP is a **single company managed PEP**. The plan manager chooses which company to hold and when to switch to another.

With a **self-select PEP**, you choose the investments in your PEP, which can be shares, trusts, bonds or a mixture of them. They are offered mainly by stockbrokers and specialist investment managers. The minimum lump sum investment is often £500 or more. Only a few of these self-select plan managers accept regular savings. A few unit and investment trust management companies allow you to choose a mix of trusts and may accept some shares, too, such as building society conversion shares. These types of self-select trusts are suitable for regular savings as well as lump sums.

An **advisory PEP** is a halfway house between a managed and self-select PEP. You decide on the investments in your PEP, but have access to advice on which to choose and when to buy and sell. These PEPs are mainly offered by stockbrokers. The minimum lump sum can be low, but is often £1,000 to £3,000.

Corporate PEPs (not to be confused with corporate bond PEPs) are set up by a company to encourage investment in its own shares by outside investors and/or its own employees – for example, a corporate PEP might be used in conjunction with a profit-sharing scheme or savings-related share option scheme (see above). Corporate PEPs can be set up as single company PEPs, but are often general PEPs (allowing you to invest up to the full £6,000 limit). As well as a number of smaller plan managers (generally stockbrokers), a few High Street banks and building societies run corporate PEPs for a large number of companies and can thus offer investors a wide choice.

The tax advantages

At present, investing through a PEP means that both income and gains on the underlying investments are tax-free. However, in its first Budget, the Labour government announced that from April 1999, the dividends earned by shares held in a PEP would no longer be completely tax-free. Your PEP manager receives net dividends together with a tax credit and, currently, the manager reclaims the amount of the credit from the Inland Revenue and adds it to your plan. From April 1999, the manager will no longer be allowed to reclaim the credit, which means that income from shares held in a PEP will be taxed at the tax credit rate, due to be set at 10 per cent from 1999. However, since that Budget announcement, the government has published its proposals for the new ISAs. If these proposals go ahead in their current form, no new PEPs will be started from April 1999 onwards – the date from which ISAs become available. Existing PEP investors may (up to a limit likely to be £50,000) switch to the new ISAs, and a six-month transitional period – i.e. to 6 October 1999 – will be allowed to facilitate this. During the transitional period, existing PEPs will retain their tax privileges (except that dividends will be taxable as described above), but from October 1999 onwards, the tax advantages will be abolished, so where money is left invested in the old PEP, income will be taxable and capital gains tax may be due when the investments are sold on gains arising from 6 October 1999 onwards. Because annual limits will be on the amount you can put into an ISA, it may be worth putting as much as you can into PEPs while the opportunity remains in order to maximise the amount you can switch into your ISA in 1999.

Most people do not pay tax on capital gains anyway, so in the early days of a PEP the tax-free (until 1999, anyway) income – which can be reinvested – is the main attraction. But, if you invest through PEPs each year, you can build up a large enough portfolio to make the exemption from capital gains tax useful too.

To take out a PEP, you must be aged at least 18 and resident in the UK. Each adult has his or her own PEP allowances. Your allowances for a tax year must be used up by the end of the year (5 April) or else they are lost. This means that, if you pay by cheque, your payment must be *received* by the plan manager on or before 5 April, assuming there is no cooling off period – i.e. the period during which you have the option to change your mind and not invest after all. Where, as is often the case, there is a seven–day cooling off period, your cheque must reach the plan manager by 28 March. If you pay by standing order or direct debit, you are treated as investing for the tax year in which the *first* payment falls, so, if you are close to the end of the tax year, a wise safeguard against delay is to make the first payment by cheque. There are no tax restrictions on when or how much you can withdraw from a PEP.

Chart 6.1 compares the growth of an investment direct in a tracker fund – a selection of shares chosen to mimic a particular share index (in this case, the FTSE 100 index) with investment in the same shares through a PEP, assuming you had invested £6,000 at the start of 1993. First, we have assumed that there are no extra charges for the PEP beyond the 1 per cent a year charge we have built into the tracker fund. This is compared with the position when there is an additional 0.5 per cent a year charge for the PEP. As you can see, this eats heavily into the tax relief.

Chart 6.1: Value of £6,000 invested in shares (FTSE 100 Index) from January 1993 to July 1997

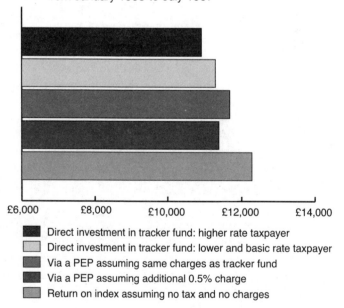

Legend	
■	Direct investment in tracker fund: higher rate taxpayer
□	Direct investment in tracker fund: lower and basic rate taxpayer
■	Via a PEP assuming same charges as tracker fund
■	Via a PEP assuming additional 0.5% charge
□	Return on index assuming no tax and no charges

What PEPs cost

If you are investing in a unit trust or investment trust, using your PEP allowance makes good sense, because very often there is no extra charge for the PEP arrangement. But, when you invest direct in shares, there are usually extra charges for a PEP. These can eat heavily into your investment and may even outweigh the tax advantage if you are a basic rate or lower rate taxpayer.

Charges vary a lot between different plan managers. For example, there could be a setting-up fee, an annual charge (e.g. from 0.5 to 1.5 per cent of the value of your PEP, plus VAT), a charge each time a dividend is added to your plan, a fee if you want to receive a company's report and accounts or attend a shareholders' meeting and a charge if you want to switch to another PEP manager. These charges may be on top of normal dealing fees levied when you buy and sell the shares in your PEP, though some plan managers offer reduced dealing charges to PEP holders. One of the best sources of information about PEPs, including the charges, is the *Chase de Vere PEP Guide*.★

Individual Savings Accounts (ISAs)

On 2 December 1997, the government published a consultative paper outlining its plans for new Individual Savings Accounts (ISAs), which had been foreshadowed in the July 1997 Budget. The proposals may be altered as a result of the consultation process, but assuming they go ahead as announced, ISAs will take the following form:

- Like PEPs, ISAs are not an investment in their own right. They are a tax-efficient 'wrapper' allowing you to benefit from tax advantages when investing in a wide range of investments.
- Through your ISA you will be able to invest in shares, unit trusts and so on. Unlike PEPs, there will be very few restrictions on which shares and other investments are eligible. You will also be able to invest in cash and National Savings. In addition, you will be able to use the account to take out life insurance. You choose the mix of investments.
- There will be no minimum investment for the purpose of the tax rules (ISA providers might, however, be able to set their own minima).
- There will be a maximum annual limit on the amount paid into the ISA. This could be £5,000.

- There will be a maximum lifetime limit on the amount which can be paid in overall. This could be £50,000.
- There are likely to be limits on the amount put towards cash and life insurance each year. These limits could be £1,000 each.
- There will be no income tax or capital gains tax on income and gains made by investments held in the ISA. Dividends from shares will carry a 10 per cent tax credit which, during the first five years of the scheme, can be reclaimed and added to the ISA.
- You can withdraw money and investments from your ISA at any time without losing the tax privileges.
- As with PEPs, ISAs will be run by plan managers.
- You will be able to invest in only one ISA each year, but you can switch to a different ISA manager.
- PEP and TESSA investments may be transferred to ISAs.
- ISAs will be available through a wide range of outlets, possibly including supermarket checkouts and High Street stores.
- There will be a prize draw each month with 50 winners having £1,000 added to their ISA.

Chapter 7

Which shares for you?

SHARES are not a single type of investment: they come in several forms which are technically different from one another. And, whatever the technical shape, all shares – but especially ordinary shares – can display very different characteristics, making them as diverse as the companies which issue them. This makes the shares of one company more suitable for one investor with a particular aim than another. The vast majority of individual shareholders have experience only of ordinary shares in 'blue chip' companies, and although a good spread of these can make a very sound investment, other types of shares open up different opportunities.

Chart 7.1: Different types of share

Shares

Technical differences	Differences in character
Ordinary shares	Blue chip
Voting	Growth stocks
Non-voting	High yield stocks
Preference shares	Defensive
Irredeemable	Recovery stocks
Redeemable	Cyclical stocks
Cumulative	Highly rated stocks
Convertible	Highly geared shares
	Smaller companies
	Penny shares
	Takeover targets
	Demerger targets
	The foreign element

Ordinary shares

Ordinary shares are the most common form of shares. They carry the highest risk and in return they stand to take the greatest share of any rewards.

The rewards

Not all ordinary shares pay an income. It may be many years before a new company starts to pay dividends. Even some mature companies pay no income, it being accepted practice to plough income back into the company to produce further growth.

Where shares do produce an income, dividends are usually paid out twice a year with an 'interim dividend' at the six-month stage and a 'final dividend' at the year-end. The final dividend is generally larger than the interim payment.

Dividends on ordinary shares are not of a set amount and are not guaranteed: they can be reduced or even missed altogether. The directors of the company decide how much will be paid out in dividends and this depends largely on the company's profits for the year.

It would be unusual and worrying if a company distributed all its profits to shareholders. Usually, a substantial proportion is retained to be reinvested in the business. On the other hand, directors are generally reluctant to announce a cut in dividends, as this suggests that the company might be in difficulty. The directors may be equally cautious about announcing a large increase in dividends for fear that it will prove impossible to sustain the higher payments in future years. Therefore, the dividends of well-established companies tend to be fairly stable, showing modest growth over the years.

In general, shareholders expect the greatest reward to be growth in the value of their shares, reflecting the underlying value of the company.

The risks

Should the company go bust, as an ordinary shareholder – one of the owners of the company – you are last in line to get any money back and may lose your entire investment. People to whom the company owes money (creditors) will be first in line to claim; they may include the tax authorities, pension schemes, employees, banks, holders of corporate bonds and, far down the line, customers who may have paid for goods they have not received.

Certain creditors take priority over others – for example, the costs of winding up the company are met before any creditors receive payment; then come priority debts which rank equally with one another and include PAYE due to the Inland Revenue over the last 12 months, VAT due to Customs & Excise over the same period, contributions outstanding to the pension fund if any, and so on. Secured creditors, whose loans were made on condition that they had a claim on specific assets of the company, take priority over unsecured creditors, whose claim is more general.

After the creditors come the shareholders, but here also there is a pecking order. Preference shareholders will have first claim (see page 91). The very last to get any money back are the ordinary shareholders.

Even if all the company's assets are sold, there may well not be enough in the kitty to pay the creditors, let alone the shareholders. The good news is that, as a shareholder, the most that you lose is what you invested in the shares, assuming they were fully paid up. You cannot be called on to stump up more, because all companies listed on the Stock Exchange must be 'limited'. This means that your liability is limited to the paid-up value of your shares. If the shares you own are only partly paid, you can be called on to pay the remaining instalments.

Example

In October 1996, Hotel plc floated on the Stock Exchange, issuing ordinary shares at 80p a share. The shares were in partly paid form with 60p payable on issue and the remaining 20p per share due one year later in October 1997.

In June 1997, Gavin bought 1,000 Hotel shares in the open market for 72p a share. In August, the company suddenly went into receivership, following major doubts over the reliability its products. On winding up, the company's assets were found to fall far short of the amount owing to creditors. The shareholders were called on to pay the oustanding 20p per share instalment to help towards paying the creditors.

Hotel proved a disastrous investment for Gavin. Apart from the £720 originally paid for the shares, he had also to hand over a further £200, making a total loss of £920.

Voting rights

In most cases, as a holder of ordinary shares, you have the right to exercise some control over the company which you jointly own with all the other shareholders. This is done through a system of votes which you cast at the company's annual general meeting (or extraordinary meetings) or by post. Your vote can be used to approve the annual report and accounts, appoint and reappoint directors, and influence any matters which affect the shareholders' interests. You have a right to speak at the company's general meetings, voicing your opinions on the running of the company or putting questions to the directors about their actions, the state of the company, future prospects for trading, and so on.

In theory, at least, the voting system puts the shareholders in the driving seat. In practice, you have to be a very large shareholder (or part of a group of shareholders who have agreed to act in concert) in order to wield this power effectively. The large institutional shareholders, such as insurance companies, pension funds and the investment funds of the major churches, can often bring some influence to bear – for instance on the standards applied in running the company and by encouraging the company to take an ethical or environmentally sound approach in its business activities.

Watch out for the minority of ordinary shares which either carry no voting rights or give you only restricted rights. This must be made clear in the title of the shares: these might be called 'A' shares, 'N/V' (non-voting) or 'R/V' (restricted voting). It is very unusual these days for a company to issue new non-voting or restricted voting shares, but some survive (e.g. Daily Mail, Eldridge Pope and John Laing), generally in companies where the founding family retains a large shareholding. Originally, the purpose of non-voting and restricted voting shares was to raise new capital without losing control of the company, but this approach meets with disapproval nowadays. Institutional investors, in particular, are unwilling to invest in a company without having the right to influence the running of it.

Non-voting and restricted voting shares are often cheaper than their equivalents which come with full voting rights – for example, Daily Mail voting shares closed at 1815p on 4 November 1997, whereas the non-voting shares were priced at 1710p, but this does not make them a bargain. Unless the company is persuaded to enfranchise the shares, when you come to sell they will still suffer the same drawback and, as a result, will still tend to be priced at a lower level. However, with some companies the bulk of trading is in non-voting shares, so you have little choice but to invest in them if you want a stake in that company.

Preference shares

Preference shares – which are widely used by many companies (e.g. Bank of Scotland, Carlton Communications, Shell) – are less risky than ordinary shares but the degree to which you share in the rewards of the company is restricted. In many respects, preference shares behave more like corporate bonds (see Glossary) and other fixed interest investments than like ordinary shares. Their main appeal is to investors seeking income. Preference shares offer a higher income than, say, British Government stocks (see Glossary) but this premium reflects the fact that preference shares are more risky.

The rewards
Most preference shares pay a fixed rate of dividend. Often, this is pitched at a relatively high level, making preference shares a good choice if you are seeking income. 'Participating' preference shares, which are not common, pay extra dividend on top of the fixed amount. The extra is some set proportion of the dividend being paid to ordinary shareholders.

Preference share dividends are not guaranteed but are given preference over any income for ordinary shareholders. No income can be declared on the ordinary shares until the preference dividends have been paid in full.

A company may make more than one issue of preference shares, in which case it has to rank the different issues in order of preference.

Most preference shares are 'cumulative'. This means that, if the dividend is skipped or only partly paid, the unpaid amount accumulates and is carried forward in time. No new dividend on any class of the company's shares can be declared until the arrears on the cumulative preference shares have been cleared.

As with ordinary shares, preference share prices rise and fall, so there is scope for making some capital gain on the shares as well as income, although the price of preference shares tends to be more stable than that of ordinary shares. Because the income is fixed and reasonably certain, investors may be prepared to sacrifice gain for the sake of higher income.

Preference shares also behave to some extent like other fixed interest investments – this is particularly so for redeemable preference shares, which have a set lifetime, after which the face value (called the 'par value' – see Glossary) of the stock is repaid. As interest rates in the general economy rise, the price of preference shares will tend to fall, with the result that the fixed income represents a higher percentage of the price paid for the stock. Conversely, when general interest rates fall, preference share prices are likely to rise to bring their return into line.

The risks

If the company goes bust, preference shareholders are entitled to the return of their capital before the ordinary shareholders can be paid anything. However, preference shareholders still stand behind the creditors, so they might not get back anything at all. Cumulative preference shareholders may find arrears of unpaid dividends cannot be paid after all.

Some preference shares are secured against specific assets. If the sale of the assets does not meet the preference shareholders' claim in full, the balance ranks equally with the claims of the ordinary shareholders.

As with ordinary shareholders, preference shareholders can be called on to pay any instalments of the original share price which are as yet unpaid because the shares were issued in partly paid form.

Voting rights

Preference shares do not normally give their holders the right to vote at general meetings, except in very rare circumstances when an issue on the agenda might be of particular importance to this class of shareholder – for example, if the preference dividend is to be skipped, or if the company proposes to make further issues of preference shares which will rank ahead of those already in existence.

Convertible preference shares and convertible bonds

Convertible preference shares are more common than straightforward preference shares and, in many ways, are similar to convertible corporate bonds. Both let you swap your preference shares or bonds for ordinary shares in the company at a fixed price at some future time. The opportunity to convert may run for a set period or may be restricted to one or more set dates.

'Convertibles', as these two types of investment are collectively called, are fascinating hybrids, combining some of the stability of fixed interest investments with the greater excitement of ordinary shares.

The rewards

As with a normal preference share, a convertible offers you a fixed income (though not guaranteed to be paid) either indefinitely if the stock is irredeemable, or until the stock is redeemed on some set future date. Convertible corporate bonds are basically the same, except that a bondholder is a creditor of the company with a contractual right to receive the promised interest payments.

When there is a long time to run until the conversion date(s), convertibles will behave much like any other fixed income investment. In other words, the general level of interest rates will be the major influence on return and, therefore, price movements.

However, as the conversion date(s) approach, the potential for making a profit by swapping the convertible for ordinary shares will become an increasingly important factor. The price of the convertible will come under the sway of the movement in the underlying share price.

Blue chip shares

There is no precise definition of a 'blue chip' share, but the term is used to mean the shares of large, well-established, soundly run companies. They are often household names, such as Unilever, Marks & Spencer, BP, British Telecom and so on.

Being well established, blue chip shares usually pay dividends: these tend to be fairly stable or regularly increasing. Over the long term (i.e. ignoring the inevitable short-term dips in the market), the share price is expected to climb steadily, reflecting the continuing prosperity of the company. When the market changes direction, starting an upturn or turning down, blue chip shares are often among the first to rise or fall, because large institutions are big buyers and sellers of blue chip shares and are quick to adjust the size of their holdings in response to market movements.

The character of blue chip shares tends to be dependable but unexciting. Generally, they give you a good, solid investment base, but you are unlikely to make dramatic profits. One reason for this is the vast amounts of money which institutional investors have to invest. To

Example

Charlotte is retired and has a portfolio of investments which provide an income to supplement her pensions. One of the stocks she is currently considering is 7 per cent cumulative preference shares in India plc. The stock is irredeemable. In 2007, she would have the option to swap the preference shares for ordinary shares in India at a rate of 50 ordinary shares for each nominal £100 of preference stock. The nominal value is the face value of the stock, which is not the same as its market price, which currently stands at £77 for each £100 nominal of stock.

If Charlotte buys this stock, the 7 per cent dividends (which are paid in twice-yearly instalments) represent a before-tax return of 9.3 per cent at the preference share price of £77. This comfortably beats what she could get in the building society, though of course preference shares are a bit more risky.

India's ordinary shares currently stand at 83p a share. If Charlotte were to exercise the conversion rights, given the current share price, she would give up £77 of preference stock for ordinary shares valued at just £41.50. That would not be a good deal but, if the ordinary share price rose to more than 154p between now and 2007, the swap would be worthwhile. The amount by which the price of the ordinary shares has to rise to show a profit on conversion is called the 'conversion premium', which in this case is $((77/41.50) - 1) \times 100 = 85.5\%$.

create large enough and liquid enough shareholdings, the institutions are forced to concentrate on these big companies. As a result, they become the major focus of analysts' research.

The institutional investment managers generally know all there is to know about them and there is little scope for the small investor to stumble across something new ahead of the rest of the market. The exception has been the privatisation issues, where small investors have often been given priority over institutions in the allocation of newly issued stock. Similarly, building society conversions have placed new stock directly in the hands of individuals, leaving the institutions out in the cold. This has given small investors the chance to make a profit when institutions try to get up to weight in the new stocks by buying at virtually any price.

Shares being shares, even blue chips are not without risk. One of the most spectacular collapses of a blue chip company was Rolls-Royce in 1971. Rolls-Royce was caught out by rapidly rising costs after it had signed contracts to supply aero engines at fixed prices. The share price plummeted, falling to 7p at one point, the company went bust and the company was only rescued by being nationalised. Since then Rolls-Royce has made a comeback and the re-privatised version is again one of the UK's major companies.

In more recent times, the collapse of Barings Bank in 1995 was another reminder that even blue chip investments can give a nasty shock. Barings was a dignified City bank, established over 230 years before and boasting the Queen among its customers. It was brought to its knees by the actions of one rogue trader who was able to run up a loss of £860 million through investing in derivatives, effectively gambling on future movements in the Japanese stockmarket. The bank was salvaged through a takeover by a Dutch financial group, ING.

Blue chip companies are not synonymous with the FTSE 100 Index (a market index based on the largest 100 companies on the London Stock Exchange) but, if you opt for a blue chip portfolio, FTSE 100 companies will appear prominently in your shareholdings.

Growth stocks

Growth stocks are the dream of most investors. You are looking for a company with a glowing future. The share price will be very resilient, shrugging off downturns in the market, and scaling ever higher peaks. Dividends may be small or non-existent, but that is unimportant. The company is reinvesting its profits and so fuelling further growth.

The trick is to spot these companies before they really take off. In past years, some of the companies involved in computing and new media, such as Microsoft, have fitted the bill. More recently, biotech companies have been tipped as the up and coming darlings of the stock market, but they have yet to fulfil their promise.

Growth stocks are likely to be found among newer industries, but also crop up in more established sectors, for example, following a new drug discovery, the invention of new equipment, a major find of some natural resource, a breakthrough into a new and previously undeveloped market, or the rise of a new fashion (though beware of a fall from grace if the company or its products later cease to be trendy).

Table 7.2: The FTSE 100 companies on 5 September 1997

3i Group	Cadbury Schweppes	Land Securities	Royal Sun Alliance Insurance Group
Abbey National	Carlton Communications	LASMO	Royal Bank of Scotland
Alliance & Leicester	Centrica	Legal & General Group	Safeway
Allied Domecq	Commercial Union	Lloyds TSB Group	Sainsbury
Asda Group	Dixons Group	Lucas Varity	Schroders
Associated British Foods	EMI Group	Marks & Spencer	Scottish & Newcastle
BAA	Energy Group	Mercury Asset Management	Scottish Power
Bank of Scotland	Enterprise Oil	National Grid Group	Severn Trent
Barclays	General Accident	National Power	Shell Transport & Trading
Bass	General Electric Company	National Westminster Bank	Siebe Siebe
BAT Industries	GKN	Next	SmithKline Beecham
BG	Glaxo Wellcome	Orange	Smiths Industries
Blue Circle Industries	Granada Group	Pearson	Standard Chartered
BOC	Grand Metropolitan	P&O	Tate & Lyle
Boots	Great Universal Stores	PowerGen	Tesco
British Aerospace	Guardian Royal Exchange	Prudential Corporation	Thames Water
British Airways	Guinness	Railtrack	TI Group
British Land	Halifax	Rank	Tomkins
British Petroleum	Hanson	Reckitt & Coleman	Unilever
British Sky Broadcasting Group	Hays	Reed International	United News & Media
British Steel	HSBC Holdings	Rentokil Initial	United Utilities
British Telecom	Imperial Chemical Industries	Reuters Holdings	Vodafone Group
BTR	Imperial Tobacco Group	Rio Tinto	Whitbread
Burmah Castrol	Kingfisher	RMC	Wolseley
Cable & Wireless	Ladbroke Group	Rolls-Royce	Zeneca

Source: FTSE International

High yield stocks

Essentially, these are the reverse of growth stocks. They are the shares of companies with a good, solid – some would say stolid – business, with a history of paying stable and relatively high dividends. These companies are not expected to sparkle in the growth stakes, but that does not matter if you are an investor mainly concerned with seeking an income. Often high yield stocks will be defensive shares (see below) and may be blue chip shares too.

Defensive shares

Defensive shares are those which tend to hold their value even when the stock market is falling. They are often in sectors where the goods or services being provided are fairly essential, for example, water, gas and basic foodstuffs. They are stocks with a beta value (see Chapter 8) of less than one.

Since demand for these companies' products or services is fairly stable whatever the performance of the economy as a whole, their profits are pretty stable, too. Therefore, the return on the shares is likely to centre mainly on steady dividends rather than dramatic capital gains, which makes defensive stocks a possibility for inclusion if you want an income-oriented, relatively low-risk portfolio.

Recovery stocks

These are shares which are in the doldrums at present but which you hope will revive in due course. There are various reasons why the shares might be performing poorly:

- the company might be one that is heavily influenced by the economic cycle (see 'Cyclical stocks' below). For example, producers of luxury goods generally see a slump in demand when the economy is in recession. Once activity picks up, consumers start to buy again and profits pick up
- the company may have hit a bad patch – for example, losing a major customer or giving ground to a new competitor. With time and good management, the business may re-establish its position and the shares return to favour
- the company might be permanently in the rough. Perhaps because demand has changed or the management is poor, there may be little

likelihood of a recovery. The company could bump along the bottom indefinitely or it might even go under.

It makes sense to take a good look at the company before buying recovery shares in order to establish what nature of business you are dealing with and how realistic the prospects for recovery really are.

Cyclical stocks

These shares are very sensitive to the economic cycle and their price will tend to move early when the economy is approaching a turning point. Typical cyclical industries are house building, car manufacture, consumer durables (such as fridges and TVs) and capital goods (things used for the production of other things, such as furnaces and packing machines). When the economy is in recession, cyclical stocks will be good recovery stocks to look out for since they can be expected to rise rapidly once the economy picks up.

Highly rated stocks

These are stocks whose price is very high compared with current earnings, indicating that investors expect the company to do very well in future. If you share this optimism and consider that the share price has further scope for increase, these could be good growth stocks. But beware a tumble in price if investors' confidence evaporates – e.g. on bad news about the company or its sector.

Highly geared shares

These are the shares of companies which have a high level of borrowing compared to the money raised through shares. Borrowing is more tax-efficient than shares as a way of raising capital and through the effect of gearing (see Glossary), in good times, borrowing enhances the return to shareholders who can expect to see dividends (if paid) and an increase in the prices of shares. But if the return the company gets from its activities is lower than the cost of its borrowing – either because profitability falls or interest rates rise – the company is vulnerable to heavy losses and even bankruptcy.

Smaller companies

The motive for investing in smaller companies is generally the search for growth stocks. You have a greater chance of very large capital gains if you can get in on the ground floor and invest while a company is still new and relatively unknown. 'Adam Smith' tells an anecdote in his book, *The Money Game,** of a man who shrewdly invested $20,000 in shares in a small firm called International Tabulator, which grew to become the corporate giant IBM, one of the world's most successful growth companies. (But there was a sting in the tail: the inheritors of these millions of dollars' worth of shares were cautioned never to sell and have lived very frugally despite being paper millionaires.)

In addition, you have more chance of stumbling on opportunities missed by the big institutional investors because they devote relatively little of their resources to researching smaller companies.

However, investing in smaller companies exposes you to greater risks than sticking to established businesses:

- The management of a new company are untried. Do they have the necessary skills to exploit their ideas or opportunities successfully?
- Does the company have access to enough capital? Many companies with great ideas have foundered because working capital has not kept pace with the expansion of the company.
- Will the shares catch on? The company may be successful but if it remains small its shares might not get much attention, so it could be difficult for you to sell the shares or sell at a realistic price when you want to realise your profits.

Investing in smaller companies can be fun, but it is not the place for money which you depend on or cannot afford to lose.

Penny shares

Penny shares are the ultimate growth or recovery gamble. The shares are extremely cheap, but that is because very few people want to invest. Although they do often cost literally pennies, it is not that which tells you that penny shares are of lowly value. Investment regulators have defined penny shares as those where the spread between the buying and selling price is 10 per cent or more of the price you buy at. For example, if you can buy at 7p and sell at 6.3p or less, the share is a penny share. A wide spread like this tells you that the trading is thin and warns you that it might be hard to sell at all.

Penny shares come about, typically, because a company has suffered a major crisis some time in the past from which its share price has never recovered. You might invest in penny shares for two reasons:

- you believe that the company's original business is capable of recovery and will make a comeback at some stage, possibly in the hands of new management
- you hope that new managers will take over the company in order to take advantage of its stock market quotation and, within the 'shell' of the old company will develop completely new – and hopefully profitable – business interests. In order to do this, the new managers might call on shareholders to stump up some extra cash through rights issues.

Either way, penny shares are pure speculation, rather than investment. Very few companies do make it. There are some prominent tip sheets giving guidance on penny share opportunities. Interestingly, the *Investors Chronicle* found that these were among the poorest performing of the share tipsters in 1996.

Takeovers, mergers and demergers

At one time, searching out potential takeover prospects was very popular. With large conglomerates such as Hanson on the prowl, you could make a killing if you had shares in a company which suddenly became the target of a takeover bid.

Many conglomerates themselves have also given investors a good ride. In the 1980s, it was very fashionable for certain companies to provide growth by taking over other companies (often dubbed 'asset situations') and then reorganising their activities, selling off some assets and segments (a process viewed either as laudable rationalisation or, less charitably, as 'asset-stripping') and absorbing the rest. Sometimes this would produce powerful and efficiently combined new organisations. At other times, it produced a diversity of incompatible segments with management spread thinly across them all. However, so strong was the fashion that many financial institutions set up dedicated mergers and acquisitions (M&A) departments, whose function was akin to that of a dating agency. M&A analysts would study companies to spot likely marriage partners, approach one or both (or more if the marriage was to be polygamous) of the candidates and, if the potential partners liked the idea, set about tying the knot in exchange for a fat fee.

Times change and fashions too. Mergers still happen, but are no longer the fad. Instead, the trend is towards demerger. Instead of waiting to be taken over, companies are reviewing their structures for themselves to see whether a split into their component parts would improve future growth and profitability. The buzz word is 'focus' – companies should focus on their core activities. Shareholders find that where they had one shareholding they are now being offered shares in two or more component companies – as for instance happened with the splitting of British Gas into BG (focusing on pipeline and exploration) and Centrica (gas supply and the retail arm). If focusing does work, the new shareholdings should collectively give a better return than the former consolidated holding. However, small shareholders may be left with very small – and uneconomic – holdings in each component company.

The foreign element

Investing overseas, particularly in emerging markets, can look an attractive route to capital growth. However, buying foreign shares direct can be a nightmare. In the developed world, stock exchanges are generally well regulated and have up-to-date systems for trading and settlement. But in emerging markets, such as India and many Pacific Rim countries, buying shares is fraught with hazards. Settlement may still involve handwritten documents being physically delivered. Share certificates may be carelessly handled – remember the stories of share certificates being trampled underfoot in the streets of Bombay – entries on share registers may take many months and, worse still, if dishonesty is rife, your ownership of the shares might not be recorded at all. Fortunately, there are other ways to invest abroad.

Some foreign companies are quoted on the London Stock Exchange – for example, Norsk Hydro (an integrated Norwegian oil company) and Nestlé (a Swiss food production group) – and you can buy their shares in the same way as any other quoted share.

Alternatively, you may be able to buy depository receipts. These are not shares as such, but they are proof of your ownership of shares quoted on a foreign exchange and held on deposit on your behalf. This is often a more secure and less troublesome way to become a shareholder than attempting to buy direct on the relevant foreign stock exchange.

Another possibility is to buy shares in a UK company which derives a significant part of its profits from overseas operations. Finally, you could buy units in a unit trust or shares in an investment trust specialising in a particular geographical area (see Chapter 9).

Chapter 8

Risk

THE wider context of risk was discussed in Chapter 2. Here we focus on *capital* risk. Capital risk is the main reason why an investment in shares is likely to give you a much better return than leaving your money in the building society. The higher return is your reward for taking on the extra risk. It is a fundamental rule of the investment world that greater risks attract greater rewards.

Types of risk

The return from shares is made up of two parts. Most – though not all – established companies pay dividends to their shareholders. Dividends are generally paid at six-monthly (or quarterly) intervals. For ordinary shareholders, dividends are not fixed: they can be reduced or even missed. This risk will be particularly important to anyone who has invested in shares in order to provide an income.

Most investors in shares are much more concerned about capital risk – the risk that the price of their shares will fall, producing a loss if the shares are sold. Capital risk comes in a number of forms:

- **company risk** – the share price falls because of events specific to the company: a strike by its workers, for example, the loss of a key executive, or poor sales performance
- **sector risk or industry risk** – the price of your shares and those of other companies in the same sector fall because of events affecting the whole industry, geographical region or other basis on which the sector has been defined: shortage of a particular commodity used in the industry, for example, a health scare, or a natural disaster such as an earthquake affecting a whole region

- **market risk** – the fall in share price is part of a general slide in the whole stockmarket, for example, because the economy is moving into a cyclical recession or the inflationary outlook worsens
- **exchange rate risk** – if you invest in shares denominated in a different currency, however well the shares perform, you have an additional layer of risk because the exchange rate may move against you between the time you buy and the time you sell (assuming that you convert the sale proceeds back into your own currency).

So far, we have talked of risk only in terms of the possibility of something going wrong – the downside risk. However, risk is a symmetrical concept. There is also the upside risk that you might make gains. Capital risk refers to the volatility of a share price both upwards and downwards. The amount of volatility can be measured, giving a yardstick for assessing and comparing risk.

Using information about risk

Professional investors use several statistical measures of risk. Two of the most common are standard deviation (sometimes called volatility) and beta. Standard deviation looks at how widely a share price swings around its average level. Beta measures the extent to which a share price moves independently of the stock market as a whole.

By the 1970s risk measures had found a place in US fund management but were only tentatively being explored by the big institutional investors in Britain. Nowadays, such measures are common tools of the trade. In a similar way, most private investors, although taking account of risk in a rule-of-thumb way, have so far had little exposure to precise measures of risk. This looks likely to change. Nowadays, risk measures are being included as standard in several personal finance publications and many investment advisers believe that it is no longer acceptable to select shares or share-linked investments without some consideration of these measures.

However, it is important to be clear about what such measures can and cannot tell you. They have an immediate appeal to anyone seeking 'hard facts' on which to base a decision because they are objective and can be compared in terms of one share or investment and another. But standard deviation, beta and their statistical friends have drawbacks which limit their usefulness:

- They are all worked out from past data — typically, the standard deviation for a share will be based on the recorded share price for the last three years. Past performance is no guide to the future — this applies just as much to an assessment of risk as it does to an assessment of return. You need to think about whether you have good grounds for assuming that the future will be similar to the past. For example, suppose a company's management changed and, as a result, you expected the company to follow sounder policies in future, resulting in more stable performance. The company's measured standard deviation — based on the past — would not alter because of the change in management, but you might judge the shares to be less risky now, justifying a reduction in the risk measure.
- Risk measures are simply an observation — they tell you nothing about why the measure has the value it does. For example, a company might have a fairly high standard deviation but, if you investigated further, you might discover that this was due to a single event in the past — such as unexpected disruption of production while the company relocated — which is unlikely to be repeated. The event will continue to influence the statistics for quite a while, but you may be justified in ignoring its effect.
- Risk measures can be perverse. Intuitively, we accept that a small company with little or no track record is likely to be more risky than a large, well-established firm. Yet the standard deviation and beta for shares in a large company can be higher than they are for a smaller company in the same sector. This happens because big institutional investors concentrate on holding large companies (see page 92). When the stock market is volatile, institutional investors may be buying or selling the large companies, causing big fluctuations in their share price, while smaller companies are ignored, with the result that their share price changes little.

Risk measures can therefore be a guide when you are comparing different shares and investments but should not be accepted simply at face value. Look behind the figures to see why they have the value they do and use your judgement, taking into account all the other information you have, to assess whether the future is likely to be similar to the past or very different.

Where to find risk measures

Institutional investors have ready access to risk measures, either crunching them on in-house computers or buying the data from outside research bodies. It is not so easy for the private investor to get hold of standard deviations and betas for individual shares, but your stockbroker or financial adviser should be able to get this data for you.

Standard deviations for collective investments, such as unit trusts, are now being published in some journals – for example, *Money Management* – and are available over the Internet, e.g. from Micropal.★

Tactics for dealing with risk

Risk is a friend as well as a foe: if you are seeking higher than average returns, you are more likely to achieve this by opting for investments which are more risky than average. However, you should not put at risk any money which you cannot afford to lose or which you might need back at a fixed point in time (when prices could be low).

When it comes to shares, some are clearly more risky than others. If you choose the shares of a young company with a limited track record, you will be running a greater risk of losing some or all of your money than if you choose the shares of an established giant, such as Unilever, BP or Marks & Spencer. If you choose shares quoted on a foreign stockmarket, you expose yourself directly to exchange rate risks as well as the risks inherent in the shares themselves. You expose yourself indirectly to exchange rate risks if you choose domestic shares of companies which have substantial overseas earnings.

You can reduce your exposure to risk by building a portfolio of shares and other investments. Have some money in cash and fixed-interest investments, such as British Government stocks and corporate bonds, as well as money in shares and share-based investments. Don't invest in just one or two companies, but spread your capital across a number of different shares. Consider unit trusts and investment trusts as ways of giving you a stake in a ready-made balanced portfolio. These techniques are a straightforward application of the old adage: don't put all your eggs in one basket.

However, take care in choosing your eggs. You will not reduce risk very much if you choose investments which are exposed to similar risks. For example, holding shares in both Abbey National and

Woolwich leaves your wealth more exposed to shocks in the banking sector than if you held shares in Abbey National and National Power, say. Academic research has shown that, carefully selected, as few as half a dozen shares can produce a portfolio which can be expected to move broadly in line with the market as a whole.

Bear in mind that risk is all about uncertainty. You can measure risk, you can predict risk, you can select and mix stocks because of their particular risk profiles, but the unexpected will always happen. A company whose shares tend to increase by more than the market as a whole may suffer some domestic crisis which sends its share price tumbling. A defensive stock intended to cushion you from a slump in the market can suddenly become worthless if the company goes bust.

The risk measures

Standard deviation

The chart and table show the price movements of a fictitious share measured once every week over a period of three months. The price moves up and down but an average (in this case, an arithmetic mean) can be worked out.

The volatility of the share describes the way the share price wanders around this average price. A first step in measuring volatility is to subtract each price from the average to find the deviation. Next, you might be tempted simply to add together all these deviations but the positive values would cancel out the negative values and the end result would be zero.

So the next step is to take the square of each deviation – this turns all the deviations into positive numbers which can be added together. The average of all these squared deviations gives a measure of how widely the share prices are scattered around the average and is what statisticians call 'variance'.

However, there is one more step worth taking. Variance will look rather large compared with the original share prices and the average because the deviations were squared. Taking the square root of the variance puts the measure back into the same units as the original data. This is called the 'standard deviation' and it is used as the basic measure of share volatility.

It is important to understand the limitations of volatility measures. First, the figure you arrive at will vary according to the period over which it is measured and the frequency of share prices used – commonly, standard deviations for shares or unit trusts are worked out over a period of three years, using monthly data. Using a three-year span of data which is rolled forward month-by-month produces a fairly stable measure.

Secondly, volatility measures must be supplemented with other information. On its own, standard deviation merely describes what has happened to a share's price in the past and gives no indication of why the price has behaved in that way. Which types of risk are at work? Is the company itself inherently risky, or is it the general sector in which it is operating, or has the whole stockmarket been particularly volatile over the period in question? You need 'hard' information from company reports, newspaper articles and so on, if you are to make sense of the raw statistical measures.

Covariance and beta

Variance and standard deviation are statistical measures describing one set of data – the share price. Statistics can also be used to describe the

Chart 8.1: Measuring volatility

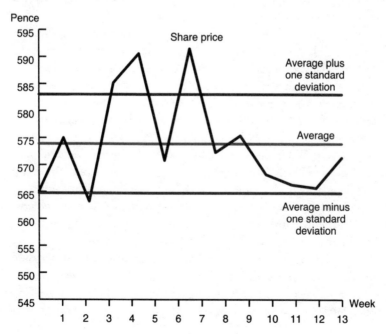

Table 8.1: Volatility of a fictitious share

Week	Share price (pence)	Share price less average	Square of share price less average
1	565.1	−8.8	77.3
2	575.0	1.1	1.2
3	563.2	−10.7	114.3
4	585.2	11.3	127.9
5	590.6	16.7	279.1
6	570.8	−3.1	9.6
7	591.5	17.6	310.0
8	572.3	−1.6	2.5
9	575.4	1.5	2.3
10	568.2	−5.7	32.4
11	566.3	−7.6	57.6
12	565.7	−8.2	67.1
13	571.3	−2.6	6.7
Average	573.9		Variance: 83.7
			Standard deviation: 9.1

relationship between two (or more) sets of data, for example, the share price and movements in the market or a sector as a whole, or the prices of two different shares.

'Covariance' can be used to describe the extent to which the share price and the market move together. A low value for the covariance suggests that no relationship exists between the two or only a very weak one. A high positive value says that the market and the share price are strongly related and that, when the market rises, the share price will tend to rise too. When the market falls, so does the share price. A high negative value for the correlation would tell you that there was an inverse relationship between the two, with the share price tending to fall when the market was rising and vice versa. But a word of warning; just because two values move together, it does not prove that there is a relationship between them. Statisticians can show that when the stork population in Norway rises, there is an increase in live births – does that prove that one caused the other?

Covariance is found by multiplying the deviations in share price by the deviations in the market values and then finding the average.

Like variance, covariance has a drawback in that the units are large compared with the original data. Dividing by the standard deviation of both the share price and the market values gives a measure, called the correlation coefficient, which is independent of units. The correlation coefficient always has a value between −1 and +1. A value of zero or close to zero tells you that there is little or no relationship between the share price and the market. The closer the coefficient gets to +1 or −1, the stronger the relationship. Table 8.2 shows the prices of a fictional share compared with a market index. The correlation coefficient works out as 0.67, suggesting a strong positive relationship between the share price movements and the market as a whole. This corresponds with what you would expect from comparing charts of the share price and the market index.

Chart 8.2: Share price movements compared with market movements

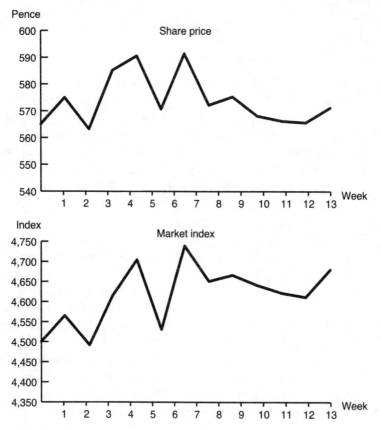

Table 8.2: Testing whether the fictitious share moves with the market

Week	Share price (pence)	Share price less average	Market index	Market index less average
1	565.1	−8.8	4,500.5	−116.6
2	575.0	1.1	4,565.2	−51.9
3	563.2	−10.7	4,491.9	−125.2
4	585.2	11.3	4,615.0	−2.1
5	590.6	16.7	4,705.0	87.9
6	570.8	−3.1	4,531.1	−86.0
7	591.5	17.6	4,739.9	122.8
8	572.3	−1.6	4,651.3	34.2
9	575.4	1.5	4,666.6	49.5
10	568.2	−5.7	4,641.4	24.3
11	566.3	−7.6	4,621.9	4.8
12	565.7	−8.2	4,611.7	−5.4
13	571.3	−2.6	4,680.5	63.4
Average	573.9		4,617.1	
Covariance	454.2			
Correlation coefficient	0.67			

Statistical techniques can be further applied to shares and markets. It is possible to work out the relationship between the return on a share and the return on the market as a whole. This can either be shown as a line on a chart or described mathematically. Chart 8.3 shows a simplified version. The slope of the line tells you how responsive the return on the share is to changes in the return on the market as a whole. Put another way, it tells you how much of the share's behaviour can be explained by the behaviour of the market as a whole. This measure of responsiveness has been given the name beta (β).

If a share has a beta equal to 1, then the return on the share moves directly in line with the return on the market as a whole. If a share has a beta of more than 1, the share tends to outperform the market and is called an 'aggressive' stock. It would be good to hold in a rising market, when the share can be expected to produce better than average returns, but it would be less attractive when the market was falling and the share produced greater than average losses.

Similarly, a share with a beta of less than 1 tends to underperform the market. It will tend to give you lower than average returns when the market is rising but smaller than average losses when the market is falling. Such stocks are called 'defensive'.

Chart 8.3: Beta

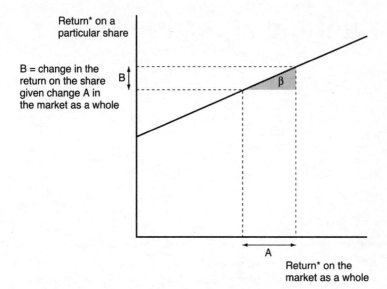

Return* on a
particular share

B = change in the
return on the share
given change A in
the market as a whole

B

β

A

Return* on the
market as a whole

* Technically, these returns are the extra return over and above that
  provided by a totally risk-free investment

Chapter 9

Building a portfolio

SHARES should play a part in most people's financial planning (see Chapter 2). But one or two shareholdings picked up through privatisations, building society windfalls or a share scheme at work are unlikely to give you the right balance of risk and return. As discussed in Chapter 8, holding too few shares leaves you over-exposed to company risk and sector risk. If your aim is long-term growth or providing an income over an extended period of time, you should ideally be looking at a reasonable spread of shares, with a diversity of companies and sectors. There are four ways of achieving this:

- build up your own portfolio
- pay for an investment manager, such as a stockbroker, to run your personal portfolio
- set up or join an investment club
- invest in a collective scheme, such as a unit trust.

Your own portfolio

There are no hard and fast rules as to how many different shareholdings you should have. Chapter 8 mentioned the work of academics who found that as few as six shares could give a portfolio with a beta of one – i.e. a portfolio which basically tracks the market as a whole. However, those shares would have to be carefully selected and not many small investors are keen to delve into the complicated statistical techniques used to estimate the beta of different portfolios.

A more general rule of thumb, widely accepted, is that you should aim for a minimum of ten different shareholdings. You do not have to buy all ten at once. For example, you might use your PEP or ISA allowances (see Chapter 6) to invest in two or three shareholdings one year, a few more the next, and so on.

The main drawback to building up your own portfolio is the cost. If you have so far acquired shares only when they were newly issued, it may come as a surprise to find that dealing costs and stamp duty will immediately swallow up around 1.5 per cent of your investment or more (see Chapter 4). Costs become especially prohibitive if you are buying shares only in relatively small amounts because of the impact of minimum commissions. In general, you should try to trade in lots of at least £1,000.

Table 9.1 shows that, even using a discount broker, charges can eat heavily into small investments. The Table assumes only that you build up ten holdings of shares and then hang on to them indefinitely. If you switch your shares from time to time, the costs will be higher. The Table also assumes that either you hold the shares yourself (except in the case of a PEP) or that, if the shares are held in a nominee account, there are no extra charges for that service.

Holding shares through a self-select PEP can be particularly costly. In addition to normal dealing costs (usually those that apply to dealing and advice), there will sometimes be an administration fee. Normally, you will have to pay a handling charge for each dividend as well as other charges for additional services, such as sending you the annual reports and accounts. If you are a higher rate taxpayer, your tax savings might come to more than the costs. If you pay tax at a lesser rate, the tax savings are unlikely to compensate for the charges and you will probably be better off holding your shares direct rather than through a PEP. The position with Individual Savings Accounts might be different – you will need to weigh up the situation once the details of these have been sorted out.

Apart from costs, before you opt for the DIY route to share ownership consider carefully whether you feel confident about selecting and monitoring shares for yourself. This requires time, access to information and some numerical skills. Don't forget the hidden costs if you subscribe to various journals, invest in a computer, buy portfolio management software, hook yourself up to the Internet, and so on. Some people are fascinated by shares and really enjoy running their own portfolio, partly as serious investment and partly as a hobby. If you are not bitten by this particular bug, others ways of holding a portfolio might be more suitable.

Table 9.1: Examples of the impact dealing costs could have on your initial portfolio

Type of dealing service used	Costs of buying and holding ten shareholdings where each purchase is:					
	£500		£1,000		£5,000	
	£	costs as % of initial portfolio	£	costs as % of initial portfolio	£	costs as % of initial portfolio
Dealing only – cut-price	75	1.5%	150	1.5%	750	1.5%
Dealing only – typical	225	4.5%	250	2.5%	750	1.5%
Dealing with advice	225	4.5%	250	2.5%	1,000	2%
Self-select PEP, including dividend handling charges for one year	575	11.5%	600	6%	1,225	2.5%

Portfolio management services

These were touched upon in Chapter 4. Stockbrokers provide portfolio management; so too do some private banks and investment advisers. If you have at least £50,000 to invest, they could be suitable.

There are two types of service: advisory and discretionary. Opting for an advisory service leaves you in the driving seat with the final say on what shares you hold, the size of holdings, how actively you trade, and so forth, but with the benefit of comment and suggestions from the portfolio manager.

With a discretionary service, you leave the manager to take these decisions on your behalf, but the manager will select stocks and trade within the framework of your own personal investment aims, attitude towards risk, quirks (e.g. regarding ethical investment), and so on, having first carried out a detailed fact-find.

The costs of portfolio management vary. In general, you will be charged normal commission on transactions within your portfolio. A few managers make no other charges, but most charge an annual management fee (plus VAT). This may be a flat rate ranging from, say, £250 up to £1,000, or a percentage of your portfolio – e.g. ½ per cent up to 1 per cent. Sometimes the cost is the same for both the advisory and discretionary routes, sometimes discretionary charges are higher. There may also be administration charges for each transaction. A survey of annual charges for an imaginary portfolio devised for the *Investors Chronicle Directory of Stockbrokers and Investment Managers*★ found that costs varied from £600 to £3,000 for an advisory portfolio and from £670 to £3,600 for a discretionary portfolio, depending on who you chose to trust with your money. In other words, expect charges to swallow anything from 0.4% to 2.4% of your portfolio.

The proof of the pudding is in the eating. Charges are justified if your investment manager produces good returns on your portfolio, but how can you assess the performance of your manager? Until recently, that was very difficult. However, in 1997, APCIMS★ and FTSE International★ together produced three indices designed to be used as standards against which you can compare the performance of your private portfolio. The three indices represent medium–risk portfolios, one aimed at producing income, one targeted on growth and one balancing both objectives. The portfolios are made up of UK shares, foreign shares, British Government stocks and corporate bonds. The mix of assets and the approach towards risk might not match your own, so care must be taken in using these benchmarks. However, the benchmark portfolios do give you a starting point for assessing the effectiveness of portfolio managers and, when choosing a manager, you should ask how they measure their performance and how they rate against these benchmarks.

If the amount you have to invest is below the threshold for managing a share portfolio, the stockbroker or adviser might still offer you a portfolio management service, but invest on your behalf in a range of unit trusts, investment trusts and/or OEICs (see page 124).

For details of how to find a stockbroker offering portfolio management services, see page 47. To find a more generalist independent financial adviser in your area, contact IFA Promotion★ or the Money Management National Register of Fee-Based Advisers★ – check direct with the advisers to find out what services they offer.

Investment clubs

An investment club is a group of people who decide to pool resources and together invest in shares (and other assets too, if they want to).

Basically, it is a small private collective investment scheme – with the advantage of no management charges. The idea crossed to Britain from the USA in the late 1950s and there are now hundreds of British investment clubs made up of family groups, friends or work colleagues.

A club is set up by a group of at least three like-minded people. The simplest way to set up and run the club is as a partnership; the laws applying to this form of organisation limit the maximum number of members to twenty.

The club adopts a formal constitution, elects officers, agrees a set of rules, chooses a bank, and so on. Members pay subscriptions into the club – often there will be an initial subscription to get the club going, followed by regular – e.g. monthly – subs. There are no limits on the amount of the subscriptions. They should be pitched at a level which suits the members – £25 a month is common.

The club meets periodically, usually monthly, to decide how to invest the money, to value the investments bought so far, swap ideas on investment strategies, and deal with other business. Investments are made through a stockbroker in the normal way. The assets of the club can be held in the nominee account of the broker or in a trust set up by the club, with members holding units in the investments in proportion to the amount they have invested.

The advantages of investment clubs are that they pool knowledge, make it easier to spread risk by investing across a larger number of shares, and that members benefit from the economies of scale from investing larger sums than they could as individuals and bring an enjoyable, social angle to investing. But it is essential that members trust each other and can reach agreement on an investment strategy; and inevitably operating as a club involves a certain amount of administration. See page 118 for how a club's early finances might look.

Proshare* produces a manual giving full guidance on setting up and running an investment club and also runs a membership organisation for clubs, providing a company information guide, regular newsletter and other benefits.

Unit trusts and other collective investments

Unless you are keen to run your own share portfolio, collective investments schemes, such as unit trusts and investment trusts, are a sensible choice for the smaller investor – anyone with, say, less than

Example

John and Ian work together and regularly meet up socially. Ian has dabbled on the stock market for several years, a hobby in which John has always shown great interest. One night, jokingly at first but with increasing seriousness, they talk about pooling resources to make some joint investments. Ian recalls hearing something about investment clubs and does some research, including buying the Proshare manual.

They decide to invite some others to join them. Ian's wife, Lucy, who has her own income is keen to join, as are three neighbours, Ken, Peter and Rebecca. The six of them form a club. Ian is the first chairman, Peter becomes secretary and Rebecca, the treasurer.

The initial subscription is £100. This gives them £600 to start with. They set an initial value of £1 on each investment unit. This means that each member starts with 100 units. Thereafter, they each put in £30 a month. They decide that they will make their first share purchase when they have accumulated £1,000.

Initially, Ian is very much the leading light, drawing on his experience of investing in shares to date. But the others are keen to learn and quickly bring new information and ideas to the group.

In the fourth month, they make their first purchase: 400 shares in Juliet plc priced at 251p per share. Since dealing costs have to be paid, the club is now showing a slight loss and the unit price falls from £1 to 98.68p. This is now the price at which new units are bought (by existing members through their regular subscription and by any new members who join). At this stage, the club is vulnerable to risk because it is holding the shares of a single company, but as the months go on the portfolio will build up.

In the fifth month, the price of Juliet plc shares has risen to 278p per share. This gives an increase in the value of members' units to £1.07p. The financial position of the group for the first five months is summarised in Table 9.2.

£30,000 to invest. They work by pooling your investment with the investments of many others. The resulting fund is used to buy a portfolio of shares and/or other investments which is run by professional investment managers.

There are numerous advantages to investing in shares in this way:

- you have none of the hassle of choosing the investments or making decisions on timing
- all the administration – placing orders, chasing share certificates, collecting dividends and so on – is done by the fund managers. This can be especially welcome if you are investing in an overseas market
- by clubbing together with lots of other investors, you benefit from the economies of scale enjoyed by large investors, enabling you to spread risks and own a diverse basket of shares and other investments at an acceptable cost.

Table 9.2: An investment club: getting started

	Month				
	1	2	3	4	5
Total cash at start of month	£0	£600	£780	£960	£120.94
New money invested	£600	£180	£180	£180	£180
Purchases	nil	nil	nil	£1,004	nil
Expenses	nil	nil	nil	£15.06	nil
Total cash at end of month	£600	£780	£960	£120.94	£300.94
Juliet plc shares					
Number of shares	nil	nil	nil	400	400
Share price	n/a	n/a	n/a	251p	278p
Value of shares	n/a	n/a	n/a	£1,004	£1,112
Total value of investments (shares and cash) at end of month	£600	£780	£960	£1,124.94	£1,412.94
Price of each unit at start of month	£1	£1	£1	£1	98.68p
New units bought	600	180	180	180	182.41
Total number of units at end of month	600	780	960	1,140	1,322.41
Price of each unit at end of month	£1	£1	£1	98.68p	£1.07

The disadvantage is that you have to pay for having your investment professionally managed.

There are both a huge choice of trust management companies to choose from and many different types of trust. Table 9.3 shows the range available; investment trusts offer a similar choice. This means that you can select the trusts that suit your attitude towards risk and investment aims – see chapter 2. You can spread your risks further by investing in a range of different trusts.

If you do not want to select the appropriate trusts for yourself, you can enlist the help of a stockbroker or other adviser. You could either seek advice but run the trust holdings yourself or you could use a portfolio management service (see page 44).

If you already have various direct holdings of shares and you would prefer to hold unit or investment trusts, instead of selling your shares yourself, you can often convert them relatively cheaply into units in a unit trust or shares in an investment trust by using a share exchange scheme. Quite a few unit trust managers and investment trust managers run such schemes.

Three main types of collective investment scheme are available in the UK, outlined below. For further information, see *Which? Way to Save and Invest*★ (also published by Which? Books). You can also get information about investing in the various collective investment schemes from the respective trade bodies: the Association of Unit Trusts and Investment Funds (AUTIF)★ and the Association of Investment Trust Companies (AITC).★

Unit trusts

You buy units which give you a share of the underlying portfolio. As new investors come into the trust and others leave, units are created and cancelled and the fund's investments increase or decrease, so the size of the fund varies with the number of investors involved and the value of your units is directly related to the value of the underlying investments in the fund.

What they cost

You buy units at the offer price and sell at the lower bid price. The spread between the two (generally around 6 per cent) is basically a charge which goes towards the cost of managing the trust fund. There is also an annual management charge of, say, 1 to 1.5 per cent. The

Table 9.3: Types of unit trust

Type of trust	How it is invested
UK equity growth	At least 80 per cent of the fund is invested in the shares of UK companies. The main objective is capital growth with moderate risk.
UK equity income	At least 80 per cent of the fund is invested in the shares of UK companies. The objective is to produce an income of more than 110 per cent of the yield on the FTSE All Share Index. Moderate risk.
UK growth and income	At least 80 per cent of the fund is invested in the shares of UK companies. The objective is to produce both capital growth and income, with the income element being in the range of 80 to 110 per cent of the yield on the FTSE All Share Index. Moderate risk.
UK smaller companies	At least 80 per cent of the fund is invested in the shares of UK smaller companies. High risk.
UK equity and bond income	At least 80 per cent of the fund is invested in UK securities, with less than 80 per cent in either UK shares or UK British Government stocks and other fixed interest investments. The aim is to produce an income of 120 per cent or more of the yield on the FTSE All Share Index. Low to moderate risk.
UK equity and bond	At least 80 per cent of the fund is invested in UK securities, with less than 80 per cent in either UK shares or UK British Government stocks and other fixed interest investments. The aim is to produce an income of 120 per cent or more of the yield on the FTSE All Share Index. Low to moderate risk.
UK gilt	At least 80 per cent of the fund is invested in UK British Government securities. Relatively low risk.
UK fixed interest	At least 80 per cent of the fund is invested in UK fixed interest securities. Relatively low risk.

Type of trust	How it is invested
International equity growth	At least 80 per cent of the fund is invested in shares. The main objective is capital growth with moderate risk.
International equity income	At least 80 per cent of the fund is invested in shares. The objective is to produce an income which is 10 per cent higher than the yield on the FTA World Index. Moderate risk.
Emerging markets	At least 80 per cent of the fund is invested in the 'emerging economies' as defined by the World Bank – includes places like India and China. High risk.
International equity and bond	Less than 80 per cent of the fund is invested in either shares or fixed interest securities. Moderate risk.
International fixed interest	At least 80 per cent of the fund is invested in fixed interest securities. Some are spread across a variety of countries; others are more concentrated on a particular geographical area. Moderate risk.
Fund of funds	The fund invests in other unit trusts. This reduces risk but may add an extra tier of charges. Relatively low to moderate risk.
Investment trust units	The fund invests in the shares of unit trusts. This reduces risk but may add an extra tier of charges. Relatively low to moderate risk.
Property	At least 80 per cent of the fund is invested in the shares of property companies or in financial securities. Moderate risk.
North America	At least 80 per cent of the fund is invested in the shares of US companies or other US securities. Moderate to high risk.
Europe	At least 80 per cent of the fund is invested in the shares of European (including UK) companies or other European securities. Moderate to high risk.
Japan	At least 80 per cent of the fund is invested in the shares of Japanese companies or other Japanese securities. High risk.

Type of trust	How it is invested
Far East including Japan	At least 80 per cent of the fund is invested in the shares of Far Eastern companies or other Far Eastern securities. High risk.
Far East excluding Japan	At least 80 per cent of the fund is invested in the shares of Far Eastern (excluding Japanese) companies or other Far Eastern securities. High risk.
Commodities and energy	At least 80 per cent of the fund is invested in commodity and/or energy securities. High risk.
Money market	At least 80 per cent of the fund is invested in deposits, bills of exchange, debentures and other assets where the amount of your original capital is protected. Low risk.
Tracker fund	The fund is designed to track the performance of a particular index – e.g. the FTSE-100. Since management is less active, charges should generally be lower. Moderate risk.
Index bear	The fund is designed to track a particular index but inversely, so that when the index is falling, the fund aims to be increasing in value. It does this by investing in derivatives. High risk.
Managed fund	Fund which invests in a range of investments, including near cash, fixed interest and shares. The idea is to switch the asset allocation as investment conditions change. Managed funds have been linked to investment-type life insurance for many years, but are new to the unit trust sector. Moderate risk.

charges for tracker funds tend to be lower – e.g. 1 per cent management charge and sometimes no front-end charge. Some trusts levy an exit charge instead of a front-end charge, so that you only pay the charge if you cash in your investment within the first few years.

Return

The income from unit trusts comes in the form of distributions and is usually paid twice a year. Distributions can be paid out or re-invested by buying new units. Trusts which re-invest the income are called 'accumulation trusts'. The income is variable, even with a trust invested in fixed interest investments. You also hope to make a capital gain by selling your units for more than they cost.

Tax

Unit trusts are taxed in the same way as shares (see Chapter 5). You can use your general PEP allowance (see Chapter 6) to invest in unit trusts.

Keeping track

Unit trust prices are widely published in serious daily and weekend newspapers and personal finance magazines. Information is also available over the Internet – e.g. from Micropal.*

Investment trusts

These are companies quoted on the Stock Exchange whose business is managing investment funds. You invest in a fund by buying the shares of the company. Since there is a fixed pool of shares, their price reflects the relative supply of and demand for the shares, rather than directly relating to the value of the underlying assets. If the shares are unpopular, the price may fall short of the value of the company's investments.

Investment trusts can be more adventurous than unit trusts when it comes to their investment policy because, since they can borrow to invest which increases the gearing of their investments (i.e. magnifies any profits or losses). With many investment trusts, you can buy warrants (see Chapter 16) instead of buying the shares direct.

What they cost

Costs arise in a variety of ways. As with all shares, there is a spread between the prices at which you buy and sell. The spread is likely to be small in the case of a large, frequently traded trust. On the other hand, shares of a small, little-known trust could have a spread of 10 per cent or more. You pay dealing charges either to a stockbroker or, if you use an investment trust savings scheme, to the trust management company – the latter is likely to be cheaper. The trust managers' charges for running the fund are an expense set against the fund.

Return

These are shares, so income is in the form of dividends that are usually paid out twice a year. The income is variable. This is the case even with a trust invested in fixed interest investments, because the particular investments held by the fund are not constant. You also hope to make a capital gain by selling your shares for more than they cost.

Some investment trusts are 'split capital trusts', which issue two classes of shares. The trust is designed to have a finite lifetime, after which it is wound up. One class of shares is entitled to all the income from the trust during its lifetime and the other class of shares is entitled to all or most of the capital when the trust is wound up.

Tax

Investment trusts are taxed as shares as described in Chapter 5. You can use your general PEP allowance (see Chapter 6) to invest in investment trusts, in which case the return is tax-free.

Keeping track

Investment trust prices are included in the share price listings published in broadsheet daily and weekend newspapers. Details are also given in many personal finance magazines, and information is also available over the Internet, as for shares (see Chapter 13 for more on all these).

Open-ended investment companies (OEICs)

As an investor, you can consider OEICs to be broadly the same as unit trusts, although technically they are different. Like investment trusts, they are companies which invest in funds but, like unit trusts, the size of the fund varies with the number of investors involved. This is achieved by creating or cancelling shares as investors come and go.

OEICs were developed largely as a way of widening the appeal of UK collective investments. Foreign investors are unfamiliar with the trust status of unit trusts and feel more comfortable with corporate status. In line with the way most Continental and US funds are priced, there is just one price, based directly on the value of the investments in the fund, at which shares in an OEIC are both bought and sold.

At the time of writing, OEICs are in their infancy, but newly created collective investment schemes are likely to adopt the OEIC model and unit trust managers may want to convert existing trusts to the new OEIC structure. Before this can happen, investors must be given the opportunity to raise any objections and a meeting of investors may be required. In most cases, it will make little or no difference to your investment whether it is classed as a unit trust or an OEIC, but in a few cases there could be an important change – e.g. if your fund focusing on mainly Japanese interests was swallowed by another group dealing with the Far East generally. So do read carefully any documents you are sent.

What they cost

There is no built-in front-end charge. All charges are shown separately.

Return, tax, keeping track

All these are the same as for unit trusts.

Chapter 10

Choosing shares

SOME 2,700 shares are listed on the main market of the London Stock Exchange and a further 252 or so are quoted on the Alternative Investment Market. How do investors decide which to own and when is the right time to buy or sell? There are four main approaches to this key area:

- fundamental analysis
- Chartism
- random walk
- quantitative ('quant') techniques.

An understanding of the approaches is important, not just to help you choose your own shareholdings and timing, but because they are also used by the professional investors who make up the bulk of the market. If you have a feel for how the professionals behave, you will have a better grasp of why stock markets move the way they do and what opportunities, if any, are left for the small investor.

Fundamental analysis

Fundamental analysis tries to establish the true worth of a company and tests whether the share price is out of step. If the share price is judged to be lower than the perceived worth per share of the company, the shares are viewed as under-valued and therefore a good buy. If the share price is higher than the perceived value per share of the company, the shares are judged as over-valued and likely to fall in price at some stage.

Crucial to the fundamental approach by analysts are two convictions, both of which are open to challenge:

- it is possible to work out a reasonably accurate value for a company's shares

- the share price will, in the end, tend towards the value based on the underlying worth of the company.

Value is measured in a wide variety of ways. Some measures focus on all or some of the net assets the company holds, while others look at the earning power of the business or the return it achieves on its capital, and yet more look at the flow of dividends to the shareholders. The figures used are derived from published accounts and analysts' own projections which carefully combine material concerning the economy as a whole, the industrial and geographical sectors the company is in and the business itself. The resulting bevy of statistics and ratios is supplemented by qualitative information about the company and its managers gleaned during visits by fundamental analysts.

This is the most widely used technique of analysing shares among professional and private investors alike. Because the ratios devised by fundamental analysts underpin so much of the behaviour of equity investors, they are considered in some detail in chapters 11 and 12.

Fundamental analysis works on the premise that markets are reasonably efficient. As new information about a company is announced, its implications will be quickly assessed, investors will adjust their views and either buy or sell the company's shares to adjust their holdings in line with their new assessment of the company, and market makers will respond by revising their prices in line with the new mood in the market. In this way, the share price will tend to encompass all knowledge about the company.

Within the scope of this 'knowledge' are investors' expectations about the company. Rather than simply responding to factual announcements as and when they occur, the players in the market will make a guess about information which they know to be due: for example, half-yearly results from the company or publication of economic statistics, such as retail sales volumes, that are likely to affect the sector in which the company operates. If the consensus of opinion turns out to be correct, the share price may not alter at all when the announcement is made, because the market will already have discounted the new information. If the consensus of opinion is wrong, the share price may move. The market will also respond to reports made by well-respected analysts who estimate the future returns from a company, and to rumours which may or may not prove to be correct.

How can you make it work for you?

What part can you, the private investor, play in all this? When prices are responding to news, there is probably little room for you, certainly where the large blue chip companies are concerned. The adjustments may take place within a matter of minutes, often long before you have any inkling of the new information. When prices are discounting information ahead of an announcement or responding to rumours, you may be able to take part. If you reckon the consensus opinion in the market is wrong, you can take your own position in the hope of making a profit after the market has adjusted on publication of the information or correction of the rumour. Smaller companies, which are not so heavily analysed by institutional investors, may give you more scope to find hidden value which could potentially feed through into the share price.

Bear in mind, though, that what matters in the market place is not being more accurate than the rest of the players, but being able to anticipate how the other players will view information. You might buy shares in a company which you are convinced will show healthy growth in a year or two. You might turn out to be right and the company may start to do very well, but it does not inevitably follow that other investors will choose to buy that company's shares.

There may be all sorts of reasons for this: for instance, the company may be too small, making it unsuitable for institutional portfolios; or the shares may be considered too illiquid to give enough certainty of being able to sell again later; or the sector may be generally unpopular for reasons unrelated to that particular company; or those in the know may have little faith in the long-term abilities of the company's managers; or it could be that other investors spotted the growth potential before you and the price at which you bought already took account of these expectations. If other investors fail to jump on to your bandwagon, the share price will not improve as you had expected and you will not be able to make the profit for which you had hoped.

More dangerous is where you jump on to somebody else's bandwagon only to find that it is out of control. There are numerous instances of the players in the stock market getting over-enthusiastic about the prospects for some venture or another – the South Sea Bubble (see Chapter 3) was one of the first, but there have been plenty more since. As long as the consensus in the market is that even better times are to come, share prices keep rising; provided you pull out in time, you can make staggering profits. But, in most cases, there comes a point at which investors lose faith in their ambitious forecasts, realising that future prospects have been exaggerated. A technical reaction sets in, there is a return to more conservative assessments of value and the share price drops. The trick for you is to anticipate the change of mood and get out before the slump.

Despite the doubts that can be cast on fundamental analysis, it remains an intuitively rational approach to selecting shares. You would not go into a shop and buy a product about which you knew nothing, not even its purpose. Similarly, it seems bizarre to buy shares in a company without knowing something about what the company does, how well it does it, what its future prospects are and whether the purchase seems to give value for money. These factors combine to give you a yardstick against which to assess the shares, even if it is not 100 per cent reliable as an indicator of whether or when you should invest.

Chartism

Chartism, or technical analysis as it is also called, ignores the fundamentals altogether and puts forward the idea that you can select shares according to the patterns you see in the movements of their prices and volumes traded.

The Chartists argue that little or no scope exists for making profits through studying the fundamentals of a company. The share price will certainly be influenced by the fundamentals of the company, but that is just a part of the picture. Share prices still go up and down, even when there is no new information. This movement is due to the psychology of the market, the way investors behave collectively. The theory goes on to assert that certain patterns of behaviour are repeated time and again. The trick is to identify a pattern as it recurs and to buy or sell as appropriate.

There is insufficient space in this book to set out the techniques of Chartism in any detail. If you would like to know more, a handy introduction to the subject is *Charters on Charting*.* Some of the more common concepts are:

- **point and figure chart:** a graph showing price movements, but instead of plotting price against time, the plots show only the direction of movement of price changes over a given size (see Chart 10.1 on page 135)

- **trend:** a general upward or downward movement of prices sustained for a reasonable period of time
- **continuation patterns:** within the context of a trend, fluctuations in price which give you the opportunity to buy or take profits but which do not upset the general trend (see Chart 10.2 on page 135)
- **reversal patterns:** price patterns which suggest that the trend of a share price, or of the market as a whole, is about to change direction. These are some of the most important features of Chartism
- **break out:** the point at which a pattern is complete and the share price either continues its former trend (in the case of a continuation pattern) or starts out on a new trend (reversal pattern)
- **resistance level:** a price level above which a share price has difficulty going. It is argued that investors start to take profits (or salvage what they can from losses) as this level is approached, thus driving the price back down
- **support level:** a price level below which a share price tends not to fall. In this case, it is argued that each time the price approaches this level, investors seize the opportunity to join the market or add to their existing shareholding, thus driving the price back up
- **double top:** a reversal pattern which indicates that a bull market is coming to an end and a bear market is about to set in
- **double bottom:** a reversal pattern which indicates that a bear market is bottoming out and a bull market is about to commence (see Chart 10.3 on page 135)
- **head and shoulders:** a reversal pattern indicating the end of a bull market and start of a bear market (see Chart 10.4 on page 136)
- **reverse head and shoulders:** reversal pattern indicating the end of a bear market and start of a bull market
- **relative strength:** ratio of a share price to a stock market index – i.e. the extent to which the stock outperforms or underperforms the market as a whole. Chartists plot this ratio over time. Changes in the ratio may help to confirm a particular pattern in the share price – for instance, if a reversal pattern suggests that now is the time to buy a stock, an increase in the relative strength ratio would strengthen that message. In addition, the extent to which relative strength swings around gives an indication of the riskiness of the shares (see Chart 10.5 on page 136)
- **volume indicators:** a buy signal from the pattern of price movements is strengthened if the volume of trading is relatively

high, suggesting that there is a lot of demand in the market. Similarly, a sell signal is more meaningful if it is accompanied by a heavy volume of trading (see Chart 10.6 on page 136).

The Chartist approach presents certain problems. First, although the behaviour of investors undoubtedly plays a part in that of the stock market in general, the size of its influence over prices, particularly in the long run, is unknown: Chartists assume that it is the major factor, but they may be wrong. Secondly, the assumption that patterns of behaviour are repeated might be wrong. Even if some repetition can be detected, over long periods of time behaviour might alter. Worse still, the 'patterns' – which are seldom entirely obvious – might simply be a case of seeing what you want to see in the normal scattering of price movements and not indicate any particular behaviour on the part of investors.

Another problem is that, if Chartism really works, then surely investors will be anticipating the actions of the market as a whole? The biggest profits will go to those people who spot a pattern early and take steps ahead of the rest of the market. But next time around, the early action will itself be anticipated, so the people to make profits will be those who act well ahead of the pattern being completed, and this process of anticipation will go on. But the earlier the action takes place, the less of the pattern will have emerged and so the less certain the Chartists can be that the particular pattern will emerge. The chances of getting it wrong escalate and Chartism ceases to be a reliable system.

Although the bulk of research carried out for institutional investors relies on fundamental analysis, most institutions do use some Chartist techniques. From the private investor's point of view, Chartism may seem appealing because the study of charts is relatively straightforward compared with the work involved in making a detailed fundamental analysis of a company.

Random walk and the efficient market hypothesis

The random walk theory grew out of academic research into the behaviour of share prices. After extensive testing, the academics concluded that future share price movements are not affected by past share prices. At any point in time, there is an equal probability of the next price movement being upwards or downwards. In other words, Chartism – whose very raison d'être is that past patterns are repeated – has no foundation.

The academics did not stop there. They went on to develop an all-embracing efficient market hypothesis which has three forms. The weak form is the same as random walk – past share prices do not influence future price movements. The semi-strong form goes a stage further and asserts that not only is a share price independent of the past but, in an efficient market, the current share price has already absorbed the impact of all published information. When new information is released, the share price almost instantaneously readjusts. The upshot of this view is that fundamental analysis – which pores over all the available information about a company in order to assess its intrinsic value – cannot work. There is no scope for an analyst to profit from his work, because everything he can glean from company reports and visits – assuming the information is also available to everyone else – has already been assessed and discounted in the share price. (Though, intriguingly, the work of the analysts is still necessary for the market to be efficient in the first place – if the fundamental analysts all downed tools, share prices would no longer quickly adjust to new information.)

In its strongest form, the efficient market hypothesis states that share prices have also absorbed all the information about a company that it is possible to know, not simply the published information. So analysts have already thought about all the possibilities for the company and the share price has discounted all these expectations too. The only thing that will have an impact on the current share price is truly random information, which – by definition – cannot be known or even expected, and that is no help to anyone when it comes to picking stocks.

In this most extreme form, the efficient market hypothesis suggests that a monkey throwing darts at the financial pages would be as good a way as any to select your shares! However, this does not mean that there is nothing to be gained from holding shares. Since share prices reflect all there is to be known about the underlying companies, over time, prices can be expected to move in an upward direction, reflecting the growth of the companies at least in line with inflation and hopefully by more. So, although you cannot with any consistency pick shares that will beat the market, you can still make a reasonable return by investing in shares and simply holding them. This is the basic philosophy which underlies 'tracker funds' – for example, unit trusts and insurance funds invested in a selection of stocks which have been carefully selected to mimic the movement of a given stock index (as an alternative to 'active fund management', where share holdings are frequently altered in the pursuit of superior returns).

Random walk and the efficient market hypothesis are all very well in theory. But, in the real world, surely there are shares which do consistently perform better than others. The academics puzzled over this awhile and came up with a whole new way of valuing shares which spawned the 'quant' analysts.

Quantitative ('quant') techniques

Quant analysts apply highly mathematical techniques to the problem of valuing shares, basing their work on an underlying model of how investors behave. The models have been revised and refined, but stem from what is known as the 'Capital Asset Pricing Model (CAPM)'.

In very simplified terms, the CAPM works as follows. It asserts that the reason why some shares consistently outperform others is risk. If you, the investor, are to hold more risky shares, you expect to be rewarded with the prospect of a higher return, called the 'equity risk premium'. You do not need to be rewarded for all the risk a share displays. Some of the risk is specific to the particular company and the sector it operates in – you can get rid of a good deal of this risk by holding a portfolio containing a range of different shares. In that way, the ups and downs of one company or sector will be offset by the downs and ups of other shares in the portfolio. But, even holding a well-diversified portfolio, you cannot get rid of the market risk – i.e. the tendency of all your shares to move up and down with the market as a whole. So the academics argue that the only risk you need to be compensated for is the market risk – which, as mentioned in Chapter 8, can be described by a measure called 'beta'.

Therefore, in the CAPM, an investor who holds a portfolio or share with a higher beta (i.e. a tendency to react more strongly to movements in the market as a whole) will expect a higher return than they would from a portfolio of shares with a lower beta (i.e. a tendency to respond more weakly to movements in the market as a whole). This relationship can be illustrated as in Chart 10.7 (page 137), which shows what the academics call a 'security market line'. On the far left of the Chart the line meets the y-axis, indicating the required return from a risk-free investment or portfolio, such as government stocks. As you move rightwards along the line, risk increases and so investors require a higher return.

The CAPM has the potential to help investors in two ways. First, if you know where the security market line lies, you can select your shares to produce a portfolio with the 'correct' combination of risk and return. If you want to invest for a higher return on your portfolio in the long run, you will have to increase the risk of your investment either by choosing shares with a higher beta or by borrowing to invest (producing an effect called 'gearing' – see the Glossary). Secondly, to the extent that there are any inefficiencies in the market, you may be able to spot shares which are incorrectly priced – any shares which lie above the security market line have a higher expected return than would be warranted by their risk rating, so they are worth buying or holding in a higher proportion than normal. (The anomaly should be short-lived, since the act of buying the shares will tend to push up their price, reducing the expected return and so bringing them back on to the security market line.) Any shares below the line offer a lower return than expected given the degree of risk and should be sold or at least reduced so that they make up a smaller than normal proportion of your portfolio. (Again, the actions of investors should correct the anomaly, since selling the shares will tend to drive the price down and so increase the expected return.)

The basic CAPM has been much modified. As discussed in Chapter 8, beta may not be a useful measure of risk, so some analysts have focused on developing 'subjective betas', which try to forecast risk rather than relying on past data. Other analysts view the CAPM as a special case in a much wider model, arguing that the return from a share is not related just to its market risk but to many factors, all of which must be built into the model.

Although widely used by professional investors, usually in combination with fundamental analysis, this type of analysis is not readily accessible to the private investor. However, the basic tenets which flow from it are useful:

- you can reduce company and sector risk by holding a well-diversified portfolio of different shares and other investments
- if you want to invest for a higher return, you must take on extra market risk either by selecting shares which respond more dynamically to movements in the market or by borrowing to invest.

Chart 10.1: Point and figure chart

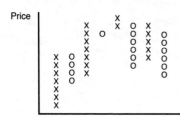

Each X shows an increase in share price of at least a given amount.
Each O shows a fall in share price of at least a given amount.
A new column is started only when the direction of the share price movement changes.

Chart 10.2: Example of a continuation pattern

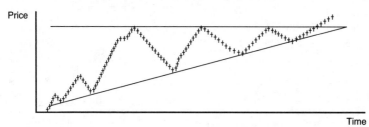

This pattern is called the triangle. The flat top is the price at which sellers of the stock believe it is fully valued. Buyers become increasingly attracted to the stock until eventually the price breaks out of the triangle.
+ is a way of showing price information. The top of the vertical is the highest price, the bottom is the lowest price and the horizontal bar indicates the mid-price.

Chart 10.3: Double bottom – a reversal pattern

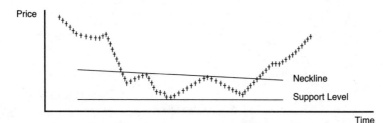

The price falls to such a low level that some people are attracted to buy. The price slips back but this attracts further buying and the share price starts to take off.
The neckline is used to estimate the minimum rise in price once the share price has reversed.

135

Chart 10.4: Head and shoulders – a reversal pattern

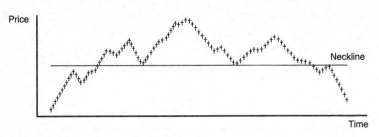

The fall from the left shoulder occurs because investors decide to realise profits. The dip in price is temporary but, as the head is approached, further profit-taking occurs and the share price starts to slide. There is a brief rally as buyers are tempted by the lower price but sellers have the upper hand and the share price resumes its fall.

Chart 10.5: Relative strength

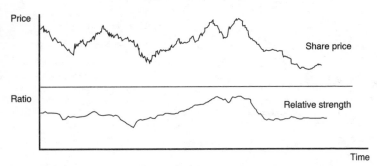

The relative strength ratio is tending to confirm the patterns seen in the share price.

Chart 10.6: Volume indicators

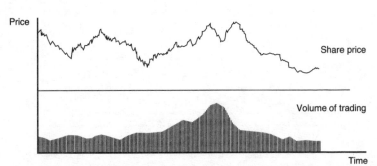

The peak in trading volume coincides with the double top formation, tending to confirm that the price movement is about to reverse.

Chart 10.7: Capital Asset Pricing Model: the relationship between risk and return

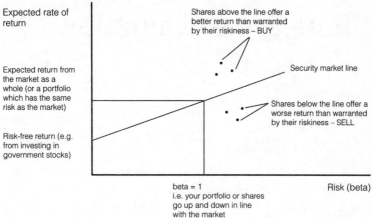

Expected rate of return

Shares above the line offer a better return than warranted by their riskiness – BUY

Expected return from the market as a whole (or a portfolio which has the same risk as the market)

Security market line

Shares below the line offer a worse return than warranted by their riskiness – SELL

Risk-free return (e.g. from investing in government stocks)

beta = 1
i.e. your portfolio or shares go up and down in line with the market

Risk (beta)

137

Chapter 11

Share price evaluation

FUNDAMENTAL analysis, as discussed in Chapter 10, tries to assess the value of a company and its shares and then asks whether the share price under-reflects or over-reflects that value. Various methods are used to work out how the underlying value is related to the current share price. Statistics being what they are, you should not treat them as the last word on whether to buy, sell or hold a share – they serve to highlight anomalies that need further research. The statistics combined with background details may help you to choose your shares and time your purchases and sales.

This chapter presents the most commonly used measures for evaluating shares – p/e ratio, dividend yield and so on – and takes a brief look at a few more specialist approaches. There are many other valuation techniques which come in and out of fashion. What they all have in common is that none can claim 100 per cent success. If they could, the people using them would be millionaires!

Price earnings ratio (p/e)

The price earnings ratio is found by dividing the current share price by the company's earnings per share. For example, suppose a company has 88 million shares outstanding, each priced at 414p, and makes annual profits of £7.5 million. The earnings per share figure is £7,500,000/88,000,000 = 8.5p and the p/e ratio is 414/8.5 = 48.7.

At one level, the p/e ratio tells you how many years' earnings the current share price is worth. So, in the example above, what you pay for the shares represents nearly 49 years' earnings. But this assumes that earnings per share will be the same year after year, which is very unlikely. More often, the p/e ratio is interpreted as giving an idea of how investors value the growth potential of a company. A high p/e ratio suggests that investors expect the company's future profits to be growing rapidly. A low p/e suggests poor growth potential.

This begs the question of what is a low or high p/e. The ratio can be interpreted only through comparison with the p/e ratios for other companies, the sector it operates within, or the market as a whole. Table 11.1 shows the p/e ratios for different stock market sectors on one day in September 1997.

Suppose a company has a p/e of around 26. Is that high or low? Compared with the stock market as a whole, it looks a little above average, given a p/e ratio for the FTSE All Share of 19.03. However, this company might be, say, Premium Trust Insurance. Given that the average p/e for the insurance sector is 8.98, the Premium Trust p/e is well above average. On the other hand, perhaps this is the p/e ratio for Enterprise Oil. The average for the oil, exploration and production sector is relatively high at 36.11, which makes Enterprise Oil's p/e on the low side.

As you can see, the p/e ratio means nothing on its own. It must be viewed in the context of the 'norm' for similar companies and in comparison with prevous p/e ratios for the particular company. What is more, the p/e is nothing more than a bald statement of fact. Premium Trust's p/e is higher than the average for the sector. The p/e does not tell you whether this is because Premium Trust has fantastic growth prospects, whether the shares are heavily in demand because the company is a takeover prospect, whether they are mistakenly over-valued, and so on. Only with further research can you come to any conclusions about whether these are worthwhile shares to buy or hold.

P/e ratios can be historic, in which case the share price is being compared with the company's profits from its most recently published accounts, or prospective, with the share price being compared with forecasts of the company's expected profits.

Be careful when comparing the p/e ratio of one company with that of another. Different companies treat tax and other items in different ways, which may result in earnings per share figures that are not strictly comparable – see page 156. Earnings need to be calculated in the same manner before p/e ratios can be meaningfully compared.

Dividend yield and dividend cover

Dividend yield is the dividend per share (usually quoted 'gross' – i.e. after adding back any tax) divided by the price per share. After

Table 11.1: Price earnings ratios for different sectors, 10 September 1997

Sector (number of companies)	P/e ratio
NON-FINANCIALS (667)	19.75
Mineral extraction (20)	20.54
Extractive industries (5)	14.29
Oil, integrated (3)	20.75
Oil, exploration & production (12)	36.11
General industrial (262)	18.08
Building & construction (35)	17.74
Building materials & merchants (30)	16.25
Chemicals (26)	19.68
Diversified industrials (15)	12.29
Electronic & electrical equipment (37)	20.67
Engineering (65)	17.54
Engineering, vehicles (13)	values are negative
Paper, packaging & printing (27)	14.57
Textiles & apparel (14)	17.21
Consumer goods (84)	19.97
Alcoholic beverages (7)	16.14
Food producers (25)	18.27
Household goods (17)	16.20
Health care (14)	26.01
Pharmaceuticals (18)	27.96
Tobacco (3)	10.70
Services (270)	21.08
Distributors (30)	19.30
Leisure & hotels (31)	21.46
Media (41)	26.55
Retailers, food (15)	16.21
Retailers, general (53)	18.00
Breweries, pubs & restaurants (22)	16.16
Support services (55)	29.17
Transport (23)	29.14
Utilities (31)	18.54
Electricity (9)	12.36
Gas distribution (2)	values are negative
Telecommunications (8)	20.38
Water (12)	9.64
FINANCIALS (103)	15.87
Banks, retail (10)	16.28

Insurance (16)	8.98
Life assurance (7)	16.69
Other financial (27)	19.10
Property (43)	28.23
INVESTMENT TRUSTS (127)	49.37
FTSE ALL SHARE (897)	19.03

Source: FTSE Actuaries Industry Sectors as published in the *Financial Times* 11/9/97

adjusting for your tax position, it gives you a measure of the amount of income you are earning for your money and is useful for income investors who want to compare the yield from their shares with the yields from other shares and other types of investment. But dividend yield alone gives you an incomplete view of your return from holding a particular share because you probably also hope to make a capital gain if you sell at some future date.

Dividend yield can also indicate how the market rates a company. A business with good profits potential will generally have a relatively high share price which will tend to produce a low dividend yield. Conversely, a company whose prospects are not well rated will tend to have a low share price which can produce a high dividend yield. In a similar vein, a high dividend yield may indicate that investors as a group expect the dividend to be cut in future and have already discounted that expectation in the share price. If they prove right and the dividend is indeed cut, the yield will resume a more 'normal' level. If the expectation is wrong and the dividend is maintained, investors will correct their position and the share price should rise, returning the dividend yield to normal.

As with p/e ratios, you can assess whether a dividend yield is abnormally high or low only by comparing with what is usual for that company based on past yield levels, the yields available on other shares in the same sector and the yield for the market as a whole.

Like p/e ratios, dividend yields can be historic – in other words, based on the most recently announced dividends – or prospective, being based on estimates of dividends shortly to be announced.

Dividend cover is the earnings per share divided by the net dividend per share. The net dividend – i.e. the amount investors receive before adding back the tax credit (see Chapter 5) – is used because the tax has already been taken into account in the earnings per share figure used in the calculation (see page 156). Dividend cover tells you what proportion of the company's earnings are being paid out to shareholders without having to dip into reserves. A value of one would mean that all the earnings were being paid out as dividends. This is unlikely to be a healthy state of affairs, not only because a fall in future profits would probably produce a cut in dividends but also because most companies re-invest at least part of their profits to fuel future growth. A dividend cover of less than one is likely to be even worse – it means that current earnings are not enough to finance the dividends and the company has had to use some of its reserves to keep up the dividend payments. A low level of cover, together with a high dividend yield, may be a sign of trouble, with the market signalling that it does not expect dividend payments to be maintained in future. Of course, you could interpret this as a buying opportunity in the hope that this will prove to be a recovery stock but you should be realistic about the risk that you might be wrong. Beyond that, there is no straightforward way to judge whether cover is adequate. Once again, it depends on the norm for that type of company. When comparing cover figures, bear in mind that different companies measure earnings per share in different ways, so figures taken from different sources might not be comparable.

A useful bit of algebra to remember is that, since cover equals earnings per share divided by dividend per share, it is also equal to:

$$1/(\text{p/e ratio} \times \text{net dividend yield}).$$

Dividend discount models

Another way to look at the price of a share is to add up all the pay-outs you expect to earn from the share and ask if the share price you will pay comes to more (in which case the shares are expensive) or less (in which case the shares are cheap).

What the shareholder earns is dividend income. Of course, not all companies pay dividends. Many plough their profits back into the business to generate more profits in future. Such growth-oriented companies are attractive even if there is no prospect of dividends in the foreseeable future, because the share price is expected to rise as the company grows, giving you the opportunity to make a handsome capital gain when you come to sell the shares. Dividend discount models cannot be used where the company does not pay dividends and are best suited to situations where your main investment aim is to receive an income.

Example

Max holds shares in Kilo plc. The company has recently announced its final dividend, bringing dividends per share for the whole year to 6.5p. This is the dividend net of tax at the savings rate (20 per cent in 1997-8), which is equivalent to a gross dividend of:

$$6.5p/0.8 = 8.1p \text{ per share}$$

(See Chapter 5 for a description of how dividends are taxed.) At the current share price of 81p, this gives a dividend yield of 8.1/81 = 10 per cent. Kilo is in the Textiles & Apparel sector, which has an average yield of 6.71 per cent, so 10 per cent looks on the high side. The published p/e ratio for Kilo is 15.4.

Max works out that the dividend cover must be $1/(15.4 \times 6.5/81)$ = 0.81. Since this is less than one, the company seems to be dipping into reserves to pay the dividend. Max does not like the look of this scenario and thinks that the company's position could worsen further. As he bought the shares some time ago at 55p, he decides to sell and take his profits now.

You cannot just add together all the dividends you expect to receive if you invest in a given share. Dividends earned this year are more valuable than dividends earned in the future. You know intuitively that this is true – if someone offered you a choice between £10 today or £10 in a year's time, in almost all cases you would choose £10 today. More formally, it can be argued that a dividend paid to you now can be invested and will thus grow in value. If you have to wait a few years to receive the dividend, you lose that growth, so there is a cost in having to wait. In addition, you may feel fairly certain of receiving a dividend this year, but who knows what will happen in future? The company's fortunes may be quite changed and dividends cut or missed altogether. If you are forecasting increasing dividends, your forecasts will tend to become increasingly unreliable the further ahead you go. In other words, the further you look into the future, the more uncertainty you have to allow for in your calculations. When adding together dividends stretching from now into the future, it is necessary to 'discount' – i.e. reduce – the future dividends to reflect their lower value to you.

The discount rate used is generally the return you could get from investing in a safe investment, such as British Government stocks, plus an 'equity risk premium'. The latter acknowledges the fact that, in order to have a chance of the higher returns that share investments offer, you are willing to take on more risk than you would by simply investing in the safer alternative of government stocks.

Adding together all the dividends, discounted in the appropriate manner, gives you the value to you today (technically, the 'present value') of the stream of dividends:

$$\text{Present value of dividends} =$$
$$D_1 + D_2/(1+r) + D_3(1+r)^2 + D_4(1+r)^3 + \ldots + D_n(1+r)^{n-1}$$

where D_1 = first dividend to be paid

$\quad\quad D_2$ = second dividend

$\quad\quad D_n$ = nth dividend

$\quad\quad r$ = discount rate (i.e. return on British Government stocks plus equity risk premium) divided by 100

If the answer you come up with equals the share price, you are paying for the shares just what they are worth to you. If it is less than the share price, the shares look over-priced and, if it is more than the share price, the shares seem a bargain.

An alternative way of using this method of evaluating shares is to set the stream of discounted dividends equal to the current share price and then solve the equation to find out what constant rate of dividends would be needed. The result can be compared with the current dividend yield or the expected future rate of dividends.

This method of evaluating the share price seems very elegant at first sight, but it is very sensitive to the assumptions you make about the size of future dividends and the discount rate you use (for example, which government stock you select and how large you think the equity risk premium should be). The calculation will also be affected by how far into the future you should look. The more years you include in your equation, the higher the total will be, although a payment many years ahead will be heavily discounted and contribute relatively little to the total. There is no right or wrong answer to the period you should use. Some professional analysts adopt a five-year horizon, some shorter, some longer. You have to use your judgement, weighing up the answers you get from the equation against your confidence in dividends being paid over the whole forecast period.

Another flaw in this method is that, even if your primary objective is investing for an income, you might still hope to make some capital gain from your shares one day, but any profit is left out of account.

Net asset value (nav)

Net asset value is a measure which stems from the balance sheet rather than from the income of either the company or its shares. It is calculated as follows:

$$\frac{\text{Book value of net assets}}{\text{Number of ordinary shares}}$$

Chapter 12 explains what you will find in the balance sheet of a company and various ways in which the information can be used. Here, it is enough to say that the assets of a company are all the things it owns – its buildings, its machinery, cash in the bank, investments and so on. Net assets are all the things the company owns less all its liabilities – basically, things it uses but which belong to other people, such as borrowed money and bills which have yet to be paid. The book value of assets is the value they are given in the balance sheet (which is not necessarily the same as their value if they were sold).

Net asset value gives you an indication of what concrete value underlies each share. However, for the majority of companies, there is no reason why the share price should bear any relationship to the net asset value. Some assets are used very productively, others not. Some businesses require lots of assets, whereas another company may be able to produce very high earnings with relatively few assets. So the mere existence of assets does not give you much idea of how well your investment in the company is going to do. An important exception is where you are buying shares in an investment trust.

The business of an investment trust is to hold a fund of shares and/or other assets and to get the best possible performance from that fund. Although the price of the investment trust's shares is determined by relative supply of and demand for the shares, there will be a strong tendency for the price to reflect the value of the underlying fund of investments. Therefore, a key measure of value used in this sector is net asset value per share. If the share price is below the net asset value, the shares are said to be trading at a discount. This makes them look an attractive buy although there is no guarantee that the discount will ever narrow or disappear. If the share price is above the net asset value, the shares are trading at a premium and look over-priced (although, if you bought them, the shares might still be at the same or a higher premium when you later sold them, so you would not necessarily make a loss).

Net asset value also becomes an important measure of value if a company is the target of a takeover bid. It gives a yardstick against which to assess the amount being offered for the business.

Net current asset value

Although, in most situations, net asset value is not a good indicator of a share's worth, there is a variant which it is claimed can be useful in spotting growth opportunities. Net current asset value per share considers only the most liquid of a business's assets – those which could very easily be converted to cash. If a company's share price is lower even than the current asset value after subtracting prior claims on those assets, such as long-term debts, contingent liabilities and so on (see Chapter 12), you will probably lose little by investing in the shares. At the very worst, if the company goes bust, there is enough in the kitty to pay off the debtors and the shareholders. And, if the company keeps going, the existing managers or perhaps new management are pretty likely at some stage to get the assets working harder and start to produce some real growth.

Shares displaying this trait – referred to as bargain issues by Benjamin Graham, who pioneered this branch of stock selection (see his book *The Intelligent Investor**) – are few and far between when the stock market is buoyant, but are likely to be more prevalent during a recession.

Chapter 12

Company reports and accounts

IF YOU want to know about a company, where better to start than the horse's mouth? Companies are required, by law, to produce a report and a set of accounts each year. And, if a company issues new shares to the public, it must publish a prospectus which provides information similar to – and often much more detailed than – that provided in an annual report and accounts.

These documents give you a good grounding in the company's activities as well as its current performance and prospects. However, they should be used with caution. Certain laws and regulations – for example, the Companies Acts and Statements of Standard Accounting Practice (SSAPs) – aim to ensure that the information presented is clear, fair and consistent. But accounts can be complex and no two companies are the same, so there is scope to present a picture in more than one light. The annual report and accounts is an important document and, if presented skilfully, a showcase for the company. Be prepared to read between the glossy lines.

What to look for in a company's report and accounts

Ultimately, what concerns you, as an investor, is how well your shares will perform – in terms of continuing to provide you with an income through the dividends and/or producing capital gains through a rising share price.

Fundamental analysts (see Chapter 10) generally agree that the single most important influence on the share price is the company's expected earnings per share. Nobody knows for sure what the company's future earnings will be. Many factors will have an impact, including the general economic situation and events affecting the industry or geographical region, but the company's own performance will usually be the key factor and the clues to future performance can be found in past financial accounts. The areas of particular importance include:

- past profitability
- how effectively investment has generated further profits
- where the company's capital comes from and how much it costs
- how many shareholders have to share in the profits.

This chapter gives only a brief introduction to understanding a set of accounts. If you want to develop your expertise in this art, a very good guide to start with is *Interpreting company reports and accounts* by Geoffrey Holmes and Alan Sugden.★ For a more detailed treatement, see *Business Accounting* (volumes 1 and 2) by Frank Wood and Alan Sangster.★ Even if you do not fancy becoming a DIY analyst, it is still right to have an understanding of the procedures and the key figures and ratios that analysts use in order to help you to get to grips with the report part of the report and accounts, as well as newpaper articles and so on about the companies in which you are interested. You will also gain a better grasp of why the market moves in a particular way when company results or new research by analysts are published.

Before considering a set of accounts in detail, a few general points need to be made. First, different companies lay out their accounts in different ways, using different headings and a different order. It is best to start by working through the summary accounts with a calculator, just reproducing the figures, so that you are clear about which items are included in which totals. Secondly, it is a standard convention to show numbers which are to be deducted (such as costs and tax) in brackets. For example, if a heading says 'Profit before taxation', a figure of '£412m' means that a profit of £412m was made. If it says '(£412m)', it means a loss of £412m was incurred.

Thirdly, the figures are just bald statements. To understand more, you need to follow up the notes scattered over the accounts which guide you to a collection of footnotes. These often give you the clearest indication about what is really going on in the business.

Finally, one figure in isolation means very little. To make sense of the accounts, you need to compare with the same figures for other periods (i.e. look at trends) or compare with another figure in the same period (i.e. look at ratios). There are numerous ratios to choose from, but the key ones are listed in Table 12.1.

Table 12.1: Important ratios when analysing accounts

Operating ratios	Financial ratios
Trading profit/turnover ('profit margin')	Debt/equity ('gearing')
Trading profit/capital employed ('return on capital employed')	Current assets/current liabilities ('current ratio')
Turnover/capital employed	(Current assets less stocks)/current liabilities ('quick ratio' or 'acid test')

The profit and loss account

Table 12.2 overleaf shows the profit and loss account for Mike plc, a fictitious company. This is a 'consolidated account' – i.e. one that collates results for all the activities in which the company is involved, including those carried out by subsidiaries. For a limited range of key figures, the report and accounts must also give a breakdown showing the contribution made by individual activities or companies within the group and by geographical area. The breakdown is worth studying to see where the strengths and weaknesses of the company lie and in which sectors any important changes have taken place throughout the year..

On examining Mike plc's profit and loss account, you might initially glean the following information.

Turnover

Turnover in 1996 was £1,750, which is higher than the £1,705 recorded for 1995. Note 1 refers you to an operational and geographical breakdown of the figures. These are also included in a five-year summary at the back of the report and accounts, which gives the picture shown in Table 12.3.

You can see straight away that the growth in turnover has been coming consistently from the two operations, November Trading and Oscar Stores. By contrast, turnover at Papa Manufacturing has fallen every year over the five-year period. Maybe Papa is in trouble – that needs further investigation as you continue through the accounts. The geographical breakdown reveals that turnover in the UK has been growing at the expense of the 'Rest of the world' activities. Trade with Continental Europe has been fairly static over the past five years. When you read the report, you find that Papa has substantial activities in Asia,

Table 12.2: Consolidated profit and loss account for Mike plc

For year ended 31 December 1996	Notes	1996 £m	1995 £m
TURNOVER			
Total	1	**1,750**	1,705
Less share of joint ventures		200	210
Continuing operations		1,500	1,485
Acquisitions	2	30	–
Other income		20	10
Costs	3	(1,588)	(1,553)
OPERATING PROFIT	4		
Continuing operations		162	152
Acquisitions		2	–
Associated undertakings		15	14
Profit before interest, currency gains and			
exceptional items	1	179	166
Exceptional profit on disposal of operations	5	15	–
Exceptional profit on disposal of fixed assets	5	2	–
Interest	6	(10)	(10)
Currency gains/(losses)	7	5	(3)
PROFIT BEFORE TAXATION			
Total profit before tax		191	153
Before exceptional items		174	153
TAXATION			
Total	8	(70)	(59)
Exceptional item	8	(3)	–
PROFIT FOR FINANCIAL YEAR			
Total profit after tax		121	94
Dividends	9	(70)	(65)
Retained profit for year		51	29
EARNINGS PER SHARE	10		
On profit for financial year		24.2p	18.8p
Less after-tax effect of exceptional items		(2.8)p	–
On profit before exceptional items		21.4p	18.8p

Table 12.3: Five-year summary of turnover for Mike plc

	1996 £m	1995 £m	1994 £m	1993 £m	1992 £m
TURNOVER BY SEGMENT					
November Trading	630	550	490	450	430
Oscar Stores	680	675	590	530	490
Papa Manufacturing	440	480	520	540	545
Total	1,750	1,705	1,600	1,520	1,465
TURNOVER BY GEOGRAPHICAL AREA					
	%	%	%	%	%
UK	43	40	41	39	37
Continental Europe	17	16	15	18	16
Rest of the world	40	44	44	43	47
Total	100	100	100	100	100

so the declining geographical share broadly coincides with the fall in Papa's turnover.

But how significant are these rises and falls? Look first at the percentage change each year rather than the change in pounds. For example, the percentage change in total turnover comparing 1996 with 1995 is $((£1,750/£1,705) - 1) \times 100 = 2.6\%$. Repeating the calculation for each year reveals the trend, making clear whether the rate of growth is steady, increasing or slowing down. But some increase would surely be expected year on year just to reflect increasing prices? You can make a very rough correction for inflation to give you some idea of the change in the volume of trading by comparing the change in turnover with the change in the Retail Prices Index. Even better would be to adjust for inflation in the three main geographical trading areas if you have ready access to the figures, but there is no point in going to great lengths on this point, since your adjustment is in any case going to be only a very crude approximation of the inflation experienced by the company. Table 12.4 shows the results of this quick analysis.

Table 12.4: Change in turnover year on year

TURNOVER BY SEGMENT	% change compared with previous year			
	1996	1995	1994	1993
November Trading	14.5	12.2	8.9	4.7
Oscar Stores	0.7	14.4	11.3	8.2
Papa Manufacturing	(8.3)	(7.7)	(3.7)	(0.9)
Total turnover	2.6	6.6	5.3	3.8
Change in Retail Prices Index (% change in averages for calendar year)	2.4	3.5	2.4	1.6

A number of facts can be drawn out from Table 12.4:

- the growth in Mike plc's turnover in 1996 was negligible once price increases are taken into account
- this was so despite the fact that November Trading experienced increasingly strong growth
- Oscar Stores saw a sharp drop in growth in contrast with the trend of previous years
- the turnover of Papa Manufacturing is shrinking each year at an increasing rate.

Table 12.4 does not say anything about why these figures are the way they are. For an explanation, you have to examine the report and accounts further.

One of the subheadings under 'Turnover' is 'Acquisitions'. It is clear that Mike plc took over one or more other businesses during the year and, if this is a net figure, may also have disposed of some businesses. Overall, acquisitions contributed £30m to the turnover for the year. Note 2 lists the companies acquired and disposed of, with the date of acquisition, the percentage of the company involved and the amount paid or realised. It includes a brief explanation of the method used to take the acquistions into the consolidated accounts and details of the impact this has had on profits for the year and on the balance sheet.

Profit
Once costs of production are deducted from turnover, you arrive at the bare profit from the company's operations. Note 3 in the accounts gives

you a breakdown of these costs – e.g. raw materials, other items which get used up during the process of production and costs of employing the staff. Note 4 explains the treatment of certain other items that affect the operating profit – for example, amounts paid out in rents for premises, the charge for leasing certain equipment and the amount paid to the company's auditors (see page 209). There is also an amount for the cost of research and development incurred by Papa Manufacturing.

The result is not the bottom line profit because the company must also pay interest on money it has borrowed. In addition, a sizeable proportion of Mike's trading is carried out overseas. This involves the company in some exchange rate dealing which gives rise to a profit or loss which needs to be taken into account. Notes 6 and 7 give details about these items.

There is also an adjustment for 'exceptional items'. These are the result of events which form part of the ordinary activities of the company but are either unusual in themselves or have had an unusually large impact on the profits for the year. It is left to some extent to companies and their auditors to decide whether an item should be singled out as exceptional or left embedded in the overall profit figure. Unfortunately, this means that different companies may treat similar items in different ways, making it harder to compare one company's accounts with those of another. Exceptional items might cover, for example, the costs of reorganising part of the company, including redundancy payments, or the profit or loss on disposing of a subsidiary or property. In the case of Mike plc, it turns out that the exceptional profit on disposal of operations arose when it sold off a subsidiary for more than its 'book value' (see page 157), and the exceptional profit on disposal of fixed assets was the result of selling an investment that it had made in another company.

One more adjustment has to be made: the deduction of tax. Once again, details are given in a note which sets out the amount of UK tax, broken down into advance corporation tax (payable when dividends are paid out – see page 56) and mainstream corporation tax, the amount of overseas taxes and any tax relief due to double taxation agreements. Where an exceptional item has had an impact on the tax bill for the year, this will be mentioned.

Finally, you arrive at the profit for the year. This is the bottom line figure which is used to calculate earnings per share. There is sometimes another adjustment to profits which occurs 'below the line' and, therefore, does not affect the earnings per share. This is the deduction or addition of any 'extraordinary items'. Once upon a time, there was a very grey area between exceptional items and extraordinary items, with plenty of scope for companies to manipulate their earnings per share figure by either including an item as exceptional or excluding it by classifying it as extraordinary. Nowadays, there are very few items which companies can claim as extraordinary. They are the expropriation of assets, such as where a government decides to nationalise a company's activities, and a fundamental change in the way the company is taxed, such as the imposition of a one-off windfall profits tax.

As with turnover, to make any sense of the profit figure you need to look at it not in isolation, but in comparison with the results for other years. Table 12.5 shows the five-year summary of profits for Mike plc, including the breakdown by segment and geographical area. Table 12.6 looks at the trends and gives a reminder of inflation over the years in question.

Table 12.6, in particular, reveals an interesting story. Although turnover was only marginally up on the year and Papa Manufacturing looked to be on a downward trend, the profit picture reveals a different

Table 12.5: Five-year summary of profits for Mike plc

	1996 £m	1995 £m	1994 £m	1993 £m	1992 £m
OPERATING PROFIT BY SEGMENT					
November Trading	80	70	63	58	55
Oscar Stores	51	51	46	42	39
Papa Manufacturing	48	45	42	40	39
Total operating profit	179	166	151	140	133
OPERATING PROFIT BY GEOGRAPHICAL AREA					
	%	%	%	%	%
UK	42	42	41	39	38
Continental Europe	14	14	14	13	14
Rest of the world	44	44	45	48	48
Total	100	100	100	100	100

Table 12.6: Change in operating profit year on year

OPERATING PROFIT BY SEGMENT	% change compared with previous year			
	1996	1995	1994	1993
November Trading	14.3	11.1	8.6	5.5
Oscar Stores	0.5	10.9	9.5	7.7
Papa Manufacturing	6.7	7.1	5.0	2.6
Total operating profit	7.8	9.9	7.9	5.3
Change in Retail Prices Index (% change in averages for calendar year)	2.4	3.5	2.4	1.6

story. Profits for November Trading and Oscar Stores have moved more or less in line with turnover. But, as turnover has fallen at Papa, its profits have been increasing and, up until the latest year, at a quickening rate. This, in turn, has led to quite reasonable growth in overall operating profit. Clearly, this needs further investigation.

Delving into the report, you discover that a few years ago the management adopted a totally new strategy at Papa Manufacturing. It had become a sprawling, high-volume but high-cost operation, producing a wide range of products but typically with only a short production run for each. The managers decided to drop the least profitable lines altogether and concentrate on those where it could be sure of long production runs, allowing the benefits of economies of scale to come through. As a result of this policy, turnover has been falling as planned and profits have shown a marked improvement.

This can be seen more clearly in Table 12.7, where the profit margin (operating profit/turnover) is shown for each segment of the business. For example, in 1996, the profit margin for Mike plc as a whole was £179m/£1,750m = 10.2%.

Table 12.7: Profit margin of Mike plc

Profit margin (i.e. operating profit/turnover) for each segment	% change compared with previous year				
	1996	1995	1994	1993	1992
November Trading	12.7	12.7	12.9	12.9	12.8
Oscar Stores	7.5	7.6	7.8	7.9	8.0
Papa Manufacturing	10.9	9.4	8.1	7.4	7.2
Total operations	10.2	9.7	9.4	9.2	9.1

The trend in profits and the profit margin is important, but you can know if the profit margin is reasonable only by comparing it with other companies engaged in similar activities. Even then, you must intepret the profit margin within the context of a company's policies. For example, if a company has decided to concentrate on taking market share from its rivals, it may well be prepared to sacrifice profits in the short run in order to achieve this. The policy can produce a low profit margin now but with the aim of increasing profits in the longer term. This is a strategy often seen in areas where a handful of very large companies compete vigorously, such as the retailing of food and of petrol.

Earnings per share

Once you have the profit figure, earnings per share may seem to be a fairly straightforward calculation, but you need to exercise a little care. First, if you are interested in the trend over the years, perhaps projecting it into the near future, you should ignore any exceptional items which, by definition, are unlikely to recur on a regular basis. Secondly, read carefully the notes concerning the number of shares used in the calculation. If a company has issued convertible loan stocks or convertible preference shares, or runs an employee share option scheme, at some stage the issued share capital will increase as the loan stocks are converted or the options taken up. You should look at earnings per share on a 'fully diluted' basis – i.e. taking into account the expected increase in issued shares. This figure will be shown in the profit and loss account.

The balance sheet

Table 12.8 gives the consolidated balance sheet for our fictitious company, Mike plc. The report and accounts will also show the balance sheet for the parent company alone (i.e. without adding in the figures for subsidiaries). Unlike the profit and loss account, which tells you what has been happening *during* the year, the balance sheet is a snapshot of affairs on one particular day – the last day of the financial year. It tells you about the financial state of the company:

- what the company owns – its assets
- what the company owes – its liabilities
- the difference between assets and liabilities belongs to the shareholders – shareholders' funds.

Analysing the balance sheet can tell you about the financial strength of the company, giving an indication of the company's ability to generate future profits. As with the profit and loss account, you can make sense of the balance sheet only by looking at trends – in other words by comparing one year's figures with another's – and ratios – and comparing the size of one figure with another.

Assets and liabilities

Assets

Assets are divided into fixed assets and current assets. Fixed assets can be tangible (for example, land, buildings, machinery, vehicles and so on) or intangible (things that do not have a physical presence, such as patents, brand names, goodwill and long-term investments).

Fixed assets are shown in the accounts at their 'book value'. In general, this is their cost when they were first bought less an amount each year for 'depreciation'. Depreciation writes off the complete value of an asset over its expected lifetime. There are various ways of doing this. The simplest is straight line depreciation, where an asset is assigned a fixed useful lifetime – such as 15 years – and its cost is written off in equal instalments over that period – in other words, knocking off one-fifteenth of its value each year. What you should realise is that the book value of the asset may not be a good indicator of the value of the asset to the company (in terms of the profit it can generate) or to another company (in terms of what it is willing to pay in order to acquire that asset).

Setting the book value of intangible assets can be extremely difficult. For example, unless a brand name has been bought from some other company, it will have no original cost, but clearly some brand names, such as 'Heinz beans', 'Coca Cola' or 'St Michael' are very valuable in terms of generating profits and this should be recognised in the balance sheet.

Current assets are cash and things which can be converted to cash fairly readily, such as your stocks (which can be sold), debtors (people who owe you money and are expected to pay up on the due dates) and short-term investments. These are all the things which the company needs in order to get on with running its business. If the company owed nothing to anybody, the shareholders would own all these assets outright, but inevitably the company also has liabilities to various people.

Table 12.8: Consolidated balance sheet for Mike plc

As at 31 December	Notes	1996 £m	1995 £m
FiXED ASSETS			
Tangible assets	11	340	330
Investments	12	43	51
Total fixed assets		**383**	**381**
CURRENT ASSETS			
Stocks	13	190	195
Debtors falling due within one year	14	280	285
Debtors falling due after one year	14	110	100
Cash and deposits	15	271	199
Total current assets		**851**	**779**
CREDITORS FALLING DUE WITHIN ONE YEAR			
Short-term borrowing	16	(75)	(60)
Other creditors	16	(400)	(370)
Net current assets		**376**	**349**
Total assets less current liabilities		**759**	**730**
CREDITORS FALLING DUE AFTER ONE YEAR			
Loans and other borrowing	17	(290)	(280)
Other creditors	17	(10)	(10)
Provisions for liabilities and charges	18	(140)	(135)
		319	305
CAPITAL AND RESERVES			
Called up equity share capital	19	120	120
Share premium account	20	50	50
Capital reserve	20	600	600
Profit and loss account	20	589	538
Gross shareholders' funds		**1,359**	**1,308**
Goodwill reserve	20	(1,040)	(1,003)
Net shareholders' funds		319	305

Liabilities

Liabilities can be divided into current liabilities and longer-term liabilities. Current liabilities generally mean debts which must be paid within one year or which could be called in at short notice. They include things like money borrowed from banks in the form of overdrafts and other short-term loans; bills of exchange used in trade to guarantee payment on a set date; trade creditors (i.e. money that the company has yet to pay to suppliers who have already provided goods or services); payments due in respect of leased equipment and so on; money owed to the tax authorities; and the amount of any dividends that have been announced but not yet paid out to shareholders. The remaining liabilities are things like longer term loans from banks and other sources; later payments under leases which cannot be cancelled; corporate bonds that the company has issued in order to raise money; tax owed on a longer timescale than one year, and so on.

Ratios

Subtracting the current liabilities from the current assets gives you an idea of how solvent the company is in the short run. A substantial positive figure is healthy, showing that the company has enough cash or near-cash to meet its debts over the next year and suggests that the company would have little trouble getting additional credit if required. An amount close to zero – or, even worse, a negative figure – would be a cause for concern. Short-term liquidity can be more neatly represented by the current ratio:

$$\text{Current ratio} = \text{current assets}/\text{current liabilities}$$

A ratio equal to one means that the current assets just equal the current liabilities. You are looking for a ratio of comfortably more than one and, in general, a current ratio of around one-and-a-half to two is considered desirable.

A very high current ratio is not necessarily a good thing. The assets of the company are supposed to be put to work in order to generate profits. A high current ratio may suggest that a lot of assets are being held in cash or near cash, which is not usually a good source of profits. There are exceptions: if the company's business is the making of financial investments, there may be times when the return on cash (i.e. interest rate) is higher than the return on other investments.

Alternatively, a company might be building up cash in order to buy other businesses – often a more efficient way of expanding than starting from scratch with its own operation. A high current ratio could also indicate that the company is carrying a high level of stocks. This could be the result of stagnating markets or the wrong pricing policy, but it could be normal for that type of business to have high stock levels.

You need to have an idea of what is the normal current ratio for that company by comparing the ratio from year to year. Any substantial changes in the ratio need to be investigated further. Unfortunately, the historic summary included in the report and accounts may not give you the figures you need to calculate the current ratio for any more than the last couple of years. You will also have to look at the report and accounts for previous years or consult another source (see Chapter 13).

So far, it has been assumed that current assets are very liquid. In fact, some might not be so readily converted into cash. In particular, stocks and work in progress could be difficult to sell in a hurry or they might have to be priced at a discount, reducing their value below that shown in the accounts. Moreover, unless the business is being closed down, the company might not want to liquidise its stocks in order to meet, say, a large loan repayment or other current liability. So perhaps the current ratio is not such a good indicator of short-term liquidity. In recognition of this, the 'quick ratio' or 'acid test' strips out stocks:

$$\text{Quick ratio} = \text{Current assets} - \text{stocks}/(\text{current liabilities})$$

The acid test is whether the company could settle all its short-term debts if they were called in today. If the quick ratio is less than one, the answer is: no. Therefore, you are looking for a quick ratio of at least one. Table 12.9 shows the liquidity position of Mike plc. The quick ratio is well above one; the current ratio is between one-and-a-half and two; both ratios have changed little since last year. The liquidity position looks very sound and there seems to be no cause for concern. Ideally, though, you would check out the position for a longer run of years and also find out what is the usual liquidity position for companies engaged in similar activities.

Under liabilities, you may find an item called 'provision for liabilities and charges'. These are items which have not yet become due for payment either within one year or later on, but which are known or expected to become due at some stage. For example, if a company is

Table 12.9: Short-term liquidity of Mike plc

	1996	1995
Current assets	£851m	£779m
Current assets – stocks	£661m	£584m
Current liabilities	£475m	£430m
Current ratio	1.79	1.81
Quick ratio	1.39	1.36

switching to a new technology and knows that this will involve substantial one-off costs when the changeover is made, it might include the costs here. Similarly, if a company pays tax only when it repatriates profits made abroad, it might include a figure here for tax if it is expecting to bring in profits of this type.

In a similar vein, you might also see an entry called 'contingent liabilities'. These are liabilities which are uncertain but could affect the company's financial position – for example, they might depend on the outcome of a court case (as in the tobacco industry, where large compensation payments could become payable if the companies are found to have promoted smoking, knowing that it was addictive as well as harmful), or could be debts (perhaps due from politically unstable countries), which might become bad ones. If contingent liabilities are large in relation to the assets of a company, less its other liabilities, you should be worried. The company is in a fragile financial state – if the contingent liabilities were to materialise, it could be in severe difficulties.

Financing the business

Shareholders' funds

Whatever remains when liabilities have been subtracted from assets represents the shareholders' funds. They include the paid-up share capital itself plus various reserves.

Paid-up share capital is the amount shareholders have invested up to the nominal value of the shares. Anything over the norminal value is part of reserves and goes into the share premium account. Rules are set down concerning how the share premium account can be used. If there are unissued shares in the company, they can be issued to existing shareholders using the share premium account, in effect, as the payment for the shares (this is a form of 'scrip issue' – see Chapter 14).

Various costs, such as the expenses of forming the company and of issuing shares, can be set against the account.

Some reserves are formed from retaining profits – for example, in the Mike plc accounts, the £51m retained profit from the profit and loss account is added to the profit and loss account entry in the balance sheet under 'Capital and reserves' (the £538m figures for 1995, plus the retained profits of £51m, comes to the £589m entry for 1996).

Some companies set foreign currency gains or losses against their reserves. If loan stock is paid off at less than its nominal value, this will also increase reserves. Other reserves arise, for example, if assets are revalued or if the company takes over another company or other assets and pays less for them than their book value – the surplus becomes part of the reserves.

If another company is taken over, the acquiring company takes the assets of the takeover target into its account at 'fair value' – i.e. the acquiring company's best estimate of the value of the assets using its own normal approach towards valuing assets (which may be different from that of the company it took over). If the price it pays comes to more than the fair value, the excess is called 'goodwill'. There are two ways of treating goodwill: either as a fixed but intangible asset to be depreciated (with depreciation being deducted each year as a cost in the profit and loss account), or as a capital sum to be written off immediately against the capital and reserves of the company. At Mike plc, the latter approach has been taken.

Borrowings

A company's operations could, in theory, be financed completely through its share capital and reserves but, in practice, borrowings in various forms will generally play some part. The two source of capital are very different.

- Shareholders' funds are risk capital. In general, the shareholders have no absolute right to any reward. Many companies do not pay any dividends at all during their early years and, even where dividends are the norm, they can be reduced or skipped if the company decides it cannot afford to pay them.
- Loan capital carries a set cost which must be met. If the company fails to pay the interest and capital repayments on a bank loan, the bank can take the company to court in order to get its money and this can drive the company into bankruptcy. Similarly, if a company

misses the interest payments due on corporate bonds or fails to redeem the bonds at the end of their lifetime, the trustees acting for the bondholders can recover the money due through the courts.

Ratios

A company with a high level of borrowing is likely to be more vulnerable than a company with a low level of debt, particularly if interest rates generally are rising. If the return from using the borrowed money is lower than the cost of borrowing, the company generates losses instead of profits. On the other hand, if the cost of borrowing is low and the returns from using the borrowed money are high, the surplus earnings from using the borrowed funds boost shareholders' profits beyond what they would have been if the company had operated without borrowed money. This effect is called 'gearing' (or 'leverage' in the USA) – see the Example on page 165. There are various ways of measuring the degree of reliance on debt. One of the most common measures is:

Debt/equity ratio = Total borrowings/Shareholders' funds

A highly geared company raises a lot of its capital through borrowing and is, therefore, following a fairly high risk strategy. A company with low gearing relies predominantly on shareholder capital to finance its operations and is, other things being equal, a lower risk venture for shareholders to get involved in. Many adjustments can be made to both the debt figure and the measure of shareholders' funds used – for example, sometimes short-term debts are ignored, the value of intangible assets might be excluded from shareholders' funds, preference shares might be treated either as debt or as shareholders' funds, and so on. Table 12.10, a very crude debt/equity ratio for Mike plc, shows Mike to be a moderately geared company, with around half its capital raised through borrowing. As such, Mike plc should be reasonably placed to cope with changes in interest rates or other 'shocks'.

The whole point of using shareholders' funds and borrowing is to generate profits. A key measure, therefore, is the amount of profit generated by the combined equity and debt capital. This is measured as:

Return on capital employed (ROCE) =
Trading profit/(Shareholders' funds + Borrowings)

163

Return on capital employed is an important measure in, for example, determining whether it is worth a company borrowing money to invest in its operations, or whether it should invest surplus cash in, say, another company's shares rather than its own operations. If the cost of borrowing is higher than the return on capital, it does not make sense to borrow. If the return on other investments, including that from buying other companies' shares, is higher than the return on capital employed, it does not make sense for a company to invest in its own operations.

Comparing across companies, return on capital employed can indicate the efficiency of a company. If the figure is unusually low, you need to know why. Many refinements can be applied to the figures used in calculating the return on capital employed and, where you are making comparisons between companies, it is important to make sure that you use a consistent approach. The crude return on capital employed for Mike plc is shown in Table 12.11.

The annual report

In addition to the financial accounts, the annual report and accounts contains written descriptions of the company's year. There will be an overview from the Chairman, usually with some indication of the company's likely future prospects, and a more detailed discussion of the operations from the Chief Executive. The Directors must also give a report, usually more dryly written and containing much information that is required by law, including:

Table 12.10: Debt/equity ratio for Mike plc

	1996 £m	1995 £m
Creditors falling due within one year		
Short-term borrowing	75	60
Creditors falling due after one year		
Loans and other borrowing (including loan stock)	290	280
Total borrowing	365	340
Shareholders' funds	319	305
Debt/equity ratio	1.1	1.1

Table 12.11: Return on capital employed for Mike plc

	1996 £m	1995 £m
Operating profit (less profit of associated operations)	164	152
Total borrowing	365	340
Shareholders' funds	319	305
Total capital employed	684	645
Return on capital employed	24.0%	23.6%

- a declaration that they take responsibility for selecting appropriate accounting policies in preparing the accounts
- details of significant events since the accounts were prepared
- names of the directors and details of their holdings of the company's shares
- details of any other holdings of the company's shares by anyone else where they amount to 3 per cent or more of the issued share capital.

The presentation of the report is usually designed to impress, with glossy photos and an upbeat tone. Try to remain objective as you read the report. Your study of the accounts will have thrown up various questions – does the report answer them satisfactorily? If not, you will need to turn to other sources for a better understanding of the company and its prospects.

Example

Table 12.12 shows selected results for two similar companies, Quebec plc and Romeo Holdings, for their two most recent financial years. In 1995, both companies had a poor year, experiencing a low return on capital but, in 1996, business picked up for both companies. Quebec relies mainly on shareholders' funds for capital, while Romeo has substantial borrowings. The result is that the earnings per share for Quebec are less volatile than those for Romeo, with less scope for large profits in good years but a smaller fall in profits in the bad years.

Table 12.12: Effect of gearing

	Quebec plc £m		Romeo Holdings £m	
	1996	1995	1996	1995
Profit before interest and taxation	140	50	238	85
Interest	(10)	(10)	(70)	(70)
Taxes	(40)	(12)	(50)	(5)
Profit for the year	90	28	118	10
Shareholders' funds	1000	1000	1000	1000
Number of shares	400 million x 250p shares	400 million x 250p shares	400 million x 250p shares	400 million x 250p shares
Total borrowings	100	100	700	700
Earnings per share	22.5p	7p	29.5p	2.5p
Debt/equity ratio (gearing)	10%	10%	70%	70%
Return on capital employed	12.7%	4.5%	14%	5%

How to obtain the report and accounts

If you are a shareholder and hold your shares direct, you will automatically be sent the annual report and accounts, together with notice of the annual general meeting and details of how to cast your vote if you are unable to attend the meeting. Some companies are now sending out summary reports and accounts, offering the full version to anyone who asks for it. The summary is unlikely to contain enough information for you to make a fair assessment of the company.

If you are a shareholder, but hold your shares through a nominee account (see Chapter 4), the report and accounts will be sent to the nominee company. Whether they are passed on to you depends on the rules of the account. There may be a charge for obtaining and passing on the report and accounts, in which case you might prefer to use one of the sources below.

For a company whose shares you do not already own, you can request a copy of the report and accounts from the company registrar, if you know who they are – if you are on the Internet, many FTSE-100 companies have a web site at which you can get details. You can also request reports and accounts from Companies House★ although there is a charge. The *Financial Times*★ runs a free service for its readers to provide the reports and accounts of many of the companies listed in its daily share reports. If you are registered for a dealing and advice service with a stockbroker, or you are a regular client of an independent financial adviser, the broker or adviser should be able to obtain and send you reports and accounts.

Chapter 13

Other sources of information

APART from a company's own report and accounts – and announcements of its interim results – there are many, many other sources of information about companies. It is not possible to list them all, so here we present just of few of the more important and more readily available sources.

Newspapers

Most serious daily and weekend newspapers print share prices, dividend yields and p/e ratios, and some carry a market report as well, commenting on companies which have issued results, are involved in takeovers, and so on. However, the main daily paper for serious share watchers in the UK is the *Financial Times* (the FT).

The FT is devoted almost entirely to reporting on financial markets and political, economic, technological and other events which might influence financial markets. The general news reports are divided mainly by geographical area – Europe, international, UK – and features focus on particular topics, such as management, information technology, small businesses. A separate section each day covers company news and frequent special surveys look at particular industries, different countries, fund management, and so on.

But what makes the FT so valuable for many investors is the wealth of statistical data published each day, covering UK shares, unit trusts, government stocks, currency markets, traded options and much more. The FT publishes its own 300-plus-page guide, *Using the Financial Pages*,★ which is well worth reading if you are new to financial statistics. Here, we take a brief look at some of the share information you will come across in the FT. You can find similar, though generally less comprehensive, information in other newspapers.

Share prices and related information

Figure 13.1 shows an extract from the FT's London Share Service. Companies traded in the UK can pay to have their details published here. The companies are divided into sectors which correspond to those used in the FTSE Actuaries share indices (see page 140). On most days, the following information is given:

- **Company name** – if more than one type of shares is listed, each class is listed on a separate line. An 'A' or 'N/V' (not in brackets) indicates non-voting shares (see Chapter 7). If shares are denoted in a currency other than sterling, the symbol for the appropriate currency follows the name of the shares – e.g. 'Norsk Hydro NKr'.

- **Notes** – various notes give you extra information – e.g. about the type of dividends payable. A useful symbol to look out for is '♣' which, in the FT, indicates that its readers can obtain a copy of the report and accounts using the free annual reports service. The FT also runs a paying service which provides a 10 to 18-page compilation of news reports, statistics and recommendations for each company marked with the symbol ♠.

Figure 13.1: Source: Financial Times

- **Share price** – this is the mid-price for the share at the close of the market on the previous day (or the last day on which the market was open). The mid-price is halfway between the price at which you can sell your shares and the price at which you can buy. There is no indication here of the spread between the buying and selling prices. The letters 'xd' (short for 'ex dividend') indicate that a dividend is due to be paid out soon. If you buy shares when the price has gone xd, you do not receive the imminent dividend; if you sell, you still receive the next dividend even though you no longer own the shares.
- **+ or –** this shows whether the closing mid-price was higher or lower than the share price published for the previous day and by how much (to the nearest 1/32). Many shares often record no change at all, so scanning this column also gives you an idea of which sectors were most actively traded the previous day.
- **52-week high and low** – these show the highest and lowest recorded (not closing) mid-prices over a rolling 52-week period.
- **Market capitalisation** – the value the stock market currently puts on the class of shares (and the company if this is the only class of shares), which is found by multiplying the closing mid-price by the number of shares issued.
- **Gross yield** – the dividends for the most recent 12 months including tax credits (see Chapter 5) divided by the closing mid-price.
- **P/e** – the price/earnings ratio (see Chapter 11) found by dividing the closing mid-price by the latest published earnings per share – this will be taken from the most recent report and accounts (see Chapter 12) or the most recent interim figures.

On Mondays, the closing data for Friday having already been shown in Saturday's edition, the FT takes the opportunity to show some other information, as shown in Figure 13.2:

- **Week % change** – the change over the week in the share price comparing Friday's closing mid-price with that for the previous Friday
- **Net dividend** – the dividend (pence per share) paid in the company's last full financial year. In most cases, this is shown net of tax at 20 per cent in 1997–8 (see Chapter 5). In a few cases, the dividend is shown gross (and marked as such).
- **Dividend cover** – earnings per share divided by the gross dividend per share (see Chapter 11).

Figure 13.2: Source: Financial Times

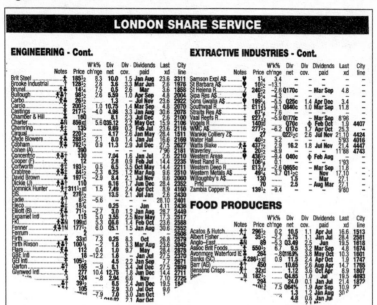

- **Dividends paid** – the months in which the interim and final dividends are paid. UK companies generally pay dividends in two instalments a year. Some companies – e.g. some oil companies and many American stocks – pay in four instalments.
- **Last xd** – the date on which the stock last went 'ex dividend' (see opposite), generally given as the day and month – for example, '11.8' means 11 August – but occasionally as the month and year – e.g. '5'96' meaning May 1996.

Share indices

Share indices are basically baskets of shares for which a collective price and other information are calculated. They give you a benchmark against which to measure the performance of a particular share or your own portfolio. There are many different indices representing, for example:

- small groups of leading shares (e.g. FT 30)
- large groups of leading shares (e.g. FTSE 250)
- smaller company shares (e.g. FTSE Small Cap)
- shares held for a particular purpose (e.g. FTSE 350 Higher Yield)

171

- particular sectors of the stock market (e.g. FTSE Actuaries Financials)
- foreign shares (e.g. Dow Jones Industrial, FT/S&P World Indices)
- non-share investments (e.g. UK gilts).

However, the two you are most likely to come across again and again are the FTSE 100 Index and the FTSE All Share Index. The FTSE 100 covers the top 100 companies on the London Stock Exchange, selected by their market capitalisation. These shares account for the largest chunk of stock market activity and so give a useful indicator of the health of the stock market as a whole. The FTSE All Share is more broadly based – though, despite its name, it does not actually cover all quoted shares. (In September 1997, it covered 897 shares.)

These indices and many more are published daily in the FT. Also very useful are the FTSE Actuaries industry sector indices – see Figure 13.3 – which give you handy baselines when comparing the performance of one company's shares against that of similar companies in the same line of business. The entries are similar to those given for individual shares:

Figure 13.3: Source: Financial Times

FTSE Actuaries Share Indices										The UK Series
Produced in conjunction with the Faculty and Institute of Actuaries										
	Sep 11	Day's chge%	Sep 10	Sep 9	Sep 8	Year ago	Div. yield%	Net cover	P/E ratio	Xd adj. ytd	Total Return
FTSE 100	4854.8	–1.0	4905.2	4950.5	4985.2	3932.6	3.40	2.04	18.03	116.44	2083.85
FTSE 250	4633.2	–0.7	4664.7	4677.0	4686.1	4432.3	3.58	1.63	21.42	106.16	1943.91
FTSE 250 ex IT	4646.4	–0.6	4675.5	4688.4	4698.6	4470.9	3.71	1.66	20.24	109.41	1955.29
FTSE 350	2345.3	–1.0	2368.1	2386.9	2401.3	1965.4	3.44	1.95	18.60	55.79	2055.78
FTSE 350 ex IT	2346.1	–1.0	2368.8	2388.1	2402.8	–	3.46	1.97	18.37	23.72	1054.68
FTSE 350 Higher Yield	2276.7	–0.7	2292.3	2305.4	2319.2	1869.6	4.59	1.78	15.28	67.52	1694.36
FTSE 350 Lower Yield	2419.0	–1.2	2448.1	2472.1	2487.1	2068.4	2.48	2.22	22.69	43.95	1732.22
FTSE SmallCap	2273.28	–0.3	2281.17	2279.55	2278.26	2179.36	3.18	1.86	21.07	47.12	1938.89
FTSE SmallCap ex IT	2254.44	–0.1	2257.51	2253.66	2252.72	2178.76	3.43	1.96	18.59	50.49	1939.87
FTSE All-Share	2294.72	–0.9	2316.01	2333.11	2346.18	1941.98	3.42	1.95	18.75	54.10	2041.23
FTSE All-Share ex IT	2295.71	–0.9	2316.85	2334.40	2347.93	–	3.46	1.97	18.38	23.18	1050.44

■ FTSE Actuaries Industry Sectors

	Sep 11	Day's chge%	Sep 10	Sep 9	Sep 8	Year ago	Div. yield%	Net cover	P/E ratio	Xd adj. ytd	Total Return
10 MINERAL EXTRACTION(20)	4824.60	–1.9	4915.96	4949.28	4996.85	3752.61	3.22	1.93	20.12	98.75	2165.43
12 Extractive Industries(5)	4177.66	–2.6	4290.15	4244.38	4213.92	4218.36	3.80	2.38	13.83	104.80	1276.98
15 Oil, Integrated(3)	5118.39	–1.9	5217.39	5265.29	5331.81	3858.36	3.32	1.85	20.35	107.40	2363.26
16 Oil Exploration & Prod(12)	3773.71	–0.6	3795.71	3814.61	3817.62	2765.54	1.55	2.30	35.16	38.65	2312.45
20 GEN INDUSTRIALS(262)	2057.11	–0.2	2061.21	2063.58	2067.37	2088.34	3.83	1.88	17.38	50.20	1180.52
21 Building & Construction(35)	1381.02	–0.3	1385.07	1385.25	1390.34	1184.90	3.26	2.17	17.69	28.21	1204.04
22 Building Matls & Merchs(30)	1835.29	–0.4	1842.83	1851.14	1861.04	1982.55	4.37	1.77	16.18	43.20	970.74
23 Chemicals(26)	2618.85	–0.5	2632.08	2636.77	2639.15	2482.33	3.90	1.64	19.58	73.10	1310.57
24 Diversified Industrials(15)	1471.60	+2.7	1433.33	1432.58	1437.74	1586.68	4.73	2.39	11.08	46.48	878.33
25 Electronic & Elect Equip(37)	2203.08	–0.1	2204.42	2218.91	2217.94	2403.00	3.72	1.63	20.66	49.49	1198.28
26 Engineering(65)	2770.42	–1.1	2800.95	2798.11	2797.92	2567.21	3.03	2.42	17.05	53.89	1750.11
27 Engineering, Vehicles(13)	3231.84	–0.1	3234.12	3228.70	3231.65	3130.77	3.14	‡	‡	71.41	1749.03
28 Paper, Pckg & Printing(27)	2193.74	–0.7	2209.90	2204.13	2197.86	2692.32	4.79	1.94	13.44		
29 Textiles & Apparel(14)	1011.85	–3.4	1046.96	1051.53	1053.12	1250.55	6.69	1.44			
30 CONSUMER GOODS(84)	4432.58	–1.3	4490.24	4565.43	4621.68	3686.43					
32 Alcoholic Beverages(7)	3212.38	–0.6	3232.57	3253.94	3258.92	2°°					
	2988.56	–1.4	3029.93	3054.90	3°°						
	¹°⁴ ⁷³	–1 7	3158 86 °¹°								

- **Sector name** – the names are self-explanatory. The figure in brackets indicates the number of different shares from which the index is constructed.
- **Value of the index** – the closing value of the index for each date shown, calculated from closing mid-prices for the constituent shares.
- **Dividend yield** – the net dividend for the index as a percentage of the level of the index, based on an average of the dividends net of tax for the constituent shares.
- **Net cover** – based on an average of the dividend cover (see Chapter 11) for the constituent shares.
- **P/e ratio** – based on an average of the p/e ratios (see Chapter 11) for the constituent shares.
- **Xd adjustment year to date** – this gives you a measure of the gross income earned by the shares in the index. When a share goes xd, its price, other things being equal, drops by an amount equal to the dividend about to be paid – this is the xd adjustment. The figure given under this heading is the sum of all these adjustments so far during the calendar year.
- **Total return** – this is a measure of the return, both in the form of income and capital gains (or losses), which you would have had so far during the calendar year if you had invested in the shares which make up the index. It assumes that dividends are reinvested.

TV and telephone

Share prices and City news can be obtained from your TV set via teletext. The Monday edition of the *Financial Times* publishes telephone numbers for FT Cityline,★ which provides information on each company via the phone. A similar service is provided by Teleshare Information Services.★

Magazines

Numerous magazines are published with the aim of keeping readers in touch with the economy, politics and business affairs. They give useful background knowledge which helps you to assess the prospects for companies and understand the performance of markets. There are also specialist journals for share owners, the most prominent of which is the weekly *Investors Chronicle*,★ published by the same group as the *Financial Times*.

Investors Chronicle carries news reports about companies and the markets, and features on, for example, spotting growth shares, prospects for particular sectors, major companies in the news, and how to value shares. The journal includes surveys (e.g. of stockbrokers), some general personal finance articles and short profiles of a wide range of popular shares and companies reporting results (see Figure 13.4). These include recommendations or comment on whether the shares are worth buying, holding or selling. There are also sections on new issues, takeovers and smaller companies, as well as a selection of useful statistics.

Other journals concentrate on particular areas of investment, such as growth stocks, smaller companies and penny shares. Some are serious works worth looking at, but others are of more dubious quality. You need to pick and choose.

If you form an investment club (see Chapter 9) and register it with Proshare Investment Clubs, you will receive a regular newsletter which covers news about investment clubs and gives guidance on investment techniques.

Figure 13.4: Source: Investors Chronicle

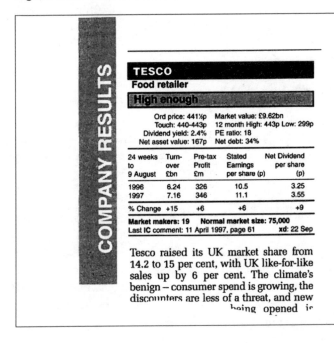

COMPANY RESULTS

TESCO
Food retailer

High enough

Ord price: 441½p		Market value: £9.62bn		
Touch: 440-443p		12 month High: 443p Low: 299p		
Dividend yield: 2.4%		PE ratio: 18		
Net asset value: 167p		Net debt: 34%		

24 weeks to 9 August	Turn-over £bn	Pre-tax Profit £m	Stated Earnings per share (p)	Net Dividend per share (p)
1996	6.24	326	10.5	3.25
1997	7.16	346	11.1	3.55
% Change	+15	+6	+6	+9

Market makers: 19   Normal market size: 75,000
Last IC comment: 11 April 1997, page 61   xd: 22 Sep

Tesco raised its UK market share from 14.2 to 15 per cent, with UK like-for-like sales up by 6 per cent. The climate's benign – consumer spend is growing, the discounters are less of a threat, and new ⌐eing opened i⌐

Reference books

Professional investors have long had access to reference works, which, in the past, were often card-based (such as Excel cards and McCarthy cards), giving essential and regularly updated data about companies – e.g. contact details, latest results, recent share price performance, analysts' forecasts, and so on. It used to be less easy for the private investor to gain access to such information. Nowadays, no one need be at a disadvantage.

One source of company details and data is reference books, which you can either subscribe to yourself or consult at a public library with a good business section. Examples are *REFS (Really Essential Financial Statistics* – a copy of which is included in the membership package for investment clubs joining Proshare★ Investment Clubs), *The Estimate Directory,★ The Hambro Company Guide★* and *Financial Times* company handbooks★ (*The Major UK Companies* and *Smaller UK Companies*) and *Hemmington Scott Company Guide.★* Some reference works are available on CD-ROM. The selection and presentation of material in each guide is different, so it is worth looking at several before deciding to buy one for yourself.

The Internet

Increasingly, you can get information about shares and companies over the Internet. If you are not already hooked up, you will need:

- a computer – you will get the best results with a multimedia PC
- a modem – choose the fastest one you can afford
- a gateway into the Internet via an access provider or a service provider (who is an access provider providing value-added services of their own, such as magazine-style web pages). You have to pay for this gateway: a monthly subscription (often between £10 and £20) and, depending on the service you choose, possibly a charge per unit of time spent on the Internet
- software enabling you to get around the Internet, such as *Internet Explorer* or *Netscape*.

Beyond that, you pay for the cost of the phone call while you are on the Internet but, in most cases, only at the local rate. The Internet is a very fast-changing medium. The table below lists some Internet sites

Figure 13.5: Source: *The Estimate Directory*

The Estimate Directory

BANKS

BANK OF SCOTLAND
Ordinary stock of 25p

Price 209
Market Cap. 2,681

SEDOL 0076454   SEAQ 45338   EPIC BSCT
FT 363   DTSM BSCT   RIC BSCT

The Mound, Edinburgh, EH1 1YZ. ☎ 031-442 7777

Activities The provision of banking, financial and related services internationally. Services include personal finance and banking, merchant banking, finance leasing, fund management, debt factoring, financial advice, insurance broking and investment.

Note broker: Cazenove & Co

Registrars Bank of Scotland 0131-442 7777

Major Shareholders
Standard Life Assurance Society   32.54%

Announcements
Interims   6/10/93
Finals   5/5/94
Report and Accounts   25/5/94
AGM   14/6/94

		Forecast Changed	Profit	2/95F EPS	DPS	Profit	2/96F EPS	DPS
BZW	H	6/11/94	460.0	23.5	5.75	530.0	27.6	6.50
Bell Lawrie White	H	6/10/94	440.0	23.4	5.80	535.0	28.8	6.60
Charterhouse Tilney Secs.	H	- 28/11/94	447.0	23.1	5.75	531.0	28.3	6.50
Collins Stewart	B	26/1/95	446.0	21.0	6.00	515.0	26.0	6.50
Credit Lyonnais Laing	H	3/11/94	440.0	22.6	6.00	474.0	24.7	6.80
Credit Suisse	-	4/1/95	-	23.2	-	-	25.3	-
Fleming Securities	H	11/10/94	435.0	22.8	5.80	500.0	28.5	6.50
Hoare Govett	H	28/11/94	460.0	24.0	5.80	520.0	27.0	6.70
James Capel	H	20/12/94	447.0	23.5	5.60	485.0	25.6	6.40
Kleinwort Benson	B	- 1/2/95	448.0	23.2	5.80	570.0	29.0	6.67
Lehman Brothers	3L	2/1/94	440.0	23.2	5.80	500.0	26.2	6.40
Lloyds Private Banking	H	29/11/94	425.0	22.0	5.70	520.0	27.0	6.40
Morgan Stanley	H	6/10/94	430.0	22.0	5.80	500.0	25.6	6.80
NatWest Securities	ADD	25/11/94	454.0	23.1	5.80	546.0	27.9	6.90
Nikko	H	5/10/94	445.0	22.8	5.65	545.0	28.1	6.25
Nomura	S	27/1/95	449.0	23.0	5.80	513.0	26.4	6.80
Panmure Gordon	S	1/11/94	437.7	21.9	5.80	526.4	26.8	6.50
S.G.S.T. Securities	S	15/11/94	460.0	23.7	5.80	515.0	26.8	6.65
Smith New Court	B	15/12/94	450.9	23.4	5.77	549.7	28.9	6.64
UBS	H	26/10/94	450.0	23.0	5.80	550.0	28.7	6.60
Warburg	H	11/1/95	433.0	22.3	5.70	470.0	24.3	6.40
Yamaichi	H	- 26/1/95	430.0	22.6	5.80	535.0	27.6	6.70
Consensus (quality YGU)		446.0	23.0	5.80	520.0	27.0	6.60
% Change on Previous Year		+66	+89	+15	+17	+17	+14
Prospective P/E and DY on consensus		17.1	9.1	3.5		7.7	3.9

Price Relative
1m   +0%
3m   +4%
12m   -1%

Year Ended 2/94

Profit	269.0	P/E	17.1
EPS	12.2	Dividend Yield	3.0
Tax Charge	39		
Dividend	5.05		

Table 13.1: Useful Internet sites

Internet address	Brief description of site
http://www.londonstockex.co.uk	Official site of the London Stock Exchange. Description of its markets, publications, press releases etc.
http://www.ftse.co.uk	Home of FTSE International, which produces most of the share indices for the UK stock markets
http://www.ft.com	Home of the *Financial Times*. News, share information service, company briefings. Search facility enables you to track information and stories about particular companies
http://www.hemscott.co.uk	Company information specialist and publisher of *The Hambro Company Guide, The Hemmington Scott Guide* and *REFS*
http://www.esi.co.uk	Electronic Share Information Ltd (esi) provides wide range of investment information, including share listings, charts etc. plus access to online share dealing facilities
http://www.pcquote-europe.co.uk http://www.dbc.com	Share charts
http://www.economist.co.uk	Home of *The Economist*, weekly journal covering economic, political and business news. Search facility enables you to track stories on specific topics
http://www.the-times.co.uk	Home of *The Times*. Search facility enables you to track stories on specific topics
http://www.news-review.co.uk	Summary of business and financial news from the UK weekend newspapers, including brokers' recommendations. Search facility enables you to track stories about specific companies
http://www.fsa.gov.uk	Home of the main financial regulator, the Financial Securities Authority (FSA – formally the Securities and Investments Board). Range of regulatory information, including investor alerts which highlight the latest scams you should beware of and tips of investing over the Internet.

which you might find useful, but new sites are being created all the time and the best way to find out what is there is to 'surf the net' e.g. by following the links from one site to another. Many financial sites give you at least some information freely, but to gain access to the most useful data, such as real-time share prices and bang up-to-date news stories, you will often have to pay a subscription to the site provider.

Your stockbroker

Of course, if you are registered with a stockbroker for a dealing and advice service (see Chapter 4), your broker should be able to provide any information you need about individual companies, sectors and markets.

Figure 13.6: Source: Electronic Share Information Ltd

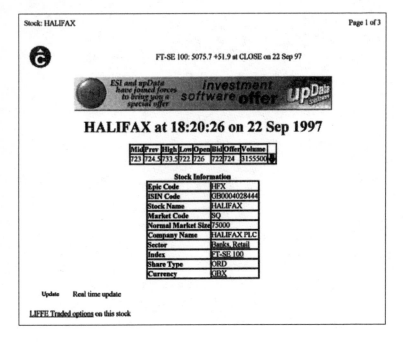

Chapter 14

Special situations

W<small>HEN</small> you invest in a building society account, say, you just sit back and let your money grow. Sometimes, you can do the same with shares, but living with equities can be more complicated. The companies you have invested in may decide, with your approval and that of the other shareholders, to alter your shares, ask you for additional finance or even offer to buy back your shares. There are restrictions on what companies can do, in particular the following.

- When a company is established, its Memorandum of Association will set out the amount of the authorised share capital. This can be altered later but only with the backing of the shareholders. A company does not necessarily issue the whole of its authorised share capital but it may not, by law, issue more than its authorised share capital.
- The rules of the London Stock Exchange aim to protect the interests of existing shareholders of companies listed on its markets. Any new issues of shares, or any issue of investments which give holders the right to acquire shares, must first be offered to the existing shareholders unless they have voted otherwise.
- The Companies Acts forbid the issue of shares at a discount to their nominal value (face value).

Some of the possible changes to your shares are purely cosmetic and require little or no action on your part. Others are more significant: the company will send you information about the proposed changes and you should read this carefully before considering how to respond. If you do not understand anything in the document, seek advice from a stockbroker.

Share splits and consolidations

If the price of a company's shares has become very large, such as several pounds per share, it can have a dampening effect on trading. There is no sound reason why this should be so, but a psychological effect is probably at work, with investors viewing the shares as expensive.

A company can eliminate the problem by making a share split. For example, suppose a company's £1 shares are trading on the stock market at £12 each. The company could make a four-for-one share split by replacing each £1 share with four new 25p shares. Other things being equal, the market price should fall to £12 / 4 = £3.

Conversely, a company could consolidate its shares to produce higher priced trading units. For example, a company with 10p shares trading at 15p each might decide on a five-for-one consolidation with every five 10p shares being called in and replaced with one new 50p share. Other things being equal, the market price should rise to 15p × 5 = 75p.

Example
The shares of Sierra Plastics plc are priced at 670p. The company views this as uncomfortably high and announces a five-for-one share split. At present the shares have a nominal value of £1 but these will be replaced by new shares with a nominal value of 20p. The pre- and post-split positions are summarised in Table 14.1.

Table 14.1: Share split at Sierra Plastics

	Post-split	Pre-split
Number of shares	5,000,000	1,000,000
Nominal value of shares	20p	£1
Ordinary share capital	£1 million	£1 million
Share premium account	£1.5 million	£1.5 million
Earnings per share	5p	25p
Stock market price	134p	670p
P/e ratio	26.8	26.8

Before the share split, Chris holds 150 shares in Sierra Plastics, worth 150 x 670p = £1,005. After the share split Chris holds 150 x 5 = 750 shares worth 750 x 134p = £1,005.

Share splits and consolidations do not make any material change to your shareholding. You have the same interest in the company and, again, other things being equal, the market value of your holding is unchanged.

From the company's point of view, a share split or consolidation has no impact on the balance sheet. However, all share-related figures, such as earnings per share and dividends per share, will have to be adjusted. The p/e ratio (see page 138) is unchanged.

A company making a share split will generally be wary of reducing the share price to too low a level. Bearing in mind that shares cannot be issued at a discount to their nominal value, the company would lose the capacity to issue new shares later if it let the market price fall below the nominal value.

Scrip issues

Chapter 12 showed the balance sheet for a fictitious company, Mike plc. The capital and reserves – the shareholders' funds – were made up of several items: the called-up issued share capital, a share premium account, capital reserves and retained profits. Only the called-up share capital is directly related to the shares which have been issued, although the price of those shares on the stock market will reflect the whole value of the company, not just the nominal share capital.

If the share price is way out of line with the nominal value and the company has considerable reserves, it may decide to turn some or all of those reserves into nominal share capital. A company's reasons for doing this tend to be psychologically driven. Following normal UK accounting practice, the dividend paid out by a company is usually related to the nominal capital of the company, not the total value of the company's balance sheet. If the company has made and retained substantial profits in the past, a dividend paid now might be a very high proportion of the nominal share capital – see the Example. Although the dividend is quite reasonable, considering the balance sheet as a whole, employees and customers might take the (erroneous) view that shareholders were being paid excessive returns at the expense of themselves. A scrip issue (also called a 'bonus issue' or 'capitalisation') boosts the value of the nominal share capital and so reduces or removes this problem. It is also a way of reducing the market price of the shares, since the number of shares in issue increases but the value of the company as a whole is unchanged.

Scrip issues tend to be popular with investors, though in fact the effect on their shareholding is purely cosmetic: they are not being given anything which they did not already own. However, sometimes there is some foundation to the shareholders' optimism – for example, the scrip issue might be interpreted as a signal either that reserves are expected to be boosted again in future through good profit performance and/or that dividends are about to be increased. This optimistic view may feed through to a rise in the share price.

As the number of shares in issue has increased, share-related statistics, such as earnings per share and dividend per share, must be adjusted. Other things being equal, there is no change to the p/e ratio.

Rights issues

A rights issue is quite different from a share split or scrip issue. The company is seeking new money. It offers new shares, initially to existing shareholders, who can choose whether or not to buy them. Whatever you do, the value of your shareholding is affected, so it is important to understand what is happening.

The new shares are virtually always offered at a discount to the stock market price of the current shares. This is a sweetener used to encourage as many shareholders as possible to take up the shares and to give some leeway in case the stock market falls between the dates on which the rights issue is announced and the new shares are taken up. (Rights issues are more common when the stock market is rising, making the chance of this happening less likely.) The size of the discount depends to a large extent on the size of the new issue. If the issue is considered to be 'light' – e.g. a one-for-ten rights issue with one new share being issued for every ten existing shares – the discount will probably be fairly small (around 10 to 15 per cent or so). If the issue is 'heavy' – say, a one-for-four issue (which would increase the number of issued shares by one quarter) – the discount would generally be larger.

As with any new issue, the company usually arranges for underwriters, in exchange for a fee, to agree to take up the whole or any part of the issue which is not bought by the shareholders. If the issue is not underwritten, the discount will tend to be larger, since the company will be even more anxious to ensure that the issue sells.

If you hold convertible loan stock or convertible preference shares

Example

Tango plc has made extremely good profits over the last few years. As a result, its retained profits have doubled. This year it has made hefty profits once again – £1 million. It would like to pay out half of this to shareholders, but £500,000 dividend on nominal share capital of just £1 million (i.e. a 50 per cent dividend) would probably stir up trouble with the trade unions, who only reluctantly agreed to a stiff wage deal this year. Tango decides to make a four-for-one bonus issue, converting a substantial part of the retained profits into nominal share capital. This increases the number of issued shares fivefold, as shown in Table 14.2.

Table 14.2: Scrip issue at Tango plc

	Post-scrip	Pre-scrip
Number of shares	5,000,000	1,000,000
Nominal value of shares	£1	£1
Ordinary share capital	£5 million	£1 million
Retained profits	£4 million	£8 million
Earnings per share	12.5p	25p
Stock market price	335p	670p
P/e ratio	26.8	26.8

No change in the overall size of the company's balance sheet has occurred nor any other changes to the company, so – other things being equal – the value of each investor's shareholding should not change.

For example, Hattie has 1,000 Tango shares initially worth 1,000 × 670p = £6,700. After the scrip issue, she has 5,000 shares worth 5,000 × 134p = £6,700, assuming no other change to the share price. In fact, Tango can now go ahead with paying out £500,000 in dividends which represents a £500,000/£5 million =10 per cent dividend. As a result of this good news, the share price jumps to 152p, giving Hattie a profit (on paper anyway) of 5,000 × (152p – 134p) = £900.

of a company which makes a rights issue, your holding of the convertible stocks or shares, or the conversion terms, will be adjusted to take account of the effect of the rights issue. The company will write to you with details.

As a holder of ordinary stock which is the subject of a rights issue, you will receive an offer document giving details of the rights offer, the reasons for it, and so on. Soon after, you will receive a 'provisional allotment letter', together with details of the time limit for taking action – say, three weeks. You have four choices:

- take up the rights
- sell your rights on the stock market
- sell part of your rights on the stock market
- do nothing.

Taking up the rights

If you decide to take up the rights, you will be investing extra money in the company. Whether this is worth doing depends, in part, on how the company intends to use the new money raised. If the cash is to fuel an expansion programme and you have confidence in the management's aims and abilities, the new shares may look to be a good investment. If the cash is to fund a redundancy programme or to reduce a high level of debt, say, the prospects for the company might be less clear and the rights issue might look less attractive.

Similarly, the impact which taking up the rights issue has on the immediate value of your shareholding depends on the way the market as a whole views the prospects for the company. If the market is optimistic, the value of your shareholding could immediately rise by more than the cost to you of the new shares. If the market is sceptical, the new shares could, initially at least, be worth less to you than you paid for them.

Example

Uniform Explorations plc has just made an unexpected large find of mineral deposits and is seeking extra cash from shareholders to fund its extraction and processing. Uniform has announced a one-for-four rights issue, offering one new share for every four existing shares – see Table 14.3.

Before the rights issue, Uniform had 1,000,000 issued shares. Their market price was 670p per share, giving a market value for the company of 1,000,000 × 670p = £6,700,000.

The new shares are offered at 530p, so they will raise 250,000 × 530p = £1,325,000 for the company. Therefore, the new market

---

capitalisation should, in theory, be £6,700,000 + £1,325,000 = £8,025,000.

The number of issued shares rises from 1,000,000 to 1,250,000, so the new share price should, in theory, be £8,025,000 / 1,250,000 = 642p. Anyone buying the shares now does not take over the entitlements to the rights issue shares, so 642p is the 'ex rights price'.

All share-based statistics – such as earnings per share (eps) – need to be adjusted to reflect the impact of the rights issue. You do not need to do these calculations yourself – the company will publish the adjusted data.

Table 14.3: Rights issue at Uniform Explorations plc

	Post-rights issue	Pre-rights issue	Change
Number of shares	1,250,000	1,000,000	250,000
Nominal value of shares	£1	£1	none
Ordinary share capital	£1.25 million	£1 million	£0.25 million
Share premium account	£2.575 million	£1.5 million	£1.075 million
Total shareholders' funds	£5.325 million	£4 million	£1.325 million
Cash and deposits held by company	£2.225 million	£0.9 million	£1.325 million
Theoretical stock market price	642p	670p	(4.2)%

George owns 800 Uniform shares valued, before the rights issue, at 800 × 670p = £5,360. He is offered 200 new shares at a price of 530p per share, in other words a total cost to him of £1,060. If he takes up the rights, he will have increased his shareholding to 1,000 shares valued at 1,000 × 642p = £6,420 – i.e. an increase of £1,060. If the market price of the shares rose to 650p, his increased shareholding would be worth 1,000 x 650p = £6,500. In that case, he would be showing a profit of £6,500 – £5,360 – £1,060 = £80 as a result of taking up the rights issue.

Deciding to take up your rights also depends on whether you have available the new cash which is being asked for, and whether increasing the proportion of your money invested in that company makes sense for your portfolio as a whole.

Selling your rights on the stock market

If you do not wish to invest more money in the company, you can instead sell your rights to the new shares. If you do this, the value of your shareholding will fall, as will the proportion of the company's shares which you hold.

You will be provisionally allotted shares according to your entitlement. This entitlement is sent to you in the form of a 'provisional allotment letter'. From the time provisional allotment letters are issued, up to the date on which the rights lapse, the rights can be sold on the stock market independently of the original shares – see the Example below. The difference between the new ex-rights price of the original shares and the price at which the rights shares are issued gives the theoretical price at which the rights will trade. The actual price of the rights could be more or less than this.

The market price of rights currently on sale is published in the *Financial Times* – see Figure 14.1. The entries are as follows:

- **issue price** – the price at which the new shares are being offered
- **amount paid up** – the amount, if any, of the issue price which has already been paid as a first instalment for the new shares. In most cases, the full price is payable later as a single lump sum and the rights are said to be trading 'nil paid'
- **latest renunciation date** – the last date on which you can sell (i.e. renounce the rights on the stock market) or opt to take up the rights yourself. After this date, the rights lapse
- **high and low** – the largest and smallest premiums (or discounts) at which the rights have traded during their short life to date
- **stock** – the name of the company making the rights issue and the name or class of shares involved if they are other than the ordinary shares
- **closing price** – the mid-price at which the rights closed on the previous day. This is shown as the premium to the issue price. For example, if the issue price was 250p, '98pm' means that the rights would be worth buying if the ex rights price of the shares was more than 250 + 98 = 348p
- **+ or −** indicates whether the closing price was higher or lower than the closing price on the previous day.

Buying and then selling rights before the new shares are allocated can produce large profits (and losses) because these are by nature highly

Figure 14.1: Source: *Financial Times*

						2¾				
	.ı'.					258½	ʼ.			.ʼ
§-	F.P.	1.				119½		-	-	
§100	F.P.	29.4		.c 1st UK		98		-	-	
§	F.P.	10.1		..ı		5¼		-	-	21.6
§145	F.P.	24.7	153·₂	.ɔtal Office Grp		153½	L4.8	2.6	3.9	9.9
§110	F.P.	119.1	124½	119½ Usher Trowbridge		120½	W3.5	3.0	3.6	11.6
§40	F.P.	5.93	43½	40½ †VFG		41½	-	-	-	26.2

† Alternative Investment Market. § Placing price. * Introduction. For a full explanation of all other symbols please refer to The London Share Service notes.

RIGHTS OFFERS

Issue price p	Amount paid up	Latest Renun. date	1996/97 High	Low	Stock	Closing price p	+or-
75	Nil	14/4	7½pm	7½pm	Cliveden	7½pm	
137	Nil	2/4	41½pm	27½pm	Grantchester	33½pm	-1
34	Nil	14/4	12½pm	7½pm	JKX Oil & Gas	12pm	
100	Nil	3/4	25pm	12½pm	PTS	12½pm	
300	Nil	9/4	35½pm	32½pm	Partco	32½pm	
55	Nil	16/4	3½pm	¾pm	Saville Gordon	¾pm	

pm premium.

FT 30 INDEX

	Mar 25	Mar 24	Mar 21	Mar 20	Mar 1º	˟' ago	*High	*Low
FT 30	2823.1	2788.9	2822.7	2833.4	^		2931.4	2668.8
Ord. div. yie'	3.93	4.05	4.00	3.9°			ʼ92	3.76
P/E ratiᶜ	˟6.90	17.15	17.36	ʼ			˕ᶜˑ	
P/E r	˟3	16.94	1˟					
FT ʼ		ˀ₀ɜı ˄						

'geared' investments. The premium at which the rights trade rises and falls in line with movements is the ex rights price of the shares. A small movement in the underlying share price translates into a large movement in the premium. For example, if the ex-rights share price increased from 348p to 358p – a rise of less than 3 per cent – the premium would also tend to move by 10p from 98p to 108p, a rise of 10.2 per cent. You have to pay dealing charges when you buy and sell rights, but no stamp duty on the purchase of rights.

Selling part of your rights

Instead of selling all your rights, you might decide to sell just enough to pay for the ones you take up. That way, you do not need to find any additional cash. Ignoring dealing costs, there is a simple formula for calculating the number of rights you need to buy:

$$\frac{\text{number of new shares offered} \times \text{rights price}}{\text{ex rights price}}$$

Example

The rights to Uniform shares have been issued. The original shares are trading at the new theoretical market price of 642p per share. There is now a market in the rights themselves which, in theory, are valued at 642p – 530p = 112p.

If George (see previous example) decides to sell his rights, the value of his shareholding will fall from 800 × 670p = £5,360 to 800 × 642p = £5,136 – i.e. a loss of £5,360 – £5,136 = £224. But the sale of his rights at 112p would raise a total of 200 × 112p = £224. In other words, George would be neither better nor worse off but he would, in effect, have sold part of his original holding of Uniform shares. (In practice, George would be slightly worse off because of the need to pay dealing charges on the sale of his rights.)

If the market in Uniform shares is bullish and the ex rights price is well above the theoretical level of 642p, the rights become more valuable and George might be able to make a good profit by selling them. For example, at an ex rights price of 650p, the rights are worth 650p – 530p = 120p. The fall in the value of George's original shareholding is only 800 x (670p – 650p) = £160. The sale of the rights raises 200 × 120p = £240, giving George an immediate profit of £80 overall.

Bear in mind that the proportion of the company's shares you hold still falls. This is important only if you have a major stake in a company. As a small shareholder in a large company, you can ignore this aspect.

Do nothing

If you ignore the rights offer and do nothing, the company will sell the unclaimed new shares and send you cash for your share of the rights sold. You have no control over the price at which they are sold.

Reducing the share capital

In some circumstances, companies decide to reduce their share capital. This can be done in three ways:

- **Reducing the nominal value of the issued share capital** – this is the mirror image of a scrip issue. With a scrip issue, reserves are converted into share capital. With a reduction in nominal share

Example

Instead of selling all his rights, George decides to sell just enough to pay for the ones he keeps. He is being offered 200 new shares. To find out how many he should buy, he does the following sum:

$$\frac{200 \times 112p}{642p} = 34.9$$

To the nearest whole number, this comes to 35. He buys 35 new shares at 530p each. This costs him 35 x 530p = £185.50. His post-rights issue holding becomes 835 shares worth 835 × 642p = £5,360.70 (i.e. maintaining the value of his original shareholding, provided the ex rights price and rights price are at their theoretical levels). He finances the purchase through the sale of the remaining 165 rights, which raise 165 × 112p = £184.80.

capital, part of the share capital is converted into reserves. A company might do this if, say, the reserves are negative because of accumulated losses, with the result that the nominal share capital is much bigger than the value (in the accounts) of the company's assets. It will often be unacceptable for the company to pay out any dividends while it has accumulated losses in its balance sheet. By using share capital to wipe out the losses, the company's balance sheet is restored to health. Instead of being used gradually to reduce the accumulated losses in the reserves, profits can once again fund a dividend.

- **Returning cash to shareholders** – if the company has large cash balances, perhaps because it has scaled down its activities, it might simply pay the surplus cash to shareholders, e.g. as a special dividend. This reduces the size of the company's balance sheet, although the nominal share capital is unchanged. Other things being equal, the share price of the company might be expected to fall, reflecting its reduced asset value.
- **Purchasing and cancelling its own shares** – this is also a way of returning cash to shareholders but, in this case, the nominal share capital falls. In a way, it is like a mirror image of a rights issue. Under a rights issue, you are invited to increase your investment in the company. With a share buy-back, you are invited to decrease your

investment. Companies' motives for buying back their own shares are various and the buy-back can be engineered in a variety of ways – see below.

The law sets out very rigorous conditions and procedures to be followed by companies which want to reduce their share capital. The aim of the regulations is to protect other people – i.e. creditors – who may also have a claim on the company's assets. For example, if there were no restraints on a company returning cash to its shareholders and if the company's prospects looked bleak, it might simply bale out the shareholders by distributing all the available cash, leaving nothing for the taxman, banks and other creditors when the crunch came. To prevent this type of scenario, companies are allowed to use only certain reserves to fund the share reduction, and other rules prevent a company buying back all of its shares.

At the time of writing, some prominent share buy-backs had been in the news: they highlight the diversity of motives and methods. For example, BG (created from the split of British Gas into BG and Centrica) announced a £1.3 billion buy-back which involved replacing shareholders' existing shares with a combination of new ordinary shares and special redeemable shares. The latter are to be bought back over a period of time at a set price. The stated reason for the buy-back was to reduce the average cost of BG's capital by increasing the proportion of debt compared with shareholders' funds in its balance sheet. Unlike share capital, the cost of debt (i.e. the interest on it) is tax-deductible and so cheaper – at least in times when interest rates are generally low.

BP, on the other hand, had seen its share capital steadily diluted over recent years, due in part to the popularity of its options to take dividends in the form of shares. Its buy-back programme aimed to restore value per share.

Another firm, Tomkins, had failed sufficiently to run down embarrassingly large cash reserves through acquisitions and reluctantly decided that the best thing to do was to return part of the surplus to shareholders through a buy-back plan. Large cash reserves are generally undesirable because they represent money which has not been put to work to generate profits and can make the cash-rich company a tempting takeover prospect for another company, which reckons it can make better use of the cash.

Takeovers

If you own shares in a company which is the target of a takeover bid, you generally have the chance to make a handsome gain. If you own shares in the company doing the taking over, the position may be less clear-cut.

In the case of a friendly takeover, the two companies involved often quietly negotiate behind the scenes and, once agreement has been reached, make a joint announcement of their intentions. A formal offer is then put to the shareholders of the company to be taken over and the management of the target company write to shareholders recommending acceptance.

Where there is no prior agreement between the companies, the battle can be bloody. Usually, the initial step is for the predator company to start buying up the shares of its takeover target on the stock market. Set rules, administered by the Takeover Panel, try to ensure that all shareholders are treated fairly. Holdings of 3 per cent or more of the share capital must be declared to the Stock Exchange and once the predator company has acquired 15 per cent of its target's shares, it must pause for one week before acquiring more. There is a second pause, once the shareholding reaches 25 per cent. When the predator owns 30 per cent of the shares, it must make a formal offer to buy the remaining share capital.

The formal offer to shareholders can be in several forms. You might be offered cash, shares in the predator company, a combination of both or a choice between cash and shares. At this stage the offer is conditional and, even if you agree to give up your shares in the target, you can change your mind. Alternatively, you could sell your shares on the stock market. While a bid is in progress, the stock market will be trying to put a value on the takeover and the shares in the target company will generally rise either to the value of the bid on the table or to a higher value, if the market as a whole puts the value of the deal at a higher level. The action really hots up if another bidder emerges.

There are no simple rules for what action you should take. There will be plenty of coverage in the business press to help you form a view and you will be bombarded with material from both the predator company (or companies) and the takeover target. If you like the predator company and reckon it will do a better job running the target than its existing managers, consider taking up any shares in the predator company that are offered. If you think the takeover target stands a good chance of fighting off the bid and you have confidence in the management's abilities, hang on to your shares. Otherwise, consider taking the cash either on offer or from selling on the market.

If the predator gains enough shares to give it over 50 per cent of the votes in the target company, the offer becomes unconditional and you must make your decision. The offer usually remains open for another two weeks or so and you must decide whether or not to accept. As a small shareholder, there is probably little point in hanging on to your shares now. If the predator gains 90 per cent of the target company's shares, it has the right to purchase compulsorily all the remaining shares, so you would then have no choice but to sell up. Note that, once you accept an unconditional offer, you cannot change your mind.

Not all takeover bids succeed. If the predator fails to gain voting control, the bid lapses and the predator must wait for at least a year before attempting another takeover bid for the same company.

Bids may also fail if the authorities step in. If the Office of Fair Trading is concerned that a takeover will give the predator company a dominant position in the market which could work against the public interest it may recommend that a bid be referred to the Monopolies and Mergers Commission (MMC). The Secretary of State for Trade decides whether the referral goes ahead and whether to accept the subsequent advice of the MMC, but the referral alone is a blow for any bidder because the MMC investigation invariably takes some months to complete. The European Commission can also block takeovers which it considers jeopardise competition in European markets. Determining the impact of a takeover on competition is not an exact science – even the definition of the market concerned can be controversial, let alone the measurement of dominance – so the outcome of referrals is seldom a foregone conclusion.

Chapter 15

Share perks

IT IS sometimes overlooked that many companies, especially in the consumer-oriented sectors, offer discounts and free gifts to their shareholders. Perks alone are not a good reason for selecting shares, which could otherwise be poor value, and, if you did concentrate only on shares which offered perks, you would build up a very unbalanced portfolio. But, if you are considering a company's shares anyway, it is worth giving some weight to the perks on offer.

Nominee accounts

Perks are a reward offered to shareholders listed on a company's share register. Increasingly, small investors are being discouraged from holding their shares direct and being persuaded instead to use a nominee account (see Chapter 4). The problem here is that the name on the share register is the name of the nominee and the perks might not be passed on to you. For example, Aberdeen Trust plc offers shareholders a 2 per cent discount on selected unit trust purchases plus membership of the Country Gentlemen's Association, but the shares must be registered in your own name. Similarly, Tottenham Hotspur gives its shareholding fans a 10 per cent discount on purchases from its Spurs Superstores and by mail order, but the perk is available for individual shareholders only. Problems also arise where perks are in the form of vouchers sent out with the annual report and accounts or dividend statements if these are not passed on to you by the nominee.

In August 1995, Proshare★ drew up a Nominee Code which it hoped nominee account providers and companies would adopt in their dealings with shareholders who invested through nominee accounts. Among other things, the code requires:

- nominee account providers to *'claim shareholder benefits and incentives on behalf of investors who request them'* and clearly declare to investors the charges for *'making any arrangements for investors to receive...perks'*
- companies to, *'on request by the nominee, and in an agreed format, make available to investors all benefits and incentives on the same basis as to shareholders in the company whose shares are not held by a nominee'*.

Unfortunately, as discussed in Chapter 4, the Proshare code has received a very mixed reception and your own perks might not be covered by it. You need to check out the policy of both your nominee and the companies concerned to see what access, if any, you have to perks from your shares.

The UK Shareholders' Association★ has proposed a solution to this problem. It suggests that shareholders should, on request, be able to require their nominee to register the shares jointly in the nominee's and the shareholder's names. This would ensure that your ultimate ownership of the shares could be recognised by the company and that you could then be given all the rights of share ownership, including any perks. The Shareholders' Association is also campaigning for regulations to prevent nominee account providers from making excessive charges for passing on rights to shareholders.

For the present, to be sure of getting your perks, you must either hold your shares direct in your own name (which could cause difficulties if you came to sell – see Chapter 4) or make enquiries at the time you invest to find out the policies of both your broker and the company. Be prepared to shop around for a different broker if you are not happy with the terms of the nominee account.

The perks on offer

One hundred or so companies offer specific perks to shareholders. Some are long-established and well known, such as the free Wimbledon Centre Court and No 1 Court tickets available to holders of debentures in the All England Lawn Tennis Ground, and Sketchley's 25 per cent discount on dry cleaning. Others are relative newcomers, such as Eurotunnel's 30 per cent discount on up to six single (or three return) journeys on Le Shuttle. One of the most novel share perks of the past was from a small seed company which, in 1984, supplied shareholders with free seeds and invited them to take part in a competition to grow the largest onion.

The value of perks varies considerably from just a few pounds to thousands – in the latter camp, you will find discounts on homes from Barratt Developments and Bellway. You need to check any restrictions applying to the perk – for example, discounts might not apply to sale items or might be available only to shareholders who attend the annual general meeting (which could be many miles away).

To qualify for the perks, you usually have to meet some qualifying terms. For example, for Wimbledon seats, you need to hold at least £500 of debentures (£2,000 for Centre Court seats); for a 1 per cent discount on a Redrow Group home, you need to hold at least 2,500 shares for at least 12 months; and, for a 10 per cent discount on British Airways flights, you need to have been on the share register on a specified date as a holder of at least 200 ordinary shares. But many offers are open to all shareholders, regardless of the size of holding, such as the Savoy Hotel's 10 per cent discount on meals and accommodation and Standard Chartered's waiver of commission on traveller's cheques.

Table 15.1 shows a selection of the perks available. For a complete list, see *Shareholder Perks* published by Premier Fund Managers Ltd.*

Table 15.1: Selection of shareholder perks in 1997

Shares	Discount	Allowed on	Minimum shareholding
The All England Lawn Tennis Ground		• One Centre Court seat ticket per day for the 1997–2001 Championships	£2,000 debentures
		• One No 1 Court seat ticket per day for the 1997–2001 Championships	£500 debentures
Allied Domecq plc		Book of vouchers giving discounts at specified pubs and restaurants and on company's products at Victoria Wine; prize draws etc.	All shareholders

Shares	Discount	Allowed on	Minimum shareholding
Barratt Developments	• £500 reduction	every £25,000 or part thereof on price of new or part exchange house in UK or USA	1,000 ordinary shares held for continuous period of 12 months
	• Discount	purchasing or renting holiday property at Barratt leisure resort in UK or Spain	
British Telecom	Discount	limited period offers to buy selected BT (and third party) products	All shareholders
Burton Group	12.5% discount	most goods from over 1,700 retail outlets	5,000 ordinary shares
Eurotunnel	30% discount	six single (or three return) journeys on Le Shuttle	1,000 shares held for at least three months
General Accident	• 10% discount	personal insurance policies	All shareholders
	• variable discount	life policies	
Lloyds TSB Group plc		Low cost share dealing service	All shareholders
Park Food Group plc	20% discount	Park Premier range of hampers	All shareholders

Source: Premier Fund Managers Limited

Chapter 16

Derivatives: indirect ways to invest in shares

YOU can play the stock market without ever actually buying a share. How? By using an investment whose price is *derived* from the value of some underlying share or portfolio of shares. Because its value is derived, this type of investment is called a 'derivative'.

Unfortunately, the word 'derivative' conjures up horror stories of the huge losses which brought down Barings Bank (see Box) and nearly did the same to Metallgesellschaft, or the £77 million loss which sent a shudder through NatWest. This highlights the fact that derivatives are risky, but overlooks the fact that the risk can be controlled and is the very element which can make derivatives useful investment tools even for the private investor.

What are derivatives?

Derivatives are any investment whose value depends on that of some other underlying investment. Chapter 14 briefly described one type of derivative: rights allocated when a company makes a rights issue and which can be traded independently in the period before the new shares are issued.

Other derivatives you will commonly come across are listed below. With the exception of warrants, they have a typical life span of up to nine months. By contrast, the original term of a warrant is usually five years or more. Common derivatives are:

- **warrants** – these are investments, often issued along with loan stock, which give the holder the right to buy shares in a company at a set price on one or more set dates in the future. In the meantime, the warrants can be bought and sold on the stock market
- **traditional options** – these are the rights to buy or sell a set number of shares in a company on (or before – though this seldom

---

How derivatives brought down a bank

Nick Leeson left two things at his Singapore desk when he went home on the evening of 23 February 1995: a note saying 'I'm sorry' and a loss of £860 million which bankrupted his employer, Barings. One 28-year-old man single-handedly brought about the collapse of this 232-year old bank by speculating with a type of derivative called 'index futures'. He used them to gamble on the future movements of the Nikkei 225 index – the main share price index for the Japanese stock market. Leeson reckoned the Japanese economy was set to grow and felt certain that the Nikkei 225 would not fall below its then current level of around 19,000 over the following three months. But disaster struck: on 17 January 1995, the Japanese city of Kobe was hit by a tremendous earthquake. In response, the stock market fell. Desperately, Leeson bought more futures, expecting the market to stabilise, but by mid-February the index had slumped to 18,000 and Leeson could no longer conceal the losses.

---

happens) a given date at a set price. Unlike warrants and traded options, they cannot be bought and sold in the interim

- **traded options** – the right, but not the obligation, to buy or sell a set number of shares in a company at a set price, or to receive cash according to the movement in a stock market index, up to a given date. In the interim, the options can be bought and sold
- **commodity futures** – the obligation to buy or sell a set quantity of a commodity at a set price at a given date in the future. In the interim, the futures can be bought and sold on the futures market
- **financial futures** – the obligation to buy or sell a set quantity of an investment or financial product – e.g. a British Government stock or a currency – at a set price on a given date in the future. The idea has also been extended to 'index futures'. Although you cannot buy or sell an index as such, you stand to pay or receive a set sum of money according to the level of the index. Like commodity futures, financial futures can be bought and sold on the futures market before the delivery date arrives.

The origin of derivatives

Derivatives began in the agricultural markets with commodity futures. In the nineteenth century, farmers from the Midwest of America were exporting their produce to Europe via the port of Chicago. They had the difficult task of predicting up to a year ahead what quantity of their produce could be sold and at what price. Similarly, customers found it hard to cope with sharp swings in the prices they had to pay. So a practice grew up of agreeing a price in advance for the delivery of a given quantity of grain or pork bellies (pigs) and so on at a date, say, six months or one year thence. A deposit (now called the 'margin') was payable at the time the contract was made, with the balance payable on delivery. Futures are still used in this way (called 'hedging') to reduce risk in commercial transactions.

However, the futures market also attracts speculators, who see the opportunity for large profits. Since only a margin is payable at the time the contract is struck, a large quantity of futures contracts can be made for a relatively small outlay. If the price of the underlying commodity rises, this will have a big impact on the value of the contract (an effect called 'gearing'). If the commodity price movement is favourable, the contract can be sold for a fat profit. On the other hand, if the commodity price moves against the speculator, large losses materialise. In fact, once the balance of payment becomes due, the losses can be far greater than the original investment (i.e. the margin).

Although speculators have a different motive from hedgers, they are equally important players in the market because they increase the liquidity of the market. Speculators make it possible for hedgers to buy and sell the contracts they need to in order to cover their commercial positions. In effect, the hedgers transfer their risks to the speculators. The hedgers are happy because they want to operate in a more certain world; the speculators are happy because high risk gives the opportunity for high returns.

In 1975, futures were extended to purely financial transactions, with contracts for the delivery of shares, government bonds and foreign currencies.

Index futures are a further development. A stock market index describes a basket of shares. In theory, an index futures contract could require the delivery of an appropriate amount of each of the constituent shares at a given future date, but this would be very awkward. So, instead, the contract is satisfied by the payment of a cash sum reflecting the difference between the level of the index in the contract and its actual level at the delivery date. For example, a FTSE 100 futures contract values each one-point difference in the index at £25.

Just like the commodity markets, the financial futures market is used by hedgers and speculators. Companies use financial futures to hedge their currency and interest rate risks when they are buying or selling overseas or agreeing to pay or receive a set price on delivery of goods or services. Similarly, fund managers – such as unit trusts, insurance companies and pension funds – use futures to offset the risk to their funds of changes in share prices, interest rates and exchange rates. Speculators look for the chance to profit and, in doing so, help to create a liquid market.

Example

Farmer Giles is a grain producer. He sells a number of contracts for delivery of £1,000 of his grain in six months' time. The deposit – the margin – payable now is just 10 per cent, i.e. £100. Ted buys one contract. He is not interested in taking delivery of the grain, but he thinks that the grain price is probably going to rise, giving him the chance to make a profit.

Three months later, the market price of grain has risen to £1,500. So Ted now has a contract to buy grain for £1,000 which could – if the price rise holds until the delivery date – be sold for £1,500, a £500 profit. But Ted does not have to wait until the delivery date. He can sell the futures contract now. If he could sell it for £500 (the full amount of the profit to be made on delivery), he would make a 500 per cent profit on his original outlay (the £100 margin) compared with just a 50 per cent profit (£500 on £1,000 outlay) if he had been buying and selling the grain itself.

On the other hand, if the grain price in the market fell to £500, Ted would have a contract which required him to take delivery on grain for £1,000 which he could sell for only £500 – i.e. a loss of £500. His investment (the margin) of £100 would have produced a 500 per cent loss, so he would have lost a good deal more than his original outlay.

Futures and options

As the example shows, futures are particularly risky, because you can lose more than your original investment. As such, they are not ideal investments for the average investor. Options provide a better vehicle. In many ways, they are similar to futures, but whereas the holder of a futures contract is obliged to buy the underlying commodity or investment when the delivery date comes round, the buyer of an options contract can choose whether or not to go ahead with delivery. Do nothing and the option simply expires, so the most you can lose is the price you paid for the contract. Certain other derivatives, such as warrants, are similar to options, limiting your losses to your whole original investment but no more.

Who should invest?

Investment in derivatives is more complicated than direct investment in shares. To understand how share or index derivatives work, you need to have a good feel for what makes the underlying share prices or indices behave the way they do. So derivatives are not for you if you are still in the early stages of becoming a shareholder.

You also need to appreciate the different roles which derivatives can play. For example, traded options can be used:

- **for speculation**: you can gamble that the price of the underlying investment will rise or fall by a given amount over a given period. This is a faster and cheaper way to speculate than by buying the underlying investments, and offers the prospect of higher returns with a known (albeit greater) degree of risk
- **for price fixing**: you can guarantee the price now at which you will be able to buy a given quantity of shares at some time within a set period. This can be useful if you do not currently have the funds available to buy the shares
- **for insurance**: if you have an existing portfolio of shares, you can use traded options to compensate you for an unexpected price movement. For example, if you think the market is at its peak, you might sell some shares to take a profit. If you simultaneously buy an option to let you buy the same shares at today's price at some future date, you will still be able to profit if the share price in fact rises further. If, as you originally suspected, the share price has peaked, you simply let the option lapse.

Depending on how you are using derivatives, you will face either an increase or a reduction in risk. You must understand the risk position.

There are more complicated techniques which involve not simply buying or selling a single derivatives contract, but using different contracts in combination. You may want to study these techniques to see how they could fit into your investment strategy.

It is inherent in the nature of derivatives that you are required to take a view over a finite, and relatively short, period of time. Therefore, temperament plays a part – are you decisive by nature?

It may be important that you monitor your investment closely and take quick action when the price of the underlying investment moves. Do your other commitments, such as work, allow you do this?

The relationship between the derivative and its underlying investment is very precise and can be described mathematically. You do not need to do the maths yourself, but it is certainly helpful to develop some understanding of what factors are in play. You can buy software to crunch the options numbers for you.

Example

The FTSE 100 Index stands at 5,030. Sophie thinks the market is due for a substantial fall in the near future. She buys two traded index options which give her the right to sell the index at 5000 at any time within the three months to December. This is called a 'December 500 put'. ('Put' indicates that this is a contract giving the right to sell; a 'call' option gives the right to buy.)

Index options are sold in standard contract sizes, based on the index multiplier – in this case, £10. Sophie pays 158 for each £10 multiple. The two contracts cost her 2 x 158 x £10 = £3,160 (ignoring dealing costs). She holds the contract to expiry, at which time the FTSE 100 index is 4,800. The value of her two contracts then is 2 x (5,000 – 4,800) × £10 = £4,000. Deducting her initial outlay, this gives Sophie a profit of £4,000 – £3,160 = £840.

If the market had fallen further, her gain would have been even larger – the potential for gain is unlimited. If instead the market had stayed level or risen, Sophie's put option would have become worthless and she would have lost her whole outlay of £3,160. This is the maximum she could have lost.

More information

An excellent introduction to the subject is *Traded options – A private investor's guide* published by LIFFE.★ LIFFE also runs training courses for private investors who are interested in options and you would be well advised to go on one of these before you start to trade. Not all stockbrokers accept orders for option trading: LIFFE publishes a list of those which do. The *Investors Chronicle*★ runs regular articles about using options and occasional features about warrants.

Chapter 17

What to do if things go wrong

SHARES are inherently more risky than deposit-based investments, such as building society accounts. In general, there is no compensation if you lose money simply because your shares fall in value. But there is an extensive regulatory system which aims to protect you from losing money because of dishonesty or poor administration – for example, your broker running off with your money, unacceptable delays in settling your business, unnecessary buying and selling of stocks in order to generate commission income.

Much of the system is about to be overhauled, so this chapter sets out the regime for protecting investors, which is expected to continue until early 1999, as well as an outline of the new regime afterwards.

There are three aspects to protecting shareholders. The first is to ensure that their investments are handled properly by the professionals, such as stockbrokers and fund managers, whom they employ. The second is to ensure that stock markets are run fairly and transparently. The third is to ensure that companies are accountable to their shareholders who are, after all, their ultimate owners.

Investor protection

At present, investors are protected through a system of regulations set up under the Financial Services Act 1986. Over the period 1997–9, the structure of the regulatory system is being revised and a new Financial Services Act is due in 1998. However, the central aims of regulators remain the same:

- **To act as a licensing authority** – it is against the law for any firm to carry on investment business without becoming a member of an appropriate regulatory body – this is called being authorised. Before being granted authorisation, the firm must meet certain conditions: for example, it must meet a minimum solvency requirement and its personnel must be deemed fit and proper.

- **To ensure high standards within the investment industry** – each regulator maintains an extensive rule book governing the way members carry on their business. The rules cover, for example, minimum levels of training and competence, advertising, the information to be given to clients and prospective customers, safeguards for clients' money and investments, segregation of departments to prevent market-sensitive information falling into the wrong hands, the handling of complaints, and so on. The regulators also put in place measures to help them to keep a check on whether rules are being kept and standards maintained – e.g. requiring reports from member firms and carrying out spot checks on their businesses.

- **To sort out problems** – each regulator must have a complaints procedure for deciding what has happened in a dispute, a system for ensuring that investors who have been unfairly treated are compensated and a system for taking disciplinary action against members who break the rules. Such action could range from warnings and fines right through to expulsion from the regulatory body, in which case the firm could no longer legally carry on its business.

During the transition from the old regulatory structure to the new, there continues to be an 'umbrella' regulator, the Financial Services Authority (FSA),★ formerly called the Securities and Investments Board (SIB). The FSA oversees the whole system, but day-to-day regulation is currently delegated to three Self-Regulating Organisations (SROs) and a number of Recognised Professional Bodies (RPBs). In addition, the FSA is responsible for regulating Recognised Investment Exchanges (RIEs), such as the London Stock Exchange. Chart 17.1 summarises the regulatory structure.

As the transition progresses, the FSA will take over completely from the SROs, which will cease to exist, and will take over the investment regulatory roles of the RPBs. It will also become responsible for the regulation of deposit-type investments and additional aspects of insurance, assuming responsibilities which currently fall to the Bank of England, the Building Societies Commission, the Department of

Chart 17.1: The transitional regulatory system

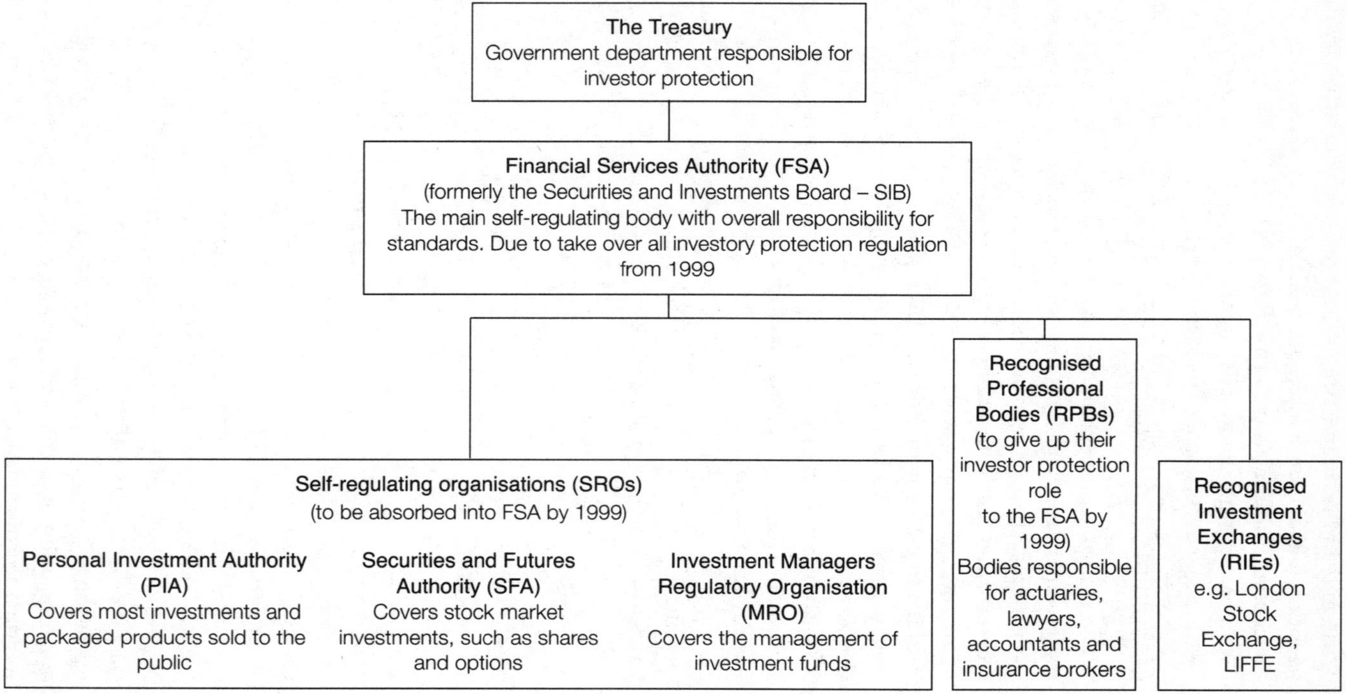

The Treasury
Government department responsible for investor protection

Financial Services Authority (FSA)
(formerly the Securities and Investments Board – SIB)
The main self-regulating body with overall responsibility for standards. Due to take over all investory protection regulation from 1999

Recognised Professional Bodies (RPBs)
(to give up their investor protection role to the FSA by 1999)
Bodies responsible for actuaries, lawyers, accountants and insurance brokers

Recognised Investment Exchanges (RIEs)
e.g. London Stock Exchange, LIFFE

Self-regulating organisations (SROs)
(to be absorbed into FSA by 1999)

Personal Investment Authority (PIA)
Covers most investments and packaged products sold to the public

Securities and Futures Authority (SFA)
Covers stock market investments, such as shares and options

Investment Managers Regulatory Organisation (IMRO)
Covers the management of investment funds

Trade and Industry and friendly society regulators. By 1999, the transition is due to be complete and the FSA will have become a single 'super regulator' for the majority of investments and savings products which are marketed and sold to the general public.

Complaints and compensation

When you go to a stockbroker, you generally come within the field of regulation looked after by the Securities and Futures Authority (SFA).★ If you have passed your money over to an investment manager, you are most likely to come within the scope of the Investment Management Regulatory Organisation (IMRO)★ or, possibly, the Personal Investment Authority (PIA).★

In general, if you have a complaint, you should first raise it with the investment firm, if necessary taking it right up to the senior management level. If this does not produce a satisfactory outcome, contact either the appropriate regulator or the regulator's complaints mechanism, as follows.

- **Securities and Futures Authority**: contact the SFA Complaints Bureau,★ which is a free conciliation service. If you are still unable to reach an agreement with the investment firm, you can go on to the Consumer Arbitration Scheme,★ for which there is a fee (£50 in 1997), refundable if you win your case.
- **Investment Management Regulatory Organisation**: the Investment Ombudsman.★ This is a free service and the outcome is not binding on you.
- **Personal Investment Authority**: the PIA Ombudsman. Again, this is a free service and the ombudsman's decision is not binding on you.

An arbitration service is a quasi-judicial system to which both you and the firm must agree to refer the case. The decision made by the arbitrator is then binding on both parties. Most ombudsmen schemes are less formal. The ombudsman has wider scope to consider all factors and to come to a commonsense judgement. The decision is not binding on you, though may be binding on the firm, depending on the terms of the scheme. This means that you can still, if you choose, pursue your case in the courts. Unfortunately, the British legal system is usually costly and slow, and the outcome of a case is seldom certain, so going to court may be viewed as a last resort.

The arbitration and ombudsmen schemes can make awards in your favour if they find that you have suffered because of some fault on the part of the investment firm. If the investment business has gone bust, the Investors' Compensation Scheme might kick in. This can cover the first £30,000 of any loss in full and 90 per cent of the next £20,000 lost – i.e. £48,000 in total.

At the time of writing, the detailed procedures for handling complaints and compensation under the new system of regulation had yet to be determined. However, it seemed likely that the various financial ombudsmen would be amalgamated – a welcome step which would mean that you had just one point of contact if you had an unresolved complaint. More ominously, there were suggestions that, since funding is finite, the compensation scheme should concentrate on those who are least able to bear a loss. This is a pragmatic approach but one which would stray from the general principle of fair redress for all.

The Internet

A particular problem exists when it comes to regulating investment businesses operating over the Internet. The same rules apply to an investment business whatever the medium through which it does its business; however, the Internet itself is not regulated. Not surprisingly, it has become a rich ground for all types of investment scam. Both the FSA★ and the Bank of England★ give advice on their own Internet sites about protecting yourself if you are considering making financial arrangement over the Internet.

The frauds to watch out for are varied. Pyramid selling schemes can be found. Some rogue firms have set up bogus Internet sites mimicking the genuine sites of bona fide investment groups with the aim of getting investors to part with their cash. Another favourite is to start rumours, particularly within the so-called 'chat rooms' where users exchange views and gossip, which aim to drive up the price of particular shares, giving the perpetrator of the rumour the chance to make a killing on the shares. The regulators try to spot these ploys and stop them, but they openly admit that the Internet is too vast to police effectively. As a result they rely heavily on tip-offs from ordinary people. If you come across something dubious on the Internet, report it to the FSA.★

Fair and transparent markets

The Financial Services Act 1986 also sets out the framework for regulating stock markets. The London Stock Exchange is a Recognised Investment Exchange (RIE) which is responsible for ensuring the fair and proper running of its stock market. Recognition is not automatic. The body running the market must show that:

- it has sufficient financial resources to carry on its business
- business is conducted in an orderly manner and investors are afforded proper protection. In particular, the exchange must stick to dealing in investments for which there is a proper market and ensure that the issuers of the investments provide investors with sufficient information for establishing the value of the investments
- it has adequate arrangements for recording transactions
- it can monitor and enforce compliance with its rules
- it has a mechanism for dealing with complaints
- it takes steps to promote and maintain high standards.

The London Stock Exchange rule book and systems, albeit refined over time, pre-date the Financial Services Act and provide a framework of regulations which govern the eligibility of companies for listing on the Stock Exchange, the reporting requirements once they are listed, procedures to be followed in the case of takeover bids, and so on. This is backed up by certain statutory rules, such as those which prohibit dealing on the basis of 'insider' information – i.e. profiting from knowledge which is not available to the body of investors as a whole.

Accountable companies

If you are to invest in a company, you have a right to know the nature of that company's business, its financial structure, recent performance, and so on. The Accounting Standards Board sets out detailed rules which must be followed in preparing financial accounts for presentation to shareholders and the wider public.

For all but very small companies, the Companies Acts require the annual financial accounts to be audited by a firm of professional accountants. They must record whether the accounts give a true and fair representation of the company's financial health.

As to the general running of the company, the shareholders are, in theory, in the driving seat. In an ideal world, ordinary shareholders would take a keen interest in the running of the company and would use their votes to signal their lack of support if they were unhappy with the directors' actions. In practice, private investors seldom exercise their votes and, even among institutional investors who generally have much more clout, only a third or so of votes are usually cast. This gives directors a great deal of leeway in running the company and setting their rewards.

To fill the vacuum left by shareholders' reluctance to exercise their votes, there have been several codes of practice attempting to regulate the way in which directors and key executives run their companies. The most recent is the Hampel Report, which aims to lay down principles rather than strictly binding rules. Its suggestions include:

- directors should stand for re-election at least every three years
- a director who resigns as a result of the company's policies should be required to explain his or her reasons to shareholders
- one third of the board of directors should be non-executive (i.e. not involved in the day-to-day running of the company)
- the majority of non-executive directors should be independent
- ideally, the chairman of the board of directors should not also be the chief executive of the company
- a non-executive director should take a lead role and act as a focus for shareholders' worries
- the board should take direct responsibility for the pay of directors
- shareholders should be given at least 20 days' notice of an annual general meeting
- at the annual general meeting, the company should give a full business presentation
- when it comes to voting, all proxy votes should be counted before the commencement of the annual general meeting and the count announced after a show of hands
- if questions put at the annual general meeting cannot be answered, the chairman should provide a written answer as soon as possible
- institutional investors should be encouraged to consider their obligation to their clients in casting their votes
- a summary of the annual general meeting should be available.

At the time of writing, the government was still considering whether the Hampel Report should be adopted, and in what form.

Self-defence for share investors

You can make it less likely that things will go wrong, if you follow these tips:

1. Use only authorised investment firms. Check that a broker or investment manager is authorised by consulting the FSA Register.*

2. Know your broker. Does the broker you've approached welcome private/small investors? What type of service are you looking for – e.g. shares, traded options? Does your broker deal willingly in that type of business?

3. Make sure your broker/investment manager knows you. If you are looking for an execution-only service, your broker needs to know very little about you. But, if the broker is to manage your investments, make sure that he or she asks enough about you to understand your investment aims, your available resources, relevant personal circumstances, your tax position and your attitude towards risk.

4. Bear in mind that, if you deal on an execution-only basis, you have only yourself to blame for poor investment decisions. If you subscribe to an advisory service, you may have some claim to redress if you were poorly advised.

5. Be informed. Understand the nature of different shares and how you expect them to help you achieve your financial aims. Ask questions if there are gaps in your knowledge.

6. Be sceptical. If a deal sounds too good to be true, then it is probably suspect. High returns always go hand-in-hand with high risk. Don't take terms like 'risk-free' and 'guaranteed' at face value – check exactly what is on offer.

7. Check how your cash and shares will be handled by the broker. They should be 'ring-fenced' so that even if the broker does go bust, your assets are safe. Does the broker have insolvency or other insurance to compensate you if your assets cannot be recovered? Or is the broker part of a much larger parent company which would underwrite any losses?

8. If you are being encouraged to hold shares through a nominee account, check whether there will be charges. Will you still benefit from your shareholder rights – are extra charges involved

211

in this? Is the account 'designated' or 'pooled'? A designated account holds only your assets. In a pooled account, your assets are lumped in with those of other investors, which is a slightly less secure arrangement.

9. How are the salesmen at your brokers paid? If they receive only commission, they may be more inclined to turn over your investments unnecessarily (a practice called 'churning').

10. Take an interest in your investments. Check paperwork, follow the markets, read company statements, cast your votes.

Glossary

Acid test A measure of liquidity derived from the balance sheet of a company which tells you whether the company has enough cash and assets which can readily be turned into cash to meet all its short-term debts. Also known as the 'quick ratio'.

ACT Abbreviation for 'advance corporation tax'.

Advance corporation tax Corporation tax which a company must hand over to the tax authorities when it pays out a dividend to shareholders. The tax can be offset against the mainstream corporation tax bill which becomes payable after the end of the company's financial year.

Aggressive stock Shares which tend to outperform the stock market as a whole, rising faster than the market when it is rising and falling faster than the market when it is falling.

AIM Abbreviation for 'Alternative investment market'.

Allotment letter Notice that you have been issued shares – e.g. as part of a 'new issue' or a 'rights issue'. The allotment letter is accepted as proof that you own the shares and can be transferred to a new owner if you decide to sell.

Alternative investment market Junior market of the London Stock Exchange on which companies can be listed more cheaply and without having to fulfil such onerous conditions as those required for a listing on the main market. AIM companies tend to be small and/or new and relatively high-risk investments.

Annuity Investment whereby you exchange a lump sum for an income either payable for life or for a set period. You cannot get your original capital back as a lump sum though it is deemed to form part of the regular income.

Approved profit-sharing scheme Scheme whereby employees acquire shares in their company in proportion to their earnings. Provided the scheme meets certain conditions, for example, the shares must be held in trust for a minimum period, the shares are not treated as part of pay, so no income tax is due on their value.

Asset In the context of a balance sheet, something which is owned by a company or owed to it.

Asset stripping The practice of selling off parts of a newly acquired company in order to realise their cash value.

Balanced portfolio A spread of different shares, and often other investments too, held in order to reduce risk to a moderate level. Sometimes used to mean a mix of shares and investments which produce both income and growth.

Balance sheet A snapshot on a specific date of a company's financial state, showing all its assets and liabilities.

Bargain A deal for the purchase or sale of shares.

Bear Someone who expects the price of a share or the stock market as a whole to fall.

BES Abbreviation for 'Business expansion scheme'.

Beta A statistical measure of risk which describes how a share's price moves in relation to the stock market as a whole or to a specific sector of the market.

Big Bang A key date in the history of the London Stock Exchange when the 'minimum commission agreement' was abolished, single capacity ceased to be a requirement and outsiders were allowed to invest in member firms. More recently, the date on which the London Stock Exchange started order book trading for FTSE 100 shares has been dubbed by some 'Big Bang Two'.

Blue chip Term (borrowed from poker where it denotes the highest value tokens) which indicates that a share or company is large and sound with an established track record.

Bonus issue The allocation of additional shares at no cost to existing shareholders. (Also called a 'scrip issue'.)

Book value The value of an asset in the balance sheet of a company (which will generally be different from its market value). Typically, this will be the original purchase price reduced by depreciation since the date of purchase.

Break out A term used in Chartism to denote the point at which a share price ceases to move according to a specified pattern and establishes or re-establishes a trend.

British Government stocks Loans you make to the government in return for regular payments of interest at a fixed rate. Most stocks are redeemable, so you receive a fixed lump sum at the end of the stock's life. In the meantime, you can sell the loan on the stock market.

Broker A professional buyer and seller of shares and other marketable securities who generally acts as an agent for an investor rather than buying and selling on his or her own account.

Bubble company Company whose share price is inflated well beyond any realistic value based on the company's prospects or assets. Eventually, the bubble bursts and the share price rapidly falls back.

Building society An organisation accepting savings and making loans which is owned by those savers and borrowers who are members.

Bull Someone who expects the price of a share or the stock market as a whole to rise.

Business expansion scheme Forerunner of the 'Enterprise investment scheme', which aimed to encourage investors to back new venture companies by offering tax incentives.

Call option A right (but not an obligation) to buy shares at a set price at any time up until the option expires on a given date.

Capital gains tax Tax on profits (in excess of inflation) which you make through selling (or otherwise disposing of) an asset for more than its value when you first bought (or otherwise acquired) it.

Capital risk The probability of losing some or all of your original investment.

Carpetbagger Someone who opens accounts with building societies mainly in the hope of becoming the recipient of windfall shares or cash if the society subsequently converts to a bank or is taken over.

Chartism System of share price analysis based on the belief that the future movement of prices can be predicted from the pattern of past price movements and selected other data.

Chinese wall An artificial intangible barrier between different parts of an organisation created in order to prevent information which could affect share prices being passed from one part of the business to another.

Collective investment Investment whereby the resources of many investors are pooled and used to buy a portfolio of shares and/or other investments. The portfolio is usually run, on behalf of the investors and in exchange for various fees and charges, by a professional investment manager. Examples of collective investments are unit trusts, investment trusts and OEICs.

Commission In the context of stockbroking, the charge (usually expressed as a percentage of the size of the deal) made by a firm for carrying out your instructions to buy or sell shares or other marketable investments.

Company A form of organisation created for the carrying on of a business which has a separate legal identity from the owners of the business.

Company registrar The person or firm responsible for maintaining a register of the owners of a company (i.e. the shareholders).

Company risk The probability of losing part or all of your original investment because of poor performance of the company whose shares you hold.

Continuation pattern A term used in Chartism to describe a pattern which indicates that the price of a share will continue the previously established trend – i.e. will continue to rise if it had previously been rising or will continue to fall if it had previously been falling.

Contract note Basically your receipt from your broker showing details of a purchase or sale of shares or other marketable investments.

'Convertible' An investment, such as loan stock or preference shares, which can be swapped for ordinary shares in a company at a set conversion rate on one or more set dates in the future.

Corporate bond Loans you make to a company in return for regular payments of interest at a fixed rate. Many stocks are redeemable, so you receive a fixed lump sum at the end of the stock's life. In the meantime, you can sell the loan on the stock market.

Corporate bond PEP A tax-efficient arrangement for investing in corporate bonds. Both income and gains from the bonds are tax-free.

Corporate PEP A tax-efficient arrangement for investing in the shares of one specific company. Until April 1999, both income and gains from the shares are tax-free.

Corporation tax Tax which a company pays on its income and gains.

Crest System of electronic share settlement used by the London Stock Exchange. It enables shares to be bought and sold without the need for paper share certificates.

CSOP Abbreviation for 'company share option plan' – a type of employee share scheme.

Cum dividend Indicates that, if you buy a share, you will be entitled to receive the next dividend payment. Conversely, if you sell a share, you are not entitled to the next (or any subsequent) dividend.

Current asset In the context of a balance sheet, generally taken to mean an asset which is cash, can be readily converted to cash or is money owed to the company which is expected to be paid within one year.

Current liability In the context of a balance sheet, amounts which the company is expected to pay out within one year.

Current ratio A measure of liquidity derived from the balance sheet of a company which tells you whether the company has enough cash and assets which can be turned into cash within the next year to meet all the liabilities which are expected to fall due over the year.

Cumulative preference share A type of share on which a company must pay dividends before making any payment to its ordinary shareholders. It differs from a standard preference share in that, if a dividend payment is missed, it is deemed to be owing and all outstanding dividend payments must be cleared before any dividends are paid on the ordinary shares.

Dealing at best Arrangement whereby your broker buys shares on your behalf at the lowest price he or she can or sells shares for you at the highest price available.

Debt/equity ratio In the context of a balance sheet, a way of measuring the extent of a company's borrowings. Also called 'gearing'.

Defensive stock A share which tends to underperform the market, rising by less than the market on its way up but falling by less than the market on its way down.

Demerger The splitting of a company into two or more component parts.

Deposit Type of investment which earns interest and where the amount of your original capital cannot fall – it either remains unchanged or increases through reinvesting the interest payments.

Depreciation In the context of a company's accounts, a cost representing the value of an asset wiped out each year through normal wear and tear.

Derivative An investment, such as options or futures, whose value depends on that of some other underlying investment.

Dilution In the context of shares, an increase in the number of shares with the capital of the company remaining unchanged or rising by a smaller proportion.

Discretionary management Service offered by brokers and investment managers whereby you leave the broker or manager to take the decisions on which investments to choose and the timing of purchases and sales.

Dividend Income payment from a share.

Dividend cover Number of times a dividend could have been paid out of current earnings. This gives some indication of how likely it is that the company will be able to maintain or increase the dividend in future years.

Dividend discount model System of share price analysis which starts from the premise that share price will tend to equal the value placed today on the future stream of dividend payments.

Dividend yield Current dividends expressed as a percentage of the current share price. The figure may be gross (before tax) or net (after tax at the rate applicable to lower-rate and basic-rate taxpayers).

Double bottom Term used in Chartism to denote a pattern which signals that a share price is about to reverse its downward trend and start instead to rise.

Double top Term used in Chartism to denote a pattern which signals that a share price is about to reverse its upward trend and start instead to fall.

Dual capacity Describes the situation where one individual or firm acts as both broker (dealing as agent for clients) and jobber (dealing on his or her own account).

Earnings per share The profits of a company divided by the number of shares – a key indicator used to estimate the value of a share.

EASDAQ Abbreviation for the European Association of Security Dealers Automated Quotation system – a pan-European stock exchange.

Efficient market hypothesis Theory which asserts that share prices encapsulate all known and expected information and assimilate new information almost instantaneously. Therefore, there is no scope for making high returns by looking for stocks which are mis-priced or for accurately predicting how share prices will move in future. The only way to achieve above-average returns is to accept more risk.

EIS Abbreviation for 'Enterprise investment scheme'.

Electronic order book System of matching buyers of shares to sellers of shares using computer software and without the need for any middleman (i.e. a market maker).

Electronic settlement System of transferring shares from sellers to buyers without the need for share certificates. Ownership is recorded by means of entries into a computer system (in much the same way as ownership of money in a bank account is recorded).

Emergency fund A personal pool of readily accessible money to be drawn on in case of emergency.

Employee share scheme Tax-efficient arrangement for giving employees shares in their company or the right to acquire shares at some set future time at a price which is fixed now.

Enterprise investment scheme Scheme which aims to encourage investors to back new venture companies by offering tax incentives.

Equity investment Any investment in shares, including direct holdings or indirect investment – e.g. by holding units in a share-based unit trust.

Equity option Investment giving you the right (but not the obligation) to buy or sell the shares of a particular company at a set price at any time up to a specified date. But you do not have to hold on to the option until that time. Instead, you can sell it in the market.

ESOP Abbreviation for company share option plan – a type of employee share scheme.

Exchange rate risk The probability of losing part or all of your original investment because of a change in the relative values of the currency in which the investment is made and your home currency.

Ex dividend Indicates that, if you buy a share, you will not be entitled to receive the next dividend payment. Conversely, if you sell a share, you are entitled to the next (but not any subsequent) dividend.

Execution-only service Service offered by a broker whereby he or she will buy or sell shares (or other investments) on your instruction but will not offer any comment or advice.

Exercise price In the context of derivatives, the price at which you can buy or sell the underlying investment.

FID Abbreviation for 'Foreign income dividend'.

Financial planning The process of structuring your investments and other financial arrangements to give you the best chance of meeting your financial responsibilities and realising your financial ambitions.

Financial Services Act 1986 An Act of Parliament which introduced a detailed scheme of regulation for investment business and came into effect from April 1988. A new Financial Services Act is due in 1998 to overhaul the system of investor protection completely.

Financial Services Authority (FSA) Name for the main regulator responsible for investor protection, formerly called the Securities and Investments Board (SIB). Over a transtional period from 1997 to 1999, the FSA will take over investor protection responsibilities from the SROs (which will cease to exist), RPBs, the Bank of England, the Building Societies Commission and the Department of Trade and Industry, and so evolve into a single 'super regulator' responsible for most investments and savings products marketed and sold to the general public.

FIRST option bonds A type of National Savings investment aimed mainly at basic-rate taxpayers.

Fixed income investment An investment – e.g. British Government stocks, many corporate bonds – offering a set amount of income. As general interest rates in the economy move up and down, the price of a fixed income investment tends to fall and rise to keep the yield (i.e. income divided by the current price) in line with the general rates.

Focus Vogue for concentrating on a company's core activities and, if necessary, shedding subsidiaries which do not fit this brief.

'Footsie index' Nickname for the FTSE 100 index.

Foreign income dividend A type of dividend (income) from shares which, like other dividends, is paid with tax deducted. However, unlike other dividends (until April 1999), the tax cannot be reclaimed by non-taxpayers.

Friendly society A mutual organisation offering investment-type insurance products, some of which are tax-free.

FSA Abbreviation for 'Financial Services Authority'.

FTSE 100 index A weighted average of 100 leading shares, which provides a handy indication of the level of and movements in the stock market as a whole.

Fully paid Describes shares where the holder has paid the full price with no instalments outstanding.

Fundamental analysis A system of share price evaluation which tries to establish the underlying value of a company based, for example, on its ability to make future profits. This is estimated by the study of a wide range of factors, such as the general economic climate, quality of management, the structure of the company's capital, and so on.

Futures contract An investment which contracts you to buy or sell an underlying investment or commodity at a set price on some specified future date. You can sell the contract before that date arrives.

Gearing In the context of a balance sheet, a way of measuring the extent of a company's borrowings. In the context of an investment, the extent to which the investment magnifies the gains or losses you can make.

General PEP A tax-efficient arrangement for investing in shares, corporate bonds, unit trusts, investment trusts and OEICs. Until April 1999, both income and gains from the investments are tax-free.

Guaranteed equity investment An investment, offered by some banks, building societies and unit trusts, which attempts to combine the security of a deposit with at least some of the rewards of equity investment.

Head and shoulders Term used in Chartism to denote a pattern which signals that a share price is about to reverse its upward trend and start instead to fall. The shape of the pattern is similar to the head and shoulders of a person, hence its name.

IMRO Abbreviation for the Investment Managers Regulatory Organisation.

Income risk The probability of losing potential income either because you have invested for a fixed return and competing interest rates rise, or because you have invested for a variable return and interest rates fall below the level of the fixed returns which had been available from competing investments.

Income tax Tax you pay on most forms of income, including the dividends from shares.

Independent financial adviser Individual or firm, authorised under the Financial Services Act, to give advice about and deal in investments, basing that advice on the full range of products and providers available.

Index option A type of traded option which, in theory, gives you the right (but not the obligation) to buy or sell an underlying portfolio of the shares which make up a particular index – e.g. the FTSE 100 – at a set price either on a set future date or at any time up to that date (depending on the type of option you buy). In the meantime, you can sell the option in the market. In practice, instead of actually buying or selling the constituent shares, you are paid cash for each point the index has moved in your favour.

Individual Savings Account A 'tax-favoured' arrangement for investing in shares and other investments due to be introduced by the Labour government from April 1999 onwards.

Inflation A sustained increase in prices.

Inflation risk The probability of the buying power of your investment falling due to a rise in general prices.

Instant access account A deposit from which you can withdraw your money without giving notice or incurring a penalty.

Institutional investors Professional investors managing large sums of money on behalf of customers or clients, for example, insurance companies, pension funds and unit trusts.

Insurance fund The pool of money resulting from the payment of insurance premiums (net of charges etc.) which an insurer invests on the stock market and in other investments.

Internet An electronic network, linking participating computers across the world and giving you access via a computer and telephone to a wide range of information and services.

Intrinsic value In the context of options, the profit (or loss) inherent in the option due to the difference between the exercise price and the current price of the underlying investment.

Investment analyst A professional working, for example, for a broker or institutional investor, whose job is to analyse shares in order to estimate the likely future return from investing in them.

Investment club A group of private investors who pool their available resources for investment in shares (and other investments) and collectively decide what to invest in and when.

Investment Managers Regulatory Organisation A self-regulating organisation under the Financial Services Act 1986, responsible for businesses running investment funds – e.g. insurance companies and unit and investment trusts.

Investment trust A company whose business is managing a fund of shares and/or other investments. You can invest indirectly in the fund by buying the shares of the investment trust.

Investors Compensation Scheme Scheme set up under the Financial Services Act 1986 to pay compensation to investors who are eligible to claim against an authorised investment business – e.g. because they have lost money through a firm's fraud or negligence – but the business has gone bust.

Irredeemable A stock – for example British Government stocks or a corporate bond – which has no eventual repayment date. The only way to get back your capital is to sell the stock in the market.

ISA Abbreviation for 'Individual savings account'.

Issue price Price at which new shares are initially sold, which is generally different from the price at which they start to trade on the stock market.

Jobber A professional buyer and seller of shares and other marketable securities who is committed to offering to buy and sell for their own account, thereby ensuring a market in the shares. These days, more commonly called a 'market maker'.

Joint stock company A company which raises its finance through the issue of shares.

Liability In the context of a balance sheet, anything which the company uses but which is owned by or owed to someone else.

Limit dealing Arrangement whereby your broker buys shares or other marketable investments for you only once the price has reached or fallen below a price you have specified, or sells the shares or other investments only once the price has reached or risen above a price you have specified.

Liquidity In the context of a balance sheet, a measure of the company's abilities to meet its debts. In the context of a market, the readiness with which investments can be bought and sold.

Loan stock Loans to, say, a government or company, which can be sold on the stock market to someone else rather than held until repaid by the original borrower.

Local authority bonds Fixed term deposits offered by local authorities (e.g. County Councils) as a way of raising money. You cannot usually get your money back before the end of the set term.

M&A Abbreviation for mergers and acquisitions. Merchant banks often have M&A departments whose job is to work for companies merging with or taking over other companies.

Managed PEP A tax-efficient arrangement for investing in shares, corporate bonds, unit trusts, and so on, where you have handed over to a professional investment manager the decisions about what to invest in and when. Until April 1999, both income and gains from the investments held in the PEP are tax-free.

Margin trading Arrangement which increases the gearing of an investment, whereby you put up only part of the cost of the investment (basically, making a down payment). Any gain or fall in the value of the investment represents a larger percentage of the capital you have invested than it would had you paid the full amount.

Market capitalisation The price of a share multiplied by the number of shares issued, giving an indication of the value investors put on the company.

Market–maker A professional buyer and seller of shares and other marketable securities who is committed to offering to buy and sell for their own account, thereby ensuring a market in the shares.

Memorandum of Association Together with the Articles of Association, a document setting out the basic rules and constitution of a company.

Merchant bank Banks which originally started up in order to raise finance for foreign trading ventures. Nowadays, they are involved in many aspects of trade and business, including raising money for companies – e.g. by organising the issue and purchase of new shares.

Merger Combining the activities, interests and running of two or more companies. In theory, the partners to the merger have equal status in the deal. In practice, one company may in effect be taking over the other(s).

Minimum commission agreement Arrangement, abandoned in 1986, whereby brokers agreed to charge customers no less than the amounts given by a set scale used throughout the broking industry. Any competition was on the basis of additional services (such as access to research) and quality of service, not price.

Monopolies & Mergers Commission An independent body (reporting to the Secretary of State for Trade and Industry) charged with assessing the impact on public interest of the activities of companies or groups of companies who have, or would have, a dominant position in the market(s) for their particular areas of business.

Mutual organisation An organisation owned by its members who, therefore, benefit from any profits made by the organisation, as opposed to an incorporated body which is owned by its shareholders, who generally expect to receive a share of profits in the form of dividends.

NASDAQ Abbreviation for the National Association of Security Dealers Automated Quotation system, a US stock exchange.

National debt Total borrowings of the government.

Nationalised industry Companies, or whole industries, in the control of the state. In effect, nationalised industries are the property of the electorate.

National Savings Range of deposit-based investments issued by the government as a way of borrowing money from the private sector.

Net asset value The value of a company's assets less its liabilities, divided by the number of ordinary shares issued. Gives a rough measure of the underlying value of the company per share and is sometimes used as an indicator of the expected share price.

Net current asset value The value of a company's cash and assets which can readily be converted to cash less its liabilities. This gives a measure of how much a company would be worth if it was wound up and the cash distributed to the shareholders. If the value is positive, the company has some intrinsic value, quite apart from any ability to generate profits. Used as an indicator of shares which are thought to have good growth potential.

New issue The process of raising new finance for a company through the public sale of shares.

Nil paid Describes shares where the price is due in one or more future instalments and nothing has yet been paid.

Nominee account Arrangement whereby someone else, usually a broker or other professional firm, holds shares or other assets on your behalf. Although you are the ultimate owner, the nominee is the legal owner, which can cause difficulties if you want to exercise ownership rights, such as voting and receiving company information and share perks.

Nominal value The face value of a share or stock. The amount you get back if the shares or stock has a finite lifetime and comes to be repaid. Also used to work out the additional money a shareholder may be called on to pay if the company goes bust and the shares were not fully paid.

OEIC (pronounced 'oik') Abbreviation for 'open ended investment company'. A collective investment similar to a unit trust.

Office of Fair Trading Government department with various responsibilities, including the monitoring of businesses to ensure they compete fairly with other firms in their market and do not jeopardise the public interest.

Official List The record of companies quoted on the main market of the London Stock Exchange.

Option Investment giving you the right (but not the obligation) to buy an underlying investment at a set price either on or up to a given date.

Order book trading System of matching buyers of shares to sellers of shares using computer software and without the need for any middleman (i.e. a market-maker).

Ordinary share Most basic form of ownership of a slice of a company, giving the shareholder the right to share in the profits, if any, remaining after all other obligations have been met. Ordinary shareholders usually have the right to vote at general meetings.

Partly paid Describes shares where the holder is required to pay the price in two or more instalments and some instalments are yet to be paid.

P/E Abbreviation for 'price/earnings ratio'.

Penny share Low-priced shares of a company which has hit rough times. The majority of these companies fail completely, but a few recover or are taken over and produce spectacular profits for their shareholders. A high-risk investment.

Pension fund Fund built up through the payment of contributions into a pension scheme or pension plans, run by a professional manager and invested in shares and/or other investments.

PEP Abbreviation for 'personal equity plan'.

PEP manager A professional – for example, a broker or unit trust management company – who organises the administration and running of a personal equity plan.

Permanent health insurance Type of insurance which replaces part of your income if you are unable to work because of a long-term illness or disability.

Permanent income-bearing shares Type of loan stock issued by building societies. The shares pay interest and are irredeemable – i.e. the only way to get any capital back is to sell the shares on the stock market.

Personal equity plan A tax-efficient arrangement for holding investments. There are two basic types: the single company version, which invests in the shares of just one company at a time; and the general version, which can be used to invest in shares, corporate bonds, unit trusts, investment trusts and/or OEICs. Until April 1999, both income and gains from the investments are tax-free.

Personal Investment Authority The self-regulating organisation responsible for policing most investment businesses which deal with the general public – e.g. insurance companies, unit trust companies and financial advisers.

PIA Abbreviation for 'Personal Investment Authority'.

PIBS Abbreviation for 'permanent income-bearing shares'.

Point and figure chart A type of graph used in Chartism which summarises information about the extent and direction of share price changes.

Portfolio A basket of different shares and/or other investments.

Portfolio management Arrangement whereby a third party – e.g. a stockbroker – runs your portfolio of shares and/or other investments on your behalf. The service may be advisory, in which case you still make the ultimate decisions about what to invest in and when, or discretionary, in which case you leave the portfolio manager to make these decisions.

Preference share Type of share whereby the holder has the right to share in a fixed amount of the profits, if any, after certain other obligations of the company have been met. Preference shareholders must be paid before the ordinary shareholders can receive anything, but do not usually have the right to vote at general meetings.

Premium bond Deposit-based investment issued by the government but, instead of interest being credited to individual accounts, it is accumulated in a prize fund and distributed to winners in a monthly draw.

Premium In the context of derivatives, the price paid for the derivative (e.g. traded option, rights etc.).

Price/earnings ratio The price of a share divided by its earnings per share. Used as an indicator of how expensive or cheap the shares are.

Private client A private investor, investing for his or her own account, as opposed to an institutional investor who acts on behalf of others.

Privatisation The process of shifting a company or industry from state ownership to private ownership by individuals and private institutions. Usually entails the issue of new shares to the public.

Profit and loss account Set of figures showing the income and expenses of a company over a given period. Any surplus of income over expenses is the profit earned for the owners which can either be paid out or reinvested.

Prospectus Document which a company is obliged to publish when offering new shares to the public. It contains similar but more detailed information to that found in a report and accounts.

Public offer The offering of new shares to the general public. An alternative is to offer new shares direct to institutional investors (called a placing), which is a cheaper and less complicated way for a company to raise money.

Put option A right (but not an obligation) to sell shares at a set price at any time up until the option expires on a given date.

Quant analysis Name given to various methods of analysing the behaviour of shares and other marketable investments, using relatively complex mathematical models to describe the relationship between expected returns and expected risk.

Quick ratio A measure of liquidity derived from the balance sheet of a company which tells you whether the company has enough cash and assets that can readily be turned into cash to meet all its short-term debts. Also known as the 'acid test'.

Quoted company A company listed on the main market of the London Stock Exchange or on some other recognised stock exchange. (But, for tax purposes, companies listed on the alternative investment market count as unquoted.)

Quote-driven market Stock market where market-makers advertise the prices at which they are willing to buy and sell shares (or other marketable investments) and wait for brokers to place their business.

Random walk Theory which asserts that the movement of a share price is completely independent of its past movements, having at any point in time an equal probability of moving up or down.

Recovery stock Shares in a company which is currently in the doldrums but expected to pick up at some time in the future.

Redeemable Description applied to a stock or share which has a set lifetime, at the end of which a capital sum is paid out.

Reinvestment relief Relief from capital gains tax available when the profits from disposing of any asset are invested in the shares of eligible unquoted UK trading companies.

Relative strength A measure used in Chartism which compares the movement of a share price with movements in the market as a whole.

Resistance level A term used in Chartism to indicate a maximum level at which a share price tends to stick At that price, sellers are tempted to take profits, so the share price tends to fall again.

Retail Prices Index The main measure of price levels in the UK. Changes in the index are widely quoted as a measure of inflation.

Retail service provider A broker acting for a client whose deals are outside the scope of the order book system of trading called SETS (e.g. because the transactions are too small).

Return The overall profit (or loss) from an investment whether in the form of income, capital or both.

Return on capital employed A balance sheet measure of the profitability of a company's activities. If the return is less than could be made from investing the capital in a deposit account, say, there is little point in investing it in the business.

Reversal pattern A term used in Chartism to describe a pattern which indicates that the price of a share will start to move in the opposite direction to the previously established trend – i.e. will start to fall if it had previously been rising or will start to rise if it had previously been falling.

Rights issue The sale of new shares by a company to its existing shareholders as a way of raising additional finance.

Risk The probability of an event. Usually interpreted as the probability of a bad outcome but, in fact, risk is symmetrical and also describes the probability of a good outcome.

ROCE Abbreviation for 'return on capital employed'.

Rolling settlement System of exchanging payment and share certificates within a short period of the date of the purchase and sale of shares (or other marketable investments) as opposed to settling up on some specified account day.

Scrip dividend The issue of free shares to existing shareholders in place of a cash dividend. Also called a 'stock dividend'.

Scrip issue The issue of free additional shares to existing shareholders (also called a 'bonus issue').

SEAQ Abbreviation for the Stock Exchange Automated Quotation system. This is a screen- based system of delivering market-makers' advertised prices and details of bargains done direct to the office computers of brokers and other professionals. It is an alternative to having a physical market place where buyers and sellers meet face to face.

Secondary share market Market in which existing shares are bought and sold. This does not raise money for the company whose shares are traded but the existence of the secondary market makes it easier for a company to raise money by issuing new shares because shareholders know that they can readily cash in their investment on the secondary market.

Sector risk The probability of losing part or all of your original investment because of factors adversely affecting the industry or geographical region in which the company, whose share you hold, operates.

Securities and Futures Authority The self-regulating organisation responsible for investment businesses dealing with marketable investments, such as shares, corporate bonds, options and futures.

Securities and Investments Board Now renamed the Financial Services Authority, the self-regulating body at the top of the Financial Services Act structure. It is responsible for the activities of the SROs and broad regulatory policy. It also authorises a few investment businesses itself.

SEDOL Abbreviation for the Stock Exchange Daily Official List, a journal published daily detailing the prices of and deals in shares quoted on the London Stock Exchange. Shares are given a standard code name (its SEDOL code) in the journal which is often used elsewhere.

Self-regulating organisations Set up under the Financial Services Act 1986, these are the bodies directly responsible for policing investment businesses. It is a criminal offence for an investment business to operate without being a member of an SRO, RPB or SIB.

Self-select PEP A tax-efficient arrangement for holding shares, corporate bonds, unit trusts, investment trusts and/or OEICs, whereby you pick the investments you wish to hold. Until April 1999, both income and gains from the investments are tax-free.

SETS System of matching buyers of shares to sellers of shares using computer software and without the need for any middleman (i.e. a market-maker).

SFA Abbreviation for the 'Securities and Futures Authority'.

Share A unit of ownership of part of a company.

Share buy-back Process whereby a company buys in and cancels its own shares, returning cash to the shareholders.

Share certificate Piece of paper giving proof that you own a given number of shares in a company. Unless they are bearer shares, proof of ownership is also recorded in the company's share register and certificates can be replaced if lost. With a bearer certificate, there is no record of who holds the shares – the certificate alone is proof of ownership and should be kept securely.

Share consolidation A way of reorganising share capital so that the original share capital is replaced with one new share being issued for a given number of existing shares. There is no change to the amount of share capital issued, but each replacement share commands a higher price than the original shares.

Shareholders' funds The assets of a company less all its liabilities. What remains belongs ultimately to the shareholders.

Share option scheme Tax-efficient arrangement for giving employees the opportunity to acquire shares in their company at a set price on some future date(s).

Share perk A reward to shareholders distinct from the return on the shares themselves. Usually, takes the form of a discount on or free gift of the company's products or services.

Share shop An outlet – e.g. a traditional stockbroker or the broking service of a High Street bank – usually heavily advertised, where you can sell shares acquired as a result of a major new issue (often a privatisation). The share shop may offer cut-price dealing.

Share split A way of reorganising share capital so that the original share capital is replaced with several new shares being issued for one existing shares. There is no change to the amount of share capital issued, but each replacement share commands a lower price than the original shares.

SIB Abbreviation for 'Securities and Investments Board'.

Single capacity Describes the situation where an individual or firm must act either as a broker (dealing as agent for clients) or as a jobber (dealing on his or her own account). They cannot act simultaneously in both roles and may switch from one role to the other only with the permission of the stock exchange.

Single company PEP A tax-efficient arrangement for investing in the shares of one company at a time. Until April 1999, both income and gains from the shares are tax-free.

SRO Abbreviation for 'self-regulating organisation'.

SSAP Abbreviation for 'Statement of Standard Accounting Practice'.

Stag A person who buys shares when they are newly issued in the hope of selling for a profit immediately the shares open for trading on the stock market.

Stamp duty Tax payable on the drawing up or exchange of certain contractual documents, including share certificates. The purchaser pays the duty.

Standard deviation A statistical measure used to describe the volatility of a share price. Because the measure is standardised, the standard deviation of one share or investment can be directly compared with that of another.

Statement of Standard Accounting Practice Statements of accounting principles and practices which companies must abide by when drawing up their accounts.

Stock Similar to shares, but whereas shares are traded in whole numbers – e.g. 1,000 shares – stock can be traded in any amount, e.g. £1,000 worth of stock.

Stockbroker A professional who advises on, and deals in, shares and other marketable securities on behalf of customers.

Stock dividend The issue of free shares to existing shareholders in place of a cash dividend. Also called a 'scrip dividend'.

Stock exchange Market where stocks and shares are traded.

Striking price In the context of derivatives, another name for the 'exercise price'. In the context of a tender issue, the price at which all the shares or stocks are sold.

Support level A term used in Chartism to indicate a minimum level at which a share price tends to stick At that price, buyers are attracted, so the share price tends to rise again.

Takeover Process whereby one company gains control of another either by mutual agreement or by a hostile bid to buy shares from existing shareholders.

Tax credit Amount of tax already paid on a share dividend (or distribution from a unit trust) which can be credited against your overall income tax bill and, until 1999, reclaimed if you are a non-taxpayer.

Tax voucher Document accompanying a share dividend (or distribution from a unit trust) which is proof that you have a tax credit to claim.

Tender issue An invitation to apply for new shares (or stock) at or above a minimum price (instead of at a fixed price). Would-be investors bid for the shares. A striking price – which all successful applicants pay – is set at the lowest level at which all the shares can be sold. Anyone who bids below this price fails to get any shares.

Time value In the context of derivatives, that part of the derivative price which is not explained by the difference between the exercise price and the current price of the underlying investment.

Traded option Investment giving you the right (but not the obligation) to buy or sell an underlying investment at a set price either on a set date or at any time up to a specified date. However, you do not have to hold on to the option until that time, but you can sell it in the market instead.

Traditional option Investment giving you the right (but not the obligation) to buy or sell the shares of a company at a set price either on a set date or at any time up to a specified date. This is a contract between you and the writer (issuer) of the option. You cannot sell the option to another party.

Transfer form Form to be completed if you sell or give your shares to someone else. Often printed on the back of a share certificate.

The Treasury Government department responsible, among other things, for the operation of the Financial Services Act 1986.

Trend An established direction of movement – e.g. of a share price.

Trustee Someone who owns assets which are to be used for the benefit of someone else in accordance with the terms of the trust arrangement.

Unit trust A collective investment where the resources of many investors are pooled and invested in a professionally managed fund of shares and/or other investments. The ownership of the fund is divided into many segments called units and you take a direct stake in the fund by buying the units.

Unlisted securities market A former junior market of the London Stock Exchange, now replaced by the Alternative investment market.

Unquoted company A company which is not listed on a stock exchange. For tax purposes, this includes companies listed on the Alternative investment market.

USM Abbreviation for the 'Unlisted securities market'.

VCT Abbreviation for 'venture capital trust'.

Venture capital trust A collective investment, similar to an investment trust, which invests in the shares of unquoted UK trading companies. Private investors are encouraged through special tax advantages to buy the shares of the venture capital trust.

Volatility Describes the degree to which a value – e.g. a share price – swings around its average over a given period of time. Used as a measure of risk.

Warrant An investment, similar to a traded call option, which gives you the right (but not the obligation) to buy the shares of a company at a set price on some set future date(s).

Windfall shares Shares issued to members when a mutual organisation, such as a building society or insurance company, converts to company status. Members typically feel that they have received something for nothing, but in fact the shares crystallise their existing ownership rights in the organisation.

With-profits insurance Form of investment-type life insurance where the return you get takes the form of bonuses which are added to your policy. Once added, bonuses cannot be taken away. A major factor influencing the level of bonuses is performance of the stock market, so this is a relatively low-risk way of gaining some exposure to equities.

xd abbreviation for 'Ex dividend'.

Addresses and publications

Association of Investment Trust Companies (AITC)
Durrant House, 8–13 Chiswell Street
London EC1Y 4YY
Tel: 0171-282 5555

Association of Unit Trusts and Investment Funds (AUTIF)
65 Kingsway
London WC2B 6TD
Unit Trust Information Service
8 am to 11 pm daily
Tel: 0171-831 0898

Association of Private Client Investment Managers and Stockbrokers (APCIMS)
112 Middlesex Street
London E1 7HY
Written enquiries only; APCIMS produces a directory of its members and the services they offer
Web site: http://www.apcims.org

Bank of England
Threadneedle Street
London EC2R 8AH
Tel: 0171-601 4444
Fax: 0171-601 4771
Web site: http://www.bankofengland.co.uk

Business Accounting
by Frank Wood and Alan Sangster
published by Pitman
From bookshops

Be Your Own Financial Adviser
Published by
Which? Books,
PO Box 44,
Hertford X, SG14 1SH
Tel: (0645) 123580
Web site: http://www.
which@which.net *and from bookshops*

Charters on Charting
by David Charters
Published by Rushmere Wynne
From bookshops

Chase de Vere PEP Guide
Published by
Chase de Vere Investments plc
Lincoln's Inn Fields
London WC2A 3JX
Tel: 0171-404 5766
Fax: 0171-831 0426

Companies House
Crown Way
Cardiff CF4 3UZ
Tel: (01222) 380801
Fax: (01222) 380517
Web site: http://www.
companies-house.gov.uk

Company REFS (Really Essential
Financial Statistics)
Published by
Hemmington Scott Publishing Ltd
City Innovation Centre
26–31 Whiskin Street
London EC1R 0BP
Tel: 0171-278 7769
Fax: 0171-278 9808
Web site: http://www.hemscott.co.uk

Electronic Share Information Ltd (ESI)
Web site: http://www.esi.co.uk

The Estimate Directory
Published by
Edinburgh Financial Publishing
3rd Floor, 124–5 Princes Street
Edinburgh EH2 4BD
Tel: 0131-473 7070
Fax: 0131-473 7080

Financial Services Authority (FSA)
Gavrelle House, 2–14 Bunhill Row
London EC1Y 8RA
Tel: 0171-638 1240
Fax: 0171-382 5900
Web site: http://www.fsa.gov.uk

FSA Register enquiries
(Address as above)
Tel: 0171-929 3652
Fax: 0171-382 5900

The Financial Times
From newsagents
Web site: http://www.ft.com

FT Cityline
Tel: 0171-873 4378
Web site: http://www.ft.com
Telephone numbers for share price
information published in Monday's
Financial Times

FT Company Handbooks
The UK Major Companies Handbook
Smaller UK Companies Handbook
Published by
Financial Times Information
Fitzroy House, 13-17 Epworth Street
London EC2A 4DL
Tel: 0171-251 3333
Fax: 0171-251 2725
Web site: http://www.info.ft.com

FTSE International
St Alphage House, Fore Street
London EC2Y 5DA
Tel: 0171-448 1800
Fax: 071-448 1804

The Hambro Company Guide/
Hemmington Scott Company Guide
Published by Hemmington Scott
Publishing Ltd – see Company REFS,
above, for details

IFA Promotion
17-19 Emery Road
Brislington
Bristol BS4 5PF
For a list of independent financial advisers
in your area, phone 0117-971 1177

Infotrade
Web site: http://www.infotrade.co.uk

Inland Revenue
See phone book under 'Inland Revenue'
for your local tax office
The Inland Revenue publishes many free
explanatory booklets, including:
IR16 and IR17 Share acquisitions by
*   directors and employees*
IR89 Personal equity plans
IR95 Approved profit sharing schemes
IR97 Approved SATE share option
*   schemes*
IR101 Approved company share option
*   plans*
IR137 The enterprise investment scheme
*   CGT14 Capital gains tax − an*
*   introduction*
CGT15 Capital gains tax − indexation
*   allowance*
SVD1 Shares Valuation Division − an
*   introduction*

The Intelligent Investor
by Benjamin Graham
Published by Harper & Row
From bookshops

Interpreting Company Reports and
Accounts
by Geoffrey Holmes and Alan Sugden
Published by Prentice-Hall
From bookshops

Investment Management Regulatory
Organisation (IMRO)
Lloyd's Chambers, 1 Portsoken Street
London E1 8BT
Tel: 0171-390 5000
Fax: 0171-680 0550
Web site: http://www.imro.co.uk

Investment Ombudsman
6 Frederick's Place
London EC2R 8BT
Tel: 0171-796 3065
Fax: 0171-726 0574

Investors Chronicle
Greystoke Place, Fetter Lane
London EC4A 1ND
Tel: *(for subscription)* (01444) 445520
Fax: (01444) 445599
By subscription or from newsagents

Investors Chronicle Directory of
Stockbrokers and Investment Managers
by Veronica McGrath
Published by Pitman
From bookshops

Investors Compensation Scheme
Gavrelle House, 2–14 Bunhill Row
London EC1Y 8RA
Tel: 0171-628 8820
Fax: 0171-382 5901

The London International Financial
Futures and Options Exchange
(LIFFE)
Cannon Bridge
London EC4R 3XX
Tel: 0171-623 0444
Fax: 0171-588 3624
Web site: http://www.liffe.com

London Stock Exchange
Old Broad Street
London EC2N 1HP
Tel: 0171-797 1372
Fax: 0171-410 6861
Web site: http://www.
londonstockex.co.uk

Micropal
Web site: http://www.micropal.co.uk

Money Management National Register
of Fee-Based Advisers
0117-976 9444

Personal Investment Authority (PIA)
7th Floor, 1 Canada Square
Canary Wharf
London E14 5AZ
Tel: 0171-418 5355
Fax: 0171-418 9300

PIA Ombudsman Bureau
Hertsmere Road
London E14 4AB
Tel: 0171-216 0016
Fax: 0171-712 8742

Proshare (UK) Ltd
Library Chambers
13–14 Basinghall Street
London EC2V 5BQ
Tel: 0171-600 0984
Fax: 0171-600 0947
Web site: http://www.proshare.org.uk

Securities and Futures Authority (SFA)
Cottons Centre, Cottons Lane
London SE1 2QB
Tel: 0171-378 9000
Fax: 0171-403 7569
Web site: http://www.sfa.org.uk

SFA Complaints Bureau and Consumer Arbitration Service
Address etc. as for SFA above

Shareholder Perks
Published by
Premier Fund Managers Ltd
25–7 Chertsey Street
Guildford
Surrey GU1 4HG
Tel: (01483) 306090
Fax: (01483) 300845

Teleshare Information Services
Web site: http://www.teleshare.co.uk/index.htm

UK Shareholders' Association
12 Burgh Heath Road
Epsom, Surrey KT17 4LJ
Tel: (01372) 726535

Using the Financial Pages (FT Guide to)
Published by Pitman
From bookshops

Which? Way to Save and Invest
Published by
Which? Books
POBox 44
Hertford X, SG14 1SH
Tel: (0645) 123580
Web site:
http://www.which@which.net
and from bookshops

Index

Page references in **bold type** indicate an entry in the Glossary